THIS NATION
AND SOCIALISM
ARE ONE

". . .Only under socialism can our homeland
enjoy the most complete unity: territorial, economic, cultural, social, political and ideological
unity; uniformity in rights and duties for all our
countrymen who are closely united and bound by
sincere mutual love and affection. Nation and
socialism are one. For us Vietnamese, love of
country now means love of socialism; it means
developing all our zeal, strength, intelligence and
talent to the building of our socialist homeland . . ."   *LE DUAN*

Le Duan

THIS NATION
AND SOCIALISM
ARE ONE

Selected Writings of Le Duan
First Secretary, Central Committee
Vietnam Workers Party

Edited with an Introduction
by Tran Van Dinh

Vanguard Books
Chicago, 1976

Copyright © 1976 by Tran Van Dinh
Printed in the United States of America
All Rights Reserved
Library of Congress Cataloging in Publication Data
Le Duan. *Edited by* Tran Van Dinh
This nation and socialism are one
Bibliography: p. 259-61
Summary: A collection of essays by the First Secretary of the
Vietnam Workers Party on building socialism in Vietnam.
1 Socialism—Vietnam   2 Vietnam—History
I Tran Van Dinh   II Title

959.7   76-52513

ISBN 0-917702-01-8

VANGUARD BOOKS
P.O. Box 3556
Chicago, Illinois 60654

On August 7, 1964, the day President Johnson ordered the bombing of North Vietnam, I was speaking at a college in California on "The Essence and the Meaning of the Vietnamese Revolution." At the end of my address, a student came to me, shook my hand and said: "Please tell the North Vietnamese not to give up." Before I could ask for her name and thank her, she ran away.

To her and to millions of unknown Americans, workers, intellectuals, students, businessmen who have supported the Vietnamese "Just Cause", this book is dedicated.

Acknowledgements and Permissions

"Revolution is the Work of the Masses" first appeared in *On the Socialist Revolution in Vietnam*, Vol. I; Foreign Languages Publishing House, Hanoi, 1965.

"Principles and Methods of Revolutionary Action" is reprinted from *The Vietnamese Revolution*, (1971) with permission from International Publishers.

"The Working Class and Socialist Industrialization" first appeared in *On the Socialist Revolution in Vietnam*, Vol. II; Foreign Languages Publishing House, Hanoi, 1974.

"The New Stage of Our Revolution and the Tasks of the Trade Unions" first appeared in *Some Present Tasks*; Foreign Languages Publishing House, Hanoi, 1974.

"Some Problems of Cadres and Organization in the Socialist Revolution" first appeared in *Some Present Tasks*, Foreign Languages Publishing House, Hanoi, 1974.

"Role and Tasks of the Vietnamese Woman in the New Revolutionary Stage" first appeared in *Some Present Tasks*; Foreign Languages Publishing House, Hanoi, 1974.

"Problems of Revolutionary Strategy" is reprinted from *The Vietnamese Revolution* (1971) with permission from International Publishers.

"Let Our Entire People Unite to Build Our Reunified and Socialist Fatherland" first appeared in the "Daily Report Annex" of the Foreign Broadcast Information Service, Vol. IV. No. 126, Annex No. 105, June, 1976.

"Platform of the Viet-Nam Lao Dong (Workers Party)" is reprinted from *Conflict in Indochina and International Repercussions: A Documentary History: 1945-1955*, by Allan B. Cole et. al., Cornell University Press, Ithaca, 1955.

"Political Theses of the Indochinese Communist Party" is reprinted from *The Long Resistance [1858-1975]*, by Nguyen Khac Vien, Foreign Languages Publishing House, Hanoi, 1975.

"A Circular Letter Sent Out by Nghe Tinh Patriots" is reprinted from *The Long Resistance [1858-1975]*, by Nguyen Khac Vien, Foreign Languages Publishing House, Hanoi, 1975.

The essays in this book are reprinted as they originally appeared in the above publications.

The photograph on the front cover shows the liberation of Da Nang, a former U.S. military base and a city in central Vietnam.

Contents

Le Duan on the Socialist Reconstruction of Vietnam

Preface

On May 1st, 1975 with the Vietnamese liberation of Saigon, a new era in world politics had begun. Uncle Ho had always reminded his people that the Vietnamese Revolution was being undertaken not only as a national revolution, but as part of a major international revolution that had begun in 1917. The Vietnamese people, while proud of their national accomplishments, have always insisted that they are firm advocates of proletarian internationalism. However, while the war had ended in Vietnam, the revolution had just begun. The task of building socialism became the responsibility of the victorious party and Le Duan has proved to be one of its most accomplished spokesmen. This, then, is the voice of a revolutionary whose right to speak comes as a result of scientific investigation and revolutionary practice.

The task of compiling and editing this study from Vietnamese was undertaken by Professor Tran Van Dinh. It was during those tumultuous days of the late 60's and early 70's when the American people were speaking out against the policies adopted by their government towards the Vietnamese and Afro-American peoples, that I mentioned to my friend Tran Van Dinh that there was a remarkable dearth of literature in the English language about the Vietnamese Revolution written by the Vietnamese. The Vietnamese people had contributed so much to liberation movements, it was imperative that the writings of the Vietnamese be made available to a broader audience. We are indeed grateful to Professor Tran Van Dinh for making this study available for the English-speaking community. This volume will be a welcome addition to the literature of modern revolutions.

A. W. Singham
Washington D.C. 1976

Introduction

*". . . The Confucian scholar on the execution
block repeated: 'I die, but I have fulfilled my
duty.' The militant communist, facing a
firing squad, said: 'I die but you will be
defeated', and thought: 'When the contradictions come to a head, we will be there and
we will win. . .'"*

Nguyen Khac Vien (1)

Vietnam is not a gift of nature. It is the work of Vietnamese
women and men who, during the last four thousand years, have
been engaged in the continuing efforts of DUNG NUOC (To Build
a Nation) and of GIU NUOC (To Defend the Nation). A dialectical
relationship exists between these two tasks: to build a nation is to
defend it, to defend it is to build it. The history of Vietnam has
proved that although the Vietnamese at all times have resisted
foreign aggression, their national resistance was successful only if
they combined the task of DUNG NUOC with that of GIU NUOC,
that is to closely relate production to defense. (2) In other words, a
social revolution, that is a class struggle which alters the mode of
production, is an indispensable and an integral part of a victorious
military resistance. One of the early examples was the victory of
the Vietnamese over the Mongols, who in the thirteenth century
three times invaded Vietnam. The most recent is the Vietnamese
wars of resistance against the French (1946-1954) and the
Americans (1956-1975).

In 1858, when the Vietnamese monarchy was decadent and
Vietnamese feudal society torn by increasing contradictions

between greedy landlords and impoverished peasants, the French colonialists attacked Vietnam. The Court at Hue put up a token resistance but quickly surrendered. The masses under the leadership of patriotic Confucian scholars continued a difficult, protracted struggle which ended in failure despite heroic individual acts and enormous sacrifices. At the end of the nineteenth century the French completely occupied Vietnam. (3) The French colonization and exploitation created new contradictions and sharpened old ones. By the early twentieth century Vietnamese society "had two basic contradictions: the contradiction between the Vietnamese nation and oppressive imperialism, and that between the broad masses and the feudal landlord classes". (4) New anti-French rebellions erupted, but again all collapsed under the bloody repression of the French police and army. The main reason for these failures was the inability of anti-French, nationalist parties to "put forth a correct political programme aimed at solving the above mentioned contradictions." (5)

Humiliated and angered by these defeats, a number of Vietnamese patriots left the country "in search for a path of national liberation, the right path for the revolution in Vietnam". (6) One of these patriots was Nguyen Ai Quoc (Nguyen the Patriot) who was to become in 1945 President Ho Chi Minh of the Democratic Republic of Vietnam. (7) Born in 1890, Ho Chi Minh studied at Quoc Hoc (National Studies) College in Hue. After a short career as a teacher, he went to France, working as a cook on a French merchant ship, in 1911. He travelled throughout the world, visiting Africa and the American east coast. From his observations of America and the conditions of the Blacks, he wrote: "Lynching" and "The Ku Klux Klan". (8)

Ho Chi Minh returned to France at the end of World War I to present the demands for Vietnam's independence at the Versailles Peace conference, but he was not heard. Continuing the search for a solution to the sufferings of his people, he followed the development of the Soviet Revolution. He was convinced that Lenin's theses on the national and colonial question was the ideological path for national liberation. (9) In December 1920, he participated in the Congress of the French Socialist Party which split into two:

the majority formed the French Communist Party (FCP) and joined the Third International, the minority kept the name Socialist Party and joined the Second International. A founding member of the FCP, Ho Chi Minh was the first Vietnamese communist.

In 1921, with the help of the FCP, he founded the League of Colonial Countries. The League published a weekly, "Le Parias", which attacked French colonial policy in Vietnam and Africa. He wrote a book: *Proces de la Colonisation Francaise* (French Colonialism on Trial) and mobilized the oppressed colonial masses to fight and to follow Marxism-Leninism. ". . . In their life of sufferings and inequality" Ho Chi Minh affirmed, "the colonial peoples find in Lenin the creator of a new life, a lighthouse showing to the whole oppressed mankind the way to liberation." (10) He constantly urged that the colonial peoples must be united with the metropolitan proletariat in joint action against the common enemy, that is, imperialism. In June 1923, he attended in Moscow the International Peasants Conference and was elected to its Executive Committee. After Lenin's death, the Communist International held its Fifth Congress in Moscow from June 17th to July 8th, 1924. Ho Chi Minh participated in its deliberations as a representative of the FCP and the colonial countries. During his stay in the USSR, he contributed articles to newspapers and magazines and wrote two books: *China and the Chinese Youth* and *The Black Race*. (11)

In December 1924 he arrived in Canton, South China to be near home and to build the revolutionary movement in Indochina. He founded the League of the Oppressed Peoples in Asia. In 1925 he organized the Vietnam Young Revolutionary Comrades Association (VNYRCA). With a communist group at the core, the purpose of the VNYRCA was to educate Vietnamese youth, preparing the grounds for the founding of a communist party in Indochina. The VNYRCA cadres, trained by Ho Chi Minh in China, returned secretly to Vietnam to agitate. In 1927 Chiang Kai-Shek staged a counter-revolution in Canton. As a result the Vietnamese were persecuted and the VNYRCA headquarters had to move to Hong Kong.

Ho Chi Minh went to Shanghai, and then to the USSR and Belgium where he attended the Anti-Imperialist War Conference.

After visiting France, Germany, Switzerland, and Italy, he left Europe for Thailand where he organized the Vietnamese community in that country. During his absence, the VNYRCA spread its activities in factories, and in May 1929 held its Congress in Macao. The Congress was attended by active communist members coming from different parts of Vietnam. In late 1929, Ho Chi Minh arrived in Hong Kong to convene the Unified Conference which merged the three communist organizations into one party. On February 3, 1930 the Vietnamese Communist Party was officially formed. In October 1930 the Party's Central Committee held its first session in Hong Kong, discussed and passed the Political Programme, and decided to change the Party's name to the Indochinese Communist Party (ICP). Young Vietnamese progressive patriots now had a Marxist-Leninist party to look to in their struggle. Many joined it, among them Le Duan (pronounced: Lee Zuan).

Le Duan was born in Quang Tri (the central part of Vietnam) in 1908. After finishing his high school education and joining the ICP, he worked in the railroad service. In 1931, he was arrested for his political activities and sentenced to twenty years hard labor. (12) In prison he continued his activism among the other inmates, among them Nguyen Luong Bang, now Vice President of the Socialist Republic of Vietnam. On May 3, 1936 the French Popular Front won a clear-cut victory in the general elections resulting in the coming to power of a Popular Front government in Paris. The new French government declared a general amnesty to political prisoners in Indochina. Freed, Le Duan devoted himself to party work which was both legal and illegal. As a cover, he opened a bookstore in Hue, the imperial city. The ICP's policy during that period (1936-1939) was on the one side to openly struggle for democratic rights, and on the other side secretly consolidate the party and mass organizations, combining legal, semi-legal, and illegal activities to fulfill their revolutionary task.

In September 1939 World War II broke out in Europe. The French colonial administration in Indochina ordered general mobilization. The elementary democratic rights gained by the workers and peasants during the Popular Front period were wiped out, and the ICP was outlawed. In November 1939 as a member of the ICP's Central Committee, Le Duan participated in a secret meeting which founded the Indochinese Anti-Imperialist National United Front, an organization aimed at unifying all peoples, all classes, against fascism and imperialism. In September 1940 Indochina was invaded by the Japanese Imperial Army. Offering no resistance, the French colonial authorities cooperated with the Japanese fascists. They arrested most of the ICP's Central Committee members. Le Duan was given a ten-year sentence and sent to the infamous Poulo Condor island penitentiary, off the coast of southern Vietnam. (13) He stayed there until August 1945 when the victory of the Revolution freed him and his comrades.

During the First Indochina War of Resistance against the French (1946-1954) Le Duan represented the ICP (which changed its name in 1951 to the Dang Lao Dong Vietnam or Vietnam Workers Party [VWP]) on the southern front as a political commissar of the people's army. At the end of the war and the signing of the 1954 Geneva Agreements temporarily dividing Vietnam into two zones pending elections for reunification to take place in 1956, Le Duan stayed on in the south for party work while most of the VWP's leading cadres were repatriated to the north.(14) In late 1956, due to errors committed in the implementation of the Land Reform, errors which both the Party and the government publicly admitted, President Ho Chi Minh took over the secretary generalship of the VWP, replacing Truong Chinh, now chairman of the National Assembly. Le Duan was recalled to the north to carry out the day to day assignments in the Party's Central Committee. In 1959 he was named Secretary General of the Central Committee of the Party and in September 1960, when the title of Secretary General was changed to First Secretary, became First Secretary of the Central Committee, Vietnam Workers Party. In that capacity he has visited other socialist countries, alone or with President Ho Chi Minh, to represent the VWP.

After the liberation of "South Vietnam" and Saigon he paid a quick visit to the south in May 1975. In the elections for a unified Vietnam National Assembly in April 1976, he was re-elected in District 2 (Hanoi) with 99.76 per cent of the vote, the highest. On

June 25, 1976 he delivered the Political Report to the National Assembly, thus officially opening the stage of Socialist Reconstruction for the whole of Vietnam.

The U.S. State Department's biographical data on Mr. Le Duan (15) calls him "a master mind behind the scenes", and a "hardliner". These descriptions, as we can see through his own writings, are not true, and are simply the manifestations of unscientific and conspiratorial habits on the part of U.S. government officials. Like his colleagues in the Party, he abides by collective decisions, after discussions and deliberations of the Central Committee. As a Marxist-Leninist who believes that Marxism-Leninism is not a dead science, but a creative philosophical and political force, he is not dogmatic. The experiences of the Vietnamese struggle since 1930 have led him to conclude that "revolution is not only a science, but also an art". It is "creation and it cannot succeed without imagination and ingenuity". He argued that "there has never been nor will there be a unique formula for making a revolution that is suited to all situations". (16)

As an individual he can be described as a "Vietnamese who is moral, loyal, patient, strong, indomitable but filled with compassion", not a superman "endowed with steel skin and copper bones" to paraphrase what he said in an address to the soldiers and people of Quang Binh province during the TET (New Year) of 1973. (17)

The aim of this work is not to praise Mr. Le Duan. Nor is it to glorify the Vietnamese Revolution which can stand by itself as one of the most important contributions to human liberation in the twentieth century in both theory and practice. It is simply to familiarize the non-Vietnamese readers with the thoughts of a man who is assuming a great responsibility together with his comrades and his party, of leading the Vietnamese revolution in its most difficult stage: the socialist reconstruction of a country devastated by thirty years of war. (18)

At the date of the publication of this book Mr. Le Duan is convening, from December 11 to December 20, 1976 in Hanoi, the capital of the reunified Vietnam, the Fourth Congress of the VWP. (19) Forty-six years have passed since the foundation by Ho Chi Minh of the Indochinese Communist Party, the predecessor of the

VWP. During that relatively short period of time the Party, with the backing of the masses, the assistance of fraternal socialist countries and the support of progressive peoples all over the world including the Americans, has led the Vietnamese to the victory over the French colonial army at Dien Bien Phu in 1954 and to the defeat in 1975 of the U.S. "special" and "limited" wars and the Kissinger B-52 diplomacy. Within a Vietnam, now independent, free and unified, the task of the VWP, under the experienced guidance of Mr. Le Duan, is to educate and mobilize fifty million Vietnamese to build the first socialist state in Southeast Asia. With reinforced national unity and continuing international solidarity, this difficult task will be equally successful.

Tran Van Dinh
October, 1976

On the Use of Vietnamese Names

In the Vietnamese usage, similar to the Chinese, a person's family name comes first, followed by her or his middle name (optional) then given names. Since there are not many family names in Vietnam, the most common being: Le, Nguyen, Tran, Phan, Ngo, Vo, Pham, Ly, Hoang, . . . a reference to family names alone would create confusion. Therefore, Vietnamese are generally known by their given names. Example: General Vo Nguyen Giap. Since Vo is his family name and Giap his given name, he is known as General Giap or, more formally, General Vo Nguyen Giap. This is the form I prefer and it will be used in this book. There is an exception however. To convey the sense of respect and admiration to a leader, people would address her or him by her or his family name only. For Example: Hai Ba Trung (the two ladies Trung referring to two sisters Trung Trac and Trung Nhi who revolted against the Chinese feudal domination of Vietnam in the first century) or President Ho or Uncle Ho for President Ho Chi Minh. He has been and is known as President Ho, not President Minh.

Le Duan on Revolution

Revolution is the Work of the Masses

I

Since human society exists its history is made and constantly pushed forward by the masses. No great event nor revolutionary change in society is possible without the active participation and support of the masses.

But the decisive role of the masses was not realized from the outset. Out of their own interests the exploiting classes blurred the historical role of the masses whom they looked upon as dunces. Formerly due to their own class viewpoint and historical conditions, philosophers could not correctly realize the role of the masses whom they regarded just as negative or passive elements at the talented men's beck and call. This wrong viewpoint led former historians to record only the feats of individuals, heroes, kings and mandarins, or well-known generals, overlooking the role of the masses.

It was not until the birth of Marxism thousands of years after that the masses were recognized as makers of history. This discovery, Marx's important contribution, was made possible by the whole process of objective historical development during which the role of the masses became more and more conspicuous. When making the anti-feudal revolution the bourgeoisie had to seek the participation of the masses, who then began to be conscious of their

---

Written on the occasion of the 13th anniversary of the founding of the Democratic Republic of Vietnam (1958).

3

own force and of the political struggle; after this revolution, they also won some democratic rights in many forms, thus drawing every one's attention to their role.

Simultaneously with the emergence and development of the great capitalist industrial production, the proletariat also came into being and grew ever stronger. The centralized labour and the struggle for daily interests, the organizational spirit, discipline and solidarity in fighting tempered in factories have gradually made the proletariat realize their huge strength and also the role of the masses. On the other hand, the more developed the capitalist society, the more acute the contradiction: the annihilation of capitalism and the certain victory of socialism are unavoidable, thus making the proletariat ever conscious of their own role and historical mission, and act more actively to impel the natural evolution of history.

The proletariat is the first class in the history of mankind to have correctly realized the huge force of the masses, and it is Marxism only, the theory of the proletariat, which can scientifically express the historical creative role of the masses.

Since there was a correct notion on the role of the masses and after it gripped hundreds of millions of people, history has changed with an unimaginable rapidity, the positive spirit and the revolutionary creativeness of the masses have shown themselves most powerful, the period of historical development has been shortened, especially in the revolutionary periods when one day is worth twenty former years. The Russian October Socialist Revolution first brought the masses to the position of masters of their own fate. And only forty years after this revolution, socialism has become a world system with over one-third of the population and over one-fifth of the territory of the globe. This is an unimaginable rapid leap in history, compared with the 150 years or 200 years capitalism had to take before it became a world system. And if we take into account that the appearance of capitalism only aims at replacing an exploiting class by another, while the regime of exploitation of man by man itself relying upon private ownership of means of production remains unchanged, whereas socialism must wipe out the exploiting regime and that of private ownership of means of production established since thousands of years, and set up the regime of social ownership of means of production in so short a period, we see more clearly the strength and extraordinary creativeness of the masses once they realize that they must rise up to make their own history. Lenin said that revolution is a great festival of the oppressed and exploited people. Never are the people so active in creating the new social system as in the revolutionary period. In such a period, people can do wonders.

Our millenary history has also proved the decisive role of the masses. For more than one thousand years our country was invaded and ruled by foreign feudalists and our people had struggled heroically against the aggressors. The glorious deeds of two Trung Sisters,(1) Heroin Trieu,(2) Ly Thuong Kiet,(3) Tran Hung Dao,(4) Le Loi,(5) Quang Trung,(6) etc. were also those of our people, but in our history the role of the masses was also overshadowed, and the masses themselves were not fully aware of their own strength. The dynasties which succeeded one another were precisely decided by the masses, but on the upshot it was the latter which were oppressed, despised, and considered as dunces.

In the period when our country was invaded by the French imperialists, many Vietnamese patriots called upon the masses to rise up and fight for independence, but they regarded them just as passive people and could not realize that the success of the national liberation was the fruit of their work. An important factor of the failure of various patriotic campaigns was that these patriots did not correctly see the decisive role and impact of the masses in the imperialist era.

Only with the founding of the Indo-Chinese Communist Party, based on Marxism-Leninism and the practical study of the Vietnamese history, could the Vietnamese communists correctly assess the role of the masses. For the first time in our history our Party has pointed out: "The revolution is the work of the masses to liberate themselves, no hero can save them; only by raising their consciousness, organizing and uniting themselves under the leadership of the vanguard unit of the working class—the Indo-Chinese Communist Party—can they liberate themselves." The Party's revolutionary programme which was set forth in 1930 to overthrow the imperialists and feudalists, establish the worker-peasant-soldier

Soviet power, and distribute land to the peasants, voiced confidence in and determination to rely upon the masses.

Facts have proved that though our economic development lagged behind imperialist France for hundreds of years, we succeeded in relying upon the immense and inexhaustible force of the masses, awaking their revolutionary positiveness, to speed up our advance by leaps and bounds. In a relatively short period we overthrew imperialism and the feudal power, liberated half the country and are taking it gradually to socialism, a higher stage of development, much more equitable, rational and beautiful social system then capitalism. Had it not been for the correct mass viewpoint, and the leadership according to the Party's mass line we could not win such great and rapid a victory.

II

Marxism-Leninism assesses that the history of mankind is that of a succession of methods of production, and of the producers and labouring people. To say that the masses create history is fundamentally to speak of the toiling masses.

In each historical stage the toiling masses differ from one another, therefore the contents of the conception of the masses also changes accordingly.

Under the millenary feudal regime the toiling masses were mainly peasants, the basic productive force of the society at that time.

Since the invasion of our country by the imperialists, in Vietnam, a colonial and semi-feudal country, the toiling masses consisted essentially of workers and peasants, with the latter accounting for the overwhelming majority. Therefore in the national-democratic revolutionary stage led by the Party the most fundamental prop for the struggle against French imperialists and reactionary feudalists was the peasants, a force which makes up 90 per cent of the population of our country.

The 1930 uprising to set up a soviet power in Nghe An was essentially an insurrection of peasants; the biggest force participating in the 1936-1939 democratic movement was also the peasants; the Nam Ky, Bac Son, etc. uprisings were fundamentally waged by the peasants; the founding of the Viet Bac free zone and the

Vietnam Armed Propaganda Unit for National Liberation relied on the peasantry and the countryside; the August 1945 general insurrection to seize power was an uprising of the entire people, but the main force was the labouring people, and the great majority of them were peasants. Our protracted Resistance War which lasted nearly nine years was basically a guerilla warfare waged by the peasants, with the countryside as the mainstay and base from which to encircle the towns, and the peasants contributing the greatest part of manpower and wealth to the Resistance War.

Realizing this great force our Party has assessed that the peasants were the main force of our national democratic revolution which was essentially a revolution of the peasants, under the leadership of the proletariat and its party.

As our Party stood firmly on the proletariat's mass standpoint it could clearly realize the broad mass character of our national democratic revolution. Our country was dominated and lost its independence, therefore every patriotic Vietnamese who approved of national independence could join the anti-imperialist force. On this national basis, we succeeded in establishing a broad unified national front including all classes, strata and patriots. The front was founded in the interest of the revolution, of the nation and also of the grassroot toiling masses. For the success of the revolution the grassroot masses could not be let alone but must have as many allies as possible, and even temporary and wavering ones must be won over. Experience has shown that only when the worker-peasant force is strengthened could we set up a firm unified national front. Inversely, if it was not strong the other strata of the people did not follow it, or wavered.

But the content of our revolution is not only national but also democratic. The aspiration of the masses, first of all the grassroot ones, was to be liberated from the imperialist and feudal yoke in order to improve their livelihood. To them patriotism means the safeguard of the existence of the nation and also of their own existence and welfare. Regarding the overwhelming majority of our people—the peasants—their dearest aspiration was to have land, and to be freed from slavery, humiliation and misery. The peasants enthusiastically took part in the revolution as they were conscious of having land once the country had been independent. It is to satisfy this requirement that they have followed the proletariat and firmly built the worker-peasant alliance under the leadership of the working class, through its Party—the Indo-Chinese Communist Party.

Without democratic rights the force of the masses could not be fostered, first of all the grassroot ones and the unified national front could not be consolidated. It is precisely to foster the most basic force of the revolution and the resistance—the peasantry—that we carried out land reform during the Resistance War to satisfy the peasants' requirements and bring the Resistance War to victory.

In short, only by standing on the class standpoint and mass viewpoint of the proletariat can we see clearly the strength of the masses, realize that the peasantry is the main force in the national democratic revolution, and grasp the class content in this revolution.

III

At present North Vietnam is gradually advancing to socialism. The revolution now underway is the most profound and greatest revolution in history. We must abolish the economy based on the exploitation of man by man, turn the scattered individual economy into a socialist collective one; build and develop the socialist economy unceasingly to improve the labouring people's living conditions and make our people advance to a happier life.

The socialist revolution requires the development of the positiveness and the extraordinary creativeness of the toiling masses which are the most basic productive force of society. To this end, we must free the mind of millions of people formerly tied up within the narrow framework of small production and private economy, and transform the individualist and selfish ideology of the strata of people who lived on exploitation. We must build a new ideology, the socialist ideology, making it gain supremacy in society and become a strong mover to impel the toiling people to transform society, nature and themselves.

Such a revolution cannot succeed if it is not made by the conscious masses with a bold revolutionary spirit.

Therefore, first of all the toiling masses must seize power and use it as the main tool to transform the old economy and production and build new ones. We must grasp the class viewpoint in the setting up of power, see to it that power really belongs to the toiling masses, who will directly manage the state machinery and the economic and cultural structures of society and turn these organizations into revolutionary organizations of the toiling masses and into means to serve the productive labour of the masses and their interests. It is wrong to think that the organizations of the state machinery can replace the masses who have to act on orders from upper levels only. Every line, guiding principle, policy, as well as the working method of the state organs which do not accord with the toiling masses' interests, will create difficulties to the socialist revolution in the North, and can harm the common revolutionary work throughout the country. Therefore, the leading cadres of our Party and state organs must realize the interests of the toiling masses, form as solid bloc with them, and proceed from their interests and common work to set forth the lines and policies and solve the inner contradictions likely to arise between the state interests and those of the masses. Only by so doing can we mobilize the revolutionary enthusiasm of the masses and push forward socialist revolution.

The toiling masses in socialist revolution are first of all the *working class*.

The socialist revolution in Vietnam as well as in all the countries throughout the world, must first and foremost rely upon the force of the working class, the most progressive and revolutionary class within the masses, the class the most representative of socialism, leading the socialist revolution and construction. Without the working class standpoint and ideology we cannot understand socialism. At present, human society has only two paths: capitalism and socialism respectively represented by the bourgeoisie, and the working class.

The position of the working class is established not only in the political and ideological fields, but mainly in the economic field; the working class is the master of enterprises, mines, industrial branches, communications and transport. Without relying upon it there can be no great industry with high technique as a material and technical basis of socialism, nor satisfactory management of industry, etc. Though our socialist industry is still weak, it is developing day by day, and must become a force leading the whole economy. Only in such a way can the tempo of economy in general develop rapidly.

To us, agriculture is playing a role of utmost importance, and is the basis to push forward all national productive branches. At present our industry cannot develop smoothly without a prosperous agriculture because the consumption market of our manufacture is essentially the home market, first of all the countryside; moreover most of the raw materials and food supplied to industry come from agriculture.

Therefore the *peasant* question is still a question of particular importance in the period of socialist revolution and construction in our country. Of more than 13 million people in North Vietnam(7) the peasants account for 12 million, and are the largest force. If we do not rely on them to build socialism, socialist construction is then the work of a few only and not of the broad masses, and therefore cannot succeed. About the Chinese peasantry Mao Tse-tung has said: "Our country has over 500 million peasants, how their situation is is very important in relation to the economic development and the strengthening of power in our country(8)". This applies to our country: in the socialist revolution in North Vietnam every work must proceed from the interests of over 13 million people, including 12 million peasants.

The extremely rich experience of China in socialist construction has given us a very new conception about the path to build socialism in the countryside. Without machines the Chinese peasants could proceed to socialism through co-operativization. Recently after a political remoulding drive, their mind being set free, they have progressed by leaps and bounds. Land productivity has shown an increase unknown in the history of the country. The Chinese peasants have voluntarily pooled money, strength and raw materials for the construction of workshops, which have mushroomed in the countryside. In the leap-and-bound upsurge they have impelled culture rapidly to develop; they have not only wiped out illiteracy, popularized elementary education, but they have also opened high-education schools and vocational schools. In the Chinese countryside at present there is an intense movement to set up people's communes.

This experience has shown that once the broad peasant masses have been re-organized and roused, and their thinking liberated, their active militancy and creativeness in socialist construction are momentous.

The Vietnamese peasants, first of all the toiling peasants, possess revolutionary traditions. Since long they have followed our Party, and are united closely with the workers within the worker-peasant alliance to make revolution. Throughout the Resistance War and land reform their political and class consciousness have been raised markedly.

Though the poor toiling peasants have seen their living conditions much more improved after land reform, in general they are still in difficulty, the per capita land holding being three sao(9) for a poor peasant, and four sao for a middle peasant, that is why they also want to advance to socialism to secure a better life. As the peasant economy is a small-production economy still relying upon the private ownership system, they still are inclined to have private property, a number of well-off peasants want to grow rich in the capitalist way, therefore we must pay attention to their education and prevent their spontaneous tendency to capitalism. But the peasants' revolutionary positiveness is the main aspect. As the Party bases in the countryside have ever been strengthened, power and the peasant mass organization become strong with every passing day and really belong to the toiling peasants, we have all the positive factors to make the peasants join the movement for mutual exchange and co-operativization, and on this basis we rationally organize the labour force, improve technique, and impel the emulation movement for agricultural production to raise the peasants' living conditions and at the same time to push forward socialist revolution.

The Party's and Government's policies to speed up production, such as the policies on trade, finance, banking, etc., must suitably serve the movement for agricultural production and co-operativization. Our industry must also serve agriculture, supplying farm implements and fertilizers to it and solving the hydraulic problem for the peasants. On the basis of increased production and improved living conditions, the socialist consciousness will more deeply permeate the toiling peasants, curb their individualism and tendency to private ownership, and the socialist revolutionary wave in the the countryside will at an appointed time, advance by leaps and bounds. If the Party's and Government's policies, and the means used by the economic and financial organs to carry them out do not meet the toiling peasants' interests, or they arouse their suspicion and disagreement, worse still, their opposition, it means we have not yet grasped the mass viewpoint in socialist revolution.

Beside the peasants' small production gradually advancing to co-operativization, handicraftsmen are also a fairly important productive force in the economy of our country. They supply the bulk of consumer goods to our people. The technique of handicraft production has a national characteristic. At present our handicraft production makes up 59 per cent of the industrial and handicraft output taken together, and caters for 465,000 toilers. The value of handicraft output is twice that of state industry output and the number of handicraftsmen is four times over the number of workers in state enterprises (statistical figures by the end of 1957).

The transformation of the small handicraft production into big socialist production is also a path to make the handicraftsmen willingly organize themselves into co-operatives and improve technique in order to ensure the production of consumer goods to meet the ever increasing needs of the people, secure jobs and the improvement of living conditions for the artisans, and the rational division of labour in our economy. We must help handicraftsmen organize themselves, improve technique and gradually mechanize their bases of production into industrial bases, utilizing machines in production. The experience gained by China in the building of small industrial bases everywhere has helped us realize the latent potentialities of our handicrafts in the process of industrial development in town and countryside.

In a country where the economy of small production still exists, the small traders are still indispensable in distribution. Their scattered trade is very favourable to the consumption of the people. In the conditions of a scattered countryside, with difficult communications and an insufficient network of state trade and purchasing and marketing co-operatives, they have the effect of impelling the rural economy forward. At present, in North Vietnam they are still in great number (over 200,000 households), their income is not high—sometimes below 30,000 dongs a month(10) each, that is below the minimum wage of a low-level producer. They are toiling people, their transformation must go through the development of production, drawing them into various economic branches and production bases. They cannot be considered as the main object to be transformed like the capitalist industrialists and traders, so with regard to them as well as the peasants and handicraftsmen, we must make them realize the advantage in organizing themselves, and embarking in socialist production, and engaging in it of their own free will. They also belong to the family of toiling masses, socialism is also their source of happiness, and the guarantee of their bright future. Previously they went together with the working class, and contributed an active part to the insurrection to seize power; today in socialist revolution, they are also an integral part of the socialist toiling masses.

Therefore in the advance to socialism, we must provide the small traders and handicraftsmen with jobs to keep them up, this is also our Party mass line in socialist revolution.

It would be an unwise policy of ours if we reduced the masses of small traders and handicraftsmen to unemployment or raise difficulties in their trade. While advancing to socialism we must see to developing production, helping the small producers realize the advantage of big production and rational division of social labour; and ensure the subsistence and job to the masses, and must not act like the capitalists who run after profit without the least attention paid to the producers' fate.

The forces of the masses in socialist revolution and construction also include the revolutionary intellectuals, the intellectuals of the workers and peasants. Socialist revolution closely links with the rapid scientific and technical development, the all-round cultural development, to which the intellectuals give a very important contribution. But like any other revolution the cultural revolution must be made by the masses. The Party's slogan "to raise the cultural level of the workers and peasants and inculcate the worker-peasant standpoint on the intellectuals" is to set the problem of building up and developing culture on the basis of the toiling masses. This is also the Party mass line.

In short, according to our mass viewpoint socialist revolution is also the work of the toiling masses. Workers, peasants, urban and rural toilers, and revolutionary intellectuals, all belong to the family of the toiling masses. Only by paying attention to their aspirations and interests, can we rouse their determination and enthusiasm, and develop their inexhaustible creativeness to overcome all difficulties and speed up the revolution.

Only by relying on the enthusiasm and revolutionary determination of the toiling masses and the powerful pressure of the revolutionary movement they wage, can we make the national bourgeois willingly transform themselves and gradually join the toilers' rank.

In socialist revolution the unified front includes the toiling classes, and the self-transformed national bourgeois who have joined the rank of the toilers. It also includes all the brother nationalities living on an equal footing in Vietnam, the believers of various religions, and the Vietnamese residing abroad, who with concerted efforts build an abundant and happy life.

Any policy weakening this front is an obstacle, sometimes a danger to socialist revolution.

At present our country is temporarily partitioned in two zones, with two opposing political and economic systems.

North Vietnam is gradually advancing to socialism but South Vietnam is under the U.S.-Diem rule. The South Vietnam people are making the national democratic revolution. Though the present situation and condition differ from the past, the revolution in South Vietnam still follows the general law of national democratic revolution. Our Party's mass viewpoint in the national democratic revolution still suits South Vietnam in the main.

President Ho Chi Minh has often taught us: Revolution is the work of the masses to liberate themselves. The force of the masses is invincible.

The history of the world as well as that of our country have proved that once the force of the masses is roused, organized, and determined to rise up, it can overcome every difficulty, and do every work.

At present in the world, under the leadership of the communist parties, thousands of millions of people are heroically struggling for peace and socialism, a happy life and a glorious future. It is precisely this great force which has stayed the imperialists' hand and made them recoil. No doubt, the future belongs to the toiling people.

At home, under the leadership of the Party, the toiling masses have done their best in every respect to fulfil the state plan and contribute to the building of socialism as a basis of the struggle for national reunification, and have achieved many brilliant successes.

It is our firm belief that grasping thoroughly the working class' mass standpoint and viewpoint and Marxism-Leninism, our entire Party which is determined to rely upon the toiling masses, rouse their consciousness, and develop their boundless creativeness, will certainly take our socialist revolution and national reunification to a glorious success.

Principles and Methods of Revolutionary Action

The victory of the revolution depends primarily on a correct determination of the general orientation and strategic objective, as well as the specific orientation and objective for each period. But just as important as defining the orientation and objective is the problem of how to carry them into effect once such decisions have been made. What road should be followed? What forms should be adopted? What measures should be used? Experience has shown that a revolutionary movement may mark time, or even fail, not for lack of clearly defined orientations and objectives, but essentially because there have been *no appropriate principles and methods of revolutionary action.*

Methods of revolutionary action are devised to defeat the enemy of the revolution, and in the most advantageous way, so that the revolution may attain its ends as quickly as possible. Here one also needs wisdom as well as courage; it is not only a science, but also an art.

Decisions over methods of revolutionary action require, more than in any other field, that the revolutionary maintain the highest creative spirit. Revolution is creation; it cannot succeed without imagination and ingenuity. There has never been nor will there ever be a unique formula for making a revolution that is suited to all situations. One given method may be adaptable to a certain

---

Written on the occasion of the 40th Anniversary of the establishment of the Indochinese Communist Party (1970).

country but unsuitable in another. A correct method in certain times and circumstances may be erroneous in other situations. Everything depends on the concrete historical conditions. Lenin said: "Marxism demands an absolutely *historical* examination of the question of the forms of struggle. To treat this question apart from the concrete historical situation betrays a failure to understand the rudiments of dialectical materialism . . . . To attempt to answer yes or no to the question whether any particular means of struggle should be used, without making a detailed examination of the concrete situation of the given moment at the given stage of its development, means completely to abandon the Marxist position."(1)

A method or form of struggle can be considered best and most appropriate only when it fully satisfies the requirements of a given concrete situation, is thoroughly suited to the conditions in which it is applied, raises the courage of the revolutionary and progressive forces and rouses them to action, permits a thorough exploitation of the enemy's weaknesses, and for all these reasons, is likely to bring about the greatest success possible, given the relation of forces prevailing at the moment.

As a result of more than a century of revolutionary struggle, the international proletariat has amassed a great wealth of valuable experience. If one has mastered the concrete historical perspective and has taken the peculiar traits of one's country into full account, then the knowledge gained about revolutionary experiences in other nations allows for greater revolutionary inventiveness in one's own country. While carrying on the struggle, our Party knows how to enrich its fund of revolutionary knowledge and develop continuously its imagination and skill in political leadership—not only by constantly assessing, summing up, and improving upon the experience gained in our revolution, but also through attentive, selective and careful study of the revolutionary experience acquired in other countries, with full attention paid to the specific conditions of the Vietnamese revolution.

It is a matter of principle that either in the daily policies or in the practice of revolutionary struggle, in whatever way and under whatever circumstances they are carried out, a revolutionary should never lose sight of the final goal. If one considers the fight for small daily gains and immediate targets as "everything" and views the final goal as "nothing" (" to sacrifice the future of the movement to the present"), then one displays the worst kind of opportunism which can only result in keeping the popular masses in eternal servitude.

However, it is by no means sufficient to comprehend only the final objective. While keeping firmly in mind the revolutionary goal, the art of revolutionary leadership lies in knowing how *to win judiciously step by step*. Revolution is the work of millions of popular masses standing up to overthrow the ruling classes, which command powerful means of violence together with other material and spiritual forces. That is why a revolution is always a long-term process. From the initial steps to the final victory, a revolution necessarily goes through many difficult and complex stages of struggle full of twists and bends, clearing one obstacle after another and gradually changing the relation of forces between the revolution and the counter-revolution until overwhelming superiority is achieved over the ruling classes. To push the enemy back and gain one success after another for the revolution, and proceed to the total defeat of the enemy and a complete victory for the revolution, is a law of revolutionary struggle.

Throughout the long road leading to the final goal, one should never fail to consider the concrete conditions of the struggle in each period. When and in what circumstances are the masses going into action? How are the various social forces aligned? What are the enemy's strong and weak points? How is he maneuvering and what are his aims? Lenin used to demand that the Communists carefully study and view with the greatest objectivity not only the situation at home but also all elements of international economics and politics, and the relation between all class forces within their country and throughout the world. Without taking full notice of all these factors of changing concrete reality, a revolutionary may at best perceive the ultimate objective of the struggle, but he will have no command over the means to achieve it. He will not find the ways, methods and practical means to reach that goal and may commit serious errors in his strategic and tactical guidance of the revolution.

Knowing how to win step by step in a judicious manner means that in various situations one sets the most appropriate concrete objectives and, on the strength of objective laws, directs the fight in such a way as to achieve the maximum success. This approach paves the way for further revolutionary advances and opens up certain prospects for ultimate victory. These steps have been taken in our revolution.

The triumph of the August Revolution would not have been possible had it not been preceded by the 1930-31 and 1936-39 movements, and the patriotic upsurge of 1940-45.

The greatest achievement of the 1930-31 movement—a gain that the subsequent atrocious white terror of the imperialists and feudalists failed to obliterate—lies in the fact that the proletariat, represented by our Party, asserted in practice the claim and ability to lead the revolution, and that it infused the peasantry with an unshakable faith in the proletariat. Thus the worker-peasant masses were inspired with confidence in their immense revolutionary stamina. The 1930-31 movement also exposed the adventurism, reformism, tendencies to compromise, vacillations and half-heartedness of the national bourgeoisie and petty bourgeoisie, as well as demonstrating the sound revolutionary line of the proletariat and the huge revolutionary capabilities of the workers and peasants. Furthermore, it revealed to our entire people the extremely reactionary nature of the landlord class and comprador bourgeoisie. That first successful step was decisively significant for the whole subsequent development of the revolution. In fact, had it not been for the fierce class conflicts of 1930-31 in which the peasants and workers displayed extraordinary revolutionary energy, the upsurge of 1936-39 would not have been possible.

The period of 1936-39, in which legal and semi-legal actions were coupled with clandestine and illegal activities, seldomly occurs in a colonial country. When the Popular Front came to power in France, the Party viewed this event as a favorable occasion to push the revolution one step forward. It was able to utilize this opportunity because it had built solid and fundamental combat positions beginning in 1930. Acting upon Lenin's recommendation, "concrete political tasks must be presented in concrete circumstances,"(2) the

Party set as the immediate tasks for the 1936-39 period the struggle against the reactionary colonialists (not as yet the defeat of colonialist rule as a whole), fascism and war, while demanding democratic liberties, a decent standard of living, and peace. The Party was fully aware that these demands were by no means the final goals, that one could never radically change the social order through reform. Only by eventually smashing the imperialist and feudalist rule through violence and winning power for the people would the revolutionary objective be achieved. However, Lenin himself said that without the democratic liberties brought about by the February Revolution of 1917 it would have been difficult to start the large-scale mass struggle that led to the October Revolution. We may refer in similar terms to the effect of the 1936-39 democratic movement on the subsequent development of the August Revolution. The intense mass agitation during this period was without precedent under French rule. Through a variety of flexible forms of organization and activity, including our utilization of the "chambers of people's representatives" and the "colonial councils" set up by the French colonists, the Party mobilized and gave political education to millions of people, especially workers and peasants. The political struggles swept through town and countryside. They spread from factories, plantations and mines to villages and hamlets and created conditions for leading the masses into the new, fierce battles of the 1940-45 period.

After the outbreak of the Second World War, the French colonialists capitulated and offered Indochina to the Japanese fascists, putting a two-fold yoke on our people's necks. During this period our Party held that oppression, exploitation and war would incite the people to ever more vigorous revolutionary action; the revolution would inevitably flare up. On President Ho Chi Minh's initiative, it founded the Viet Minh Front to bring together the broadest range of national democratic forces. At the same time, the Party began building revolutionary bases, and the first armed units started a "fight the French, drive out the Japanese" movement, expanded guerrilla warfare, and extended the partial insurrections. When, as the Party had foreseen, the Japanese betrayed the French, it made a quick shift and initiated a movement to resist the Japanese and save the nation. This was a period of seething and vigorous mass mobilization in which political forces developed intensively in all areas—rural and urban, plain and hill-forest—together with the armed revolutionary forces. Widespread preparations were made for the forthcoming general insurrection.

The glorious triumph of the August Revolution was not only the result of the national liberation movement of the 1940-45 period but also the outcome of a revolutionary process fostered and prepared through the two full dress rehearsals of 1930-31 and 1936-39.

A revolutionary struggle unfolds steadily in all spheres of social life—political, economic and cultural. Hence, constant success in each area of combat requires the mobilization and organization of the masses to undermine the enemy's successive policies and thwart every one of his schemes and maneuvers. It is necessary to point out and attain at all costs every objective possible in a given period or during a specific battle, thereby impelling the movement forward and bringing it to a higher level. Nothing succeeds like success, and each success in a given field stimulates the struggle in other fields. Starting from scratch, the movement develops to ever higher levels, driving the enemy from pillar to post, consolidating its partial gains and relentlessly expanding the revolutionary battlefield in the direction of total victory. In the Vietnamese revolution, the movement toward the seizure of power shows the distinguishing feature of an evolution from partial to general insurrections. This is indeed an application of the method of "winning step by step" to the specific conditions of our revolution.

In short, this method expresses the unity between steadiness of purpose and a clear understanding of changing concrete reality. It is the art of dialectically combining firmness of principle with flexibility of policy and applying to the work of revolutionary leadership the law of development from gradual changes to "leaps." One must show boldness and determination in setting new tasks and devising new plans. One must be able to foresee, at least in a broad outline, the results of forthcoming actions and of all possible trends of development of the objective situation. In practice, new factors and possibilities keep emerging, so that one must take them into account by changing or correcting actions and quickly working out new plans to insure that the strategic and tactical guidance keeps pace with the changing situation. Only then is it possible to pursue the fight without hesitation, a gradual process—interspersed with leaps, big and small, in the revolutionary movement and in the relations of forces—toward the crucial leap to final victory.

Lenin firmly opposed subjectivism and voluntarism, as well as all forms of political passivity. He required that the Communist parties work out their policies and tactics in such a way as to "combine complete scientific sobriety in the analysis of the objective state of affairs and the objective course of evolution with the most emphatic recognition of the importance of the revolutionary energy, revolutionary creative genius and revolutionary initiative of the masses."(3)

A revolution is not a *coup d'etat;* it is not the outcome of plots. It is the work of the masses. Hence, *the mobilization and rallying of the mass forces, the establishment and expansion of the political army of the revolution, is a fundamental and decisive problem.* This task must be approached in a vigorous and sustained way both throughout the period when a revolutionary situation has not yet appeared and the period when such a situation has arisen and matured. To realize this task, one must mingle and be active with the masses in everyday life, even within enemy organizations. One must keep abreast of the situation in the enemy's camp as well as ours, correctly appraise all schemes, moves and capabilities of the enemy, accurately assess all changes developing in his ranks, and at the same time be fully aware of the state of mind, wishes and potential power of the masses. In this way one can put forward appropriately incisive and timely slogans which will arouse the broad masses to action, direct them from lower to higher forms of struggle, ceaselessly heighten their political consciousness and help expand the army of the revolution both in scope and in depth.

On the road to the seizure of power, the only weapon available to the revolutionary masses is organization. The hallmark of the revolutionary movement led by the proletariat is its high organizational standards. All activities seeking to bring the masses to the point where they will rise up and overthrow the ruling classes revolve around this point: organize, organize, organize. The purpose of political propaganda is the organization of the masses. Only by organizing them in some way will conditions be created for educating them and building up the immense strength of the revolution. Once organized, their power will significantly increase. The masses are to be organized for combat. Conversely, through combat they are further organized and educated, and the revolutionary forces are expanded. Therefore, propaganda, organization and struggle go hand in hand and have as a common purpose the formation and growth of the political army of the masses in preparation for the decisive leap.

In every period, our Party has resourcefully organized the masses by all appropriate means and in all suitable forms. The Party knows how to interest the masses in current political events, big or small, and mobilize them to drive the enemy into confusion and passivity while building and expanding our own forces. Even when its activity requires the strictest secrecy, the Party has established varied, broad and flexible organizational forms to rally the masses for revolutionary action and guide them from lower to higher forms of struggle, thereby educating them and enlarged the revolutionary ranks. Always taking illegal action as its foundation, the Party skillfully combines it with all possibilities for legal action. In a given situation the Party may start an all-out drive for legality. It does not deceive itself with any illusions about the "legal" road to power nor spread such illusions among the masses, but seeks to provide a broader scope for the education and rallying of the masses and to augment the influence of the revolution. At such times the Party must oppose indecision and timidity just as it must guard against and combat legalism, prevent the violation of its principle of organizational secrecy, and continue building and expanding the Party and the core organizations of the masses. If one does not guard against and fight legalism in time, this situation may lead to very dangerous events, the enemy attacks the revolution, and the Party has to change quickly and completely to illegal action.

Organization and struggle, struggle and organization, again struggle—one battle leads to another. Once the masses have gone into battle, they will grow more politically conscious, and their experience will show them the truth and teach them which way to act—hence, the particular importance of *slogans*. The art of giving strategic and tactical guidance to the revolution while directing a struggle is most significantly expressed in sharp-edged and relevant slogans that keep pace with the situation.

One should not hold the oversimplified view that economic slogans are reformist while only political ones are revolutionary. There can be political slogans with a reformist character and economic ones that carry a revolutionary content. The question is: when, in what connection, and with what aim is a given slogan put forward. A genuine revolutionary party that is decisively devoted to the final goal of the revolution can in one way or another put the seal of the revolution on all slogans and all forms of organization and struggle, including minimally political ones that are necessary for rallying the masses in a situation not yet favorable for all-out revolutionary actions.

Throughout all periods and especially the period preceding the August Revolution of 1945, the Party has skillfully combined action and propaganda slogans to link immediate targets with fundamental objectives. A slogan relevant to a concrete situation makes it possible to arouse a whole movement. One vivid example is the slogan, "Get the stocks of rice and stamp our famine," put forward by our Party in the preparatory period for the August Revolution. It was issued at a time of terrible famine in Bac Bo and northern Trung Bo. It answered the most urgent aspirations of the masses, fomenting their anger and hatred and arousing them to advance with intense revolutionary fervor toward insurrection and the seizure of power.

A distinction should be drawn between propaganda and action slogans to avoid involving the masses in decisive battles either too soon or too late. Both kinds of slogans must continually be altered to conform to the evolution of the struggle. Action slogans closely connected with the daily effort must especially show extreme flexibility, even changing with each hour. As the situation develops, one must gradually raise the level of action slogans, and when the right time comes turn previous propaganda slogans into ones for direct and resolute action. It is dangerous for the revolution to lead the masses into decisive battles either too late or too soon. Under all circumstances, the most important and basic guarantee against blunders is a thorough grasp of concrete reality, both in general analysis and in every decision for action. In a revolutionary period, events develop very rapidly and intricately. Lenin pointed out: "The substitution of the abstract for the concrete is one of the greatest and most dangerous sins in the revolution."(4) He castigated those who, at a sharp turn in history, fail to adapt themselves to the new situation and cling to old slogans which were correct yesterday but are meaningless today.

For a revolution to break out and be successful, a *revolutionary situation must prevail.* A revolutionary situation is the product of the combination of a series of necessary, objective and subjective factors. One should guard against the tendency to wait passively for the revolution, as well as the hot-headed inclination to "skip intermediate stations."

Before and after the First World War, revolutionary situations and the outbreaks and triumphs of revolutions were generally connected in one way or another with the world wars provoked by imperialism. However, one should not draw the conclusion that war is either the natural source or necessary condition of revolution and that consequently one should wait for war to start before making a revolution. A revolution is first and foremost the result of class contradictions that are exacerbated to the extreme in a given country. Formerly, when imperialist wars were inevitable, they had the objective effect of accelerating the revolutionary crises in various countries. Taking advantage of this situation, the Communists advocated the "transformation of imperialist wars into revolutionary civil wars."

The present international situation differs radically from that before and after the First World War. Today, the world socialist system and the forces battling against imperialism to create a socialist society are shaping the essential content, orientation and characteristic features of the historical development of society. The possibility of breaking the weak links in the remaining parts of the imperialist chain has increased to an unprecedented degree at a time when it becomes practically feasible to prevent a world war. The fundamental interest of the proletariat, the people and the nations of the world lies in *safeguarding world peace while promoting the revolution in various countries*. These two objectives are organically linked together; each is the premise of the other. Both are perfectly attainable once the Communists, thoroughly conscious of the strategically offensive position of the world revolution, are successful in setting up a united front bringing together all currents of the world revolution, all forces fighting for peace, national independence, democracy and socialism, and are resolved to crush all imperialist aggression, repel every one of imperialism's belligerent moves and schemes, drive it back step by step, destroy it piecemeal, and eventually overthrow it entirely.

The revolution in the South of our country is an example of a correct way to march forward. It proves that a revolution can still break out and be victorious in the absence of a world war, and even as world peace has to be defended. Indeed, the intensification of the anti-imperialist revolution, far from being incompatible with the defense of peace, is proving in practice a fundamental way to attack imperialism and thus effectively safeguard world peace. Conversely, the prevention of world war and the defense of peace is also a very important way to assault imperialism and create more favorable objective conditions for the progress of the revolution in all countries.

The South Vietnamese revolution also proves that a fascist dictatorship cannot prevent the outbreak of a revolution. When the puppet administration in the South resorted to the most barbarous fascist measures against the people, this meant that they had suffered a crucial defeat in the political field. An explosive situation was developing which would surely break out into a revolution, as it did.

The existence of a revolutionary situation means that the problem of the seizure of power is immediately at hand. The manner of winning power depends on the specific conditions of each country. However, under all circumstances the only road to power lies in revolution, not reform.

Revolution is the climax of class struggle. It is always accomplished through a violent confrontation of the oppressed and ruling classes which settles the problem of political power. Violence may manifest and exert itself in various forms. In a nutshell, we may say, revolutionary violence must rely on two kinds of force, armed and political, and include two forms of struggle, military and political, and a combination of these two. The experience of the Vietnamese revolution demonstrates that in a successful revolution one must have armed forces in addition to political forces, and must know how to carry out clever military and political action according to the concrete situation prevailing in a given place and time. If the revolutionary forces, including the armed forces, are not prepared, they will not be able to resist the fierce onslaught of the enemy. However, the use of violence does not rest solely with the armed forces, nor does it only assume the form of military struggle. Political forces and political struggle are indispensable, for success cannot be won by military action and armed forces alone. It goes without saying that not all forms of political struggle are violent. The only actions that may be considered so are the *revolutionary actions undertaken by the masses outside the bounds of the state laws of the ruling class and directly aimed at overthrowing the ruling class* and seizing power for the people, once the question of political power has been raised. Revolutionary violence aimed at overthrowing the ruling class must necessarily be the *violence of the broad masses* who are oppressed and exploited. Under the leadership of the Party, they can display their strength and determination in countless ways. The best and most revolutionary method is the one that can create and organize those forms of violence most appropriate for the circumstances and can successfully mobilize the power of the masses against the ruling class, bringing about victory for the revolution under the most favorable conditions. Reluctance in starting a military struggle when the need arises or engaging in such an effort under unfavorable circumstances is a serious mistake.

In the August Revolution, our Party creatively applied the law of violent revolution and insurrection to gain power. The August Revolution combined political and military struggle. It combined elaborate preparation of the political and military forces with quick seizure of the opportune moment for inciting the masses to overthrow the imperialists and feudalists. Originating and developing in the vast revolutionary movement of the masses, the armed units for national salvation and liberation, whose prestige far outstripped their numbers and the extent of their engagements, had contributed significantly to the upsurge of the patriotic masses in the period from 1941—45. After the Soviet Union's resounding victory over the Kwangtung army of the Japanese fascists had forced them into an unconditional surrender, the Party quickly seized that unique opportunity to launch a general insurrection. It relied on the political forces of the broad rural and urban masses in combination with the revolutionary armed forces, smashing the enemy's key organs in the capital and other cities, liquidating his whole administrative network in the countryside, and seized power throughout the country.

One must have a thorough grasp of revolutionary violence, build overwhelming superiority for the revolution, and unite the broadest masses of the people on the basis of a truly firm and strong worker-peasant alliance. At the same time, one must strive to divide and isolate the enemy to the utmost, cripple his power of resistance, smash the state apparatus of the ruling class, and establish the people's power.

Besides the preparation of political and military forces, a very important problem revealed by the experience of all revolutions is the *seizure of the opportune moment.* This moment may be brought about either by revolutionary forces at home or by conditions abroad. Without sufficient revolutionary forces, it is impossible either to create a favorable opportunity or to take timely advantage of one should it develop. Therefore, it is crucial to exert a sustained effort to tip the scales in our favor and achieve decisive superiority regarding both the position and strength of the revolution. When will the fire of the revolution flare up? What spark will set off the powder keg? Once the revolution has acquired firm position and strength, and the enemy has been driven to the wall, the daily political and social life will supply us with every favorable opportunity and circumstance to encourage a great movement. The decision only depends on the leaders' perspicacity and political ability. Lenin remarked that history as a whole, and the history of revolutions in particular, is always richer in content, more varied, multiform, lively and ingenious, than is imagined by even the best parties and the most class-conscious vanguards of the most advanced classes. In the course of the revolution, it often suffices that the leaders fully possess a fundamental orientation, certain basic factors and conditions, and the boldness to act. As action evolves, possibilities and trends of development will reveal themselves. The boundless creative power of the masses who make history will provide us with the orientation and methods for solving all practical problems.

The Working Class and Socialist Industrialization

Comrades and friends,

On behalf of the Central Committee of the Vietnam Worker's Party I extend my warmest and most cordial greetings to the Second National Congress of the Vietnam Federation of Trade Unions and through it to the glorious working class all over our country.

Also on behalf of the Vietnam Workers' Party, the Vietnamese working class and people, I warmly welcome the delegates of

The World Federation of Trade Unions,

The trade unions of the brother socialist countries,

The fraternal French General Confederation of Labour, and the trade union organizations of the friendly Afro-Asian countries, who have come to take part in the present session of our National Congress of Trade Unions, and through you convey my greetings of solidarity and my best wishes to the working class and people of the brother socialist countries, the fraternal French working class and people, the working class and people of the Afro-Asian countries, and the working class and toiling people all over the world.

Comrades,

The present Congress is held at a time when the situation of the revolution in our country is undergoing changes of great importance.

Speech at the Second National Congress of the Vietnam Federation of Trade Unions held in February 1961.

It is held immediately after the successful conclusion of the Third National Congress of our Party. In application of the universal principles of Marxism-Leninism to the practice of Vietnamese revolution, the Party Congress has mapped out a correct line for the working class and all the people of our country to strive to take the North rapidly, vigorously and steadily to socialism and struggle for the liberation of our beloved South, to advance toward the peaceful reunification of our motherland on the basis of independence and democracy, to build a peaceful, united, independent, democratic, strong and prosperous Vietnam, and effectively to contribute to the strengthening of the socialist camp and to the safeguarding of peace in South-East Asia and the world.

In the light of the resolutions of the Party Congress, people throughout our country are enthusiastically and resolutely fulfilling the historical tasks set by it.

In the North, the socialist revolution and construction have recorded big achievements and are growing vigorously. We are entering a new period on the road to socialism.

In the South, the revolutionary struggle for national liberation of our compatriots is gaining ground with buoyant mettle and shaking the gloomy U.S.-Diem regime to the root. Though still encountering numerous difficulties and obstacles this struggle has an extremely bright prospect.

Our working class is the class that leads the revolution throughout our country. History has entrusted it with the glorious mission of liberating the nation and leading our country to socialism and communism. In the light of the resolutions of the Party National Congress, the present Congress of trade unions will certainly show the working class and trade union organizations the practical tasks and work to be done to transform the Party's line into the will, determination and deeds of the broad masses of workers, employees, and mobilize all of them to work heart and soul for the successful fulfillment of their glorious historical mission.

Dear comrades,

The present task of building socialism in the North is of most decisive significance for the whole development of the Vietnamese revolution and for the struggle for national reunification.

Since the restoration of peace and the complete liberation of the North we have stepped into the period of transition to socialism. We have completed the economic rehabilitation, the Three-Year Plan for economic transformation and development and for cultural development (1958-60) was successfully achieved, bringing about big revolutionary changes in the economy and life in the North of our country.

The socialist transformation of agriculture, handicrafts, private capitalist industry and commerce and small traders has won successes of decisive importance. Eighty-five per cent of peasant households are members of low-level agricultural co-operatives, 87 per cent of artisans and 82 per cent of small traders have joined co-operative organizations of various forms, the private capitalist industry and commerce as a whole have been transformed into joint state-private undertakings or co-operatives. The system of exploitation of man by man has been basically abolished and the system of individual ownership of the small producers which occupied a great part of the national economy has been turned into the system of socialist collective ownership.

On the basis of the new relations of production, the industrial and agricultural production in the past few years have also developed rapidly. The average annual rate of increase of the value of agricultural output in the Three-Year Plan was 6 per cent, of industry 21.7 per cent, and of industry turning out means of production alone 35 per cent.

The old agriculture with a monoculture is being gradually turned into a comprehensive agriculture with many branches, craft and many varieties of products.

Our industry consisted in the past only of a few small repair workshops, raw material extracting enterprises, and enterprises for preliminary processing of products; but we have now built up a light industry capable of supplying our people with the greater part of commodities. The first undertakings of heavy industry such as engineering, metallurgy, electricity, fuel, building materials, etc. have been initially set up and are developing. The industrial ratio in the aggregate value of industrial and agricultural output has increased from 30.4 per cent in 1957 to 41.3 per cent in 1960.

Efforts have been made to speed up the development of culture, education, science and technology, the training and fostering of technicians and skilled workers. The working class in the North has swollen rapidly. The material and cultural life of our people has been substantially improved.

These great achievements are proofs of the superiority of the socialist regime in the North, at the same time they constitute a great encouragement for our countrymen in the South. They create favourable conditions for the socialist laws widely to bring into play their effects, enabling the North to advance more rapidly and more powerfully on the road of socialist development.

These successes have been obtained thanks first of all to the patriotism and socialist ardour of our working class and people, and also thanks to the wholehearted assistance of the working classes and peoples of the brother socialist countries, first and foremost the Soviet Union and China. Availing ourselves of this opportunity we sincerely thank the working classes and peoples of the brother countries for their disinterested and generous aid.

At present, the socialist construction in the North is entering a new period.

The resolution of the Third National Congress of our Party has pointed out that when socialist transformation scores decisive successes socialist construction and industrialization will become our central task. It is precisely our Five-Year Plan (1961-1965) that opens up this period. The principal aim of this plan is to build the material and technical basis of socialism, carry out socialist industrialization and complete socialist transformation.

At present, we are facing a big contradiction in the process of the development of the socialist construction in the North. We have established advanced relations of production—socialist relations of production with two important forms of ownership: entire people's ownership and collective ownership, but the material and technical basis of the national economy is still very weak. Productivity is low as production still relies mostly on manual labour. The ratio of the output of modern industry in the national economy amount to only 20 per cent. With an improved but still backward farming method, agriculture which depends a great deal on nature occupies the greater part in our production. This situation is setting the economy of the North an urgent task: rapidly to accomplish socialist industrialization, and to build the material and technical foundations of socialism. A socialist economy cannot be built on the basis of a backward manual production but necessarily on the basis of a large mechanized industry. Only with a large mechanized industry can we rapidly raise labour productivity, ensure continuous enlarged reproduction and bring socialism to a complete success.

If we do not build up for our national economy a modern material and technical basis, and equip the various branches of industry, agriculture, capital construction, communications and transport, etc. with machines, to replace manual labour by mechanized labour, our economy cannot, in essence, be considered as a socialist economy.

That is precisely why our Party regards industrialization as the central task throughout the period of transition to socialism.

We have every reason to put forth the task of industrialization of our country. We have enough natural resources and labouring power. Besides, we have the powerful socialist camp with an advanced industry. With the assistance and close co-operation of our brother countries, first and foremost, the great Soviet Union and great China, the valiant working class and toiling people of our country will certainly be able to establish rapidly a national industry in accordance with our possibilities and conditions.

Our policy on industrialization consists in building a balanced and modern socialist economy which combines industry with agriculture and which has heavy industry as its basis, in giving priority to the rational development of heavy industry and at the same time striving to develop agriculture and light industry aimed at transforming our backward agricultural country into a country endowed with a modern industry, a modern agriculture, and an advanced culture and science.

To provide modern technique for the various branches of national economy it is definitely indispensable to build a heavy industry with a machine-building industry as its core. At present, an important part of our machines and equipment are supplied by the brother countries. However, for the basic and lasting benefit of our economy, we must gradually move toward self-supply for the great part of machines and equipment required by various branches of the national economy, otherwise we cannot have the initiative in the development of our national economy. Therefore in carrying out industrialization we must unfailingly stick to the principle of giving priority to the development of heavy industry.

Our industrial system must be built rationally. We need not necessarily set up all the branches of heavy industry, only the basic ones that our country must necessarily build and has conditions to develop in order to provide a material and technical basis required by industry, agriculture, capital construction, transport and communications, etc., and to direct these branches in satisfying the people's requirements in food, housing, education and circulation.

We do not have to wait until heavy industry is in full bloom before stepping up light industry and food industry. While our heavy industry is not yet developed, thanks to the assistance and co-operation of the brother socialist countries we can even base ourselves on our natural resources and our people's requirements to develop light industry and food industry, ensure the supply of staple commodities to the people and the requirements of exports.

The aid and co-operation of the brother countries is of paramount importance to our industrialization, however we must not rely too much on it but mainly on our own efforts, on the development of our national economy, on the endeavour and sacrifices of our people. We proceed from an agricultural economy to carry out industrialization. Consequently agriculture must serve as the basis for the development of industry and in its turn the developed industry becomes the main force, the lever for the development of all branches of the national economy.

Agriculture is a source supplying foodstuffs and raw materials to industry, and a market for industrial goods. Our tropical agriculture is an important source of exports in exchange for machines and equipment needed by industry. The developed agriculture also contributes to accumulating funds for industrialization.

Industry will have no basis to develop rapidly and favourably if agriculture does not develop all-sidedly, vigorously and steadily.

Vice-versa, if industry is not developed agriculture cannot expand sufficiently and vigorously.

At present, agricultural co-operativization at lower levels is completed in the main, but the material and technical basis of agriculture is still weak, labour productivity has increased but a little, as a result the co-operatives are not yet firmly consolidated. Only by expanding agricultural production on a large scale, using improved farming implements, then gradually modern machines and technique, can socialist production relations in the countryside be firmly established, and agricultural production develop rapidly. Without a developed industry to supply improved farming implements, agricultural machines, chemical fertilizers, to build irrigation works and expand transport and communications, etc. it would be impossible to set up a modern agriculture. Of course agriculture should not wait for industry, but strive to establish and strengthen the mode of collective labour and make the best of all existing possibilities of the new productive forces created by collective labour to further step up agricultural production.

Industry and agriculture are the two basic branches of production that form the unified structure of the national economy. They are closely inter-related, rely on and impel each other and serve each other's growth.

The main task of agriculture is to ensure the supply of foodstuffs to the people and also to serve the development of industry. In return industry also has the task of serving the development of agriculture in producing means of production and consumer goods. Only in this way can industry and agriculture develop rapidly and favourably. Therefore in carrying out industrialization we must endeavour to develop both industry and agriculture and should not make light of any of them.

To implement socialist industrialization a question of prime importance to be solved is socialist accumulation. Without accumulation it will be impossible to carry out enlarged reproduction on a large scale and at a quick tempo, and to build a modern industry and modern agriculture. Production and economy are the key sources for the accumulation of funds.

In the last analysis the wealth accumulated comes from productive labour. With our manual labour, backward technique and low productivity we cannot accumulate and concentrate big funds for socialist industrialization. For that reason, we have now no other way than relying ourselves on the people's revolutionary movement, and on the enthusiastic efforts of the entire people in working to increase productivity through improvement of organization of labour and of technique, making full use of the possibilities existing in production, at the same time efforts must be made to practise strict economy, resolutely to fight waste and corruption, to make use of manpower, materials and finance in the most rational way so as to be able to concentrate the necessary funds for socialist industrialization. Only by accumulating capital can we gradually endow the national economy with new technique and replace the backward manual labour by modern mechanization having a high productivity which will enable us to make bigger accumulations for the acceleration of the industrialization of our country.

Socialist industrialization is the solely correct road of development in North Vietnam. It is the only means to step up production, to rapidly expand the industrial branches to make the northern people enjoy a new, abundant and happy life and transform the North into a firm and strong base of the struggle for national reunification.

Industrialization tallies with the interests and cherished aspirations of all workers, farmers and intellectuals in our country.

The more advanced industrialization the more swollen the rank of the Vietnamese working class, the more improved the workers' livelihood and the more strengthened the leadership of the working class over the people's democratic power and other social activities.

Socialist industrialization raises the value of the peasants' labour, increases the possibility of the toiling peasants to successfully combat the age-old terrible natural calamities, improve the peasants' livelihood and consolidate the worker-peasant alliance.

Socialist industrialization affords our brain workers a favourable occasion to raise their scientific and technical standard, fully develop their capabilities, put their knowledge to the service of the people and of socialist construction and swell their rank with new intellectuals of worker, peasant and other labourer stock.

Therefore, devotedly to carry out socialist industrialization is the most important task of the working class and toiling people of the North.

A trade union is a broad mass organization of the working class; all its activities should be aimed at serving this central task.

Lenin said that in general a trade union is a school of communism, and in particular it should be a school managing socialist industry (and gradually managing agriculture) for all workers and then for all toiling people.

At present, in the North the working class leads the state and economic development and transformation. The exploiting class exists no more. The workers have become masters of factories, mines, construction sites, state farms, etc. To play this role, our working class must satisfactorily manage the economy and the enterprises, develop production rapidly, raise further labour productivity, turn out more social wealth of good quality and at low price, in order to satisfy the ever increasing needs of the society. To this end, the working class must *study to grasp modern technology, and the technique of production of modern industry.* Lenin said that to lead the management satisfactorily it is necessary to grasp the technique of production to a high degree and to possess a certain scientific standard.

The trade union must organize the study for workers and help them study; it must find every means to raise their technical and cultural level. The cadres of the organizational section and the trade union must also study to firmly acquaint themselves with the knowledge and technique of production in order effectively to take part in the management of production and of the economy, in the elaboration and fulfilment of state plans, and to carry out their task of economic management school for the working class.

Over the last few years, thanks to the efforts made by the working class and people of our country and to the wholehearted assistance of the brother countries, we have built in the North 172 centrally-run state enterprises and more than 600 local enterprises. This is a very great achievement. However, owing to the low technical standard of our cadres and workers, the yield of machines and equipment is still low, averaging less than 50 per cent, the duration of machines is not fully elaborated and correctly applied, thus causing damage and waste to machines and equipment, and even labour accident. These are mistakes and shortcomings which must be overcome.

A modern industry requires a scientific labour organization and management and a severe discipline, however our competence in these respects is still low. In our enterprises, the management of labour is not satisfactory, discipline is loose, waste of time prevails, responsibility is lacking in the protection of public property, waste and corruption are still rife; irrational regulations in the management of enterprises are not corrected in time; co-ordination is still loose between centrally-run enterprises and branches and the local ones; the business accounting system is not fully carried out, the elaboration of economic targets and technical norms is not widely applied in all enterprises.

Over the last few years, a campaign for the participation of factory and office workers in the management of enterprises has made it possible to raise their sense of being masters and has initially bettered the regulations in the organization and management of these enterprises. At present in state enterprises, congresses have been held, involving a great many office and factory workers, to discuss the situation of production and the carrying out of the plans. These are good changes. From now on, we must develop the success achieved in order constantly to improve our management, correctly apply the principle of democratic centralism in this management, fully apply the regime put forth by our Party, consisting in the management of the enterprise by the director under the leadership of the Party committee, with the participation of the workers.

The working class is duty-bound to transform the society and to this end it must constantly transform itself. The advance of industrialization will swell the rank of the working class by the admittance of new workers who were peasants, pupils, poor townsfolk or belonged to other labouring sections. This is an inevitable phenomenon. But these new workers bring in with them non-proletarian ideas of their sections of origin. The factory and office workers who lived in the old society have been badly influenced by the thinkings of the exploiting class and other non-proletarian ideologies. That is why an important regular task of the trade union is to raise the socialist consciousness of the working class, and inculcate upon it new socialist ideology and ethics, such as the sense of being masters, love of labour and respect of public property, collectivism, mutual class solidarity, respect of labour discipline, etc., the trade union must energetically struggle against the influence of bourgeois thinking, the petty-bourgeois ideology, the remnants of feudalist ideology and other non-proletarian thinkings. The trade union must help intellectuals transform themselves further in order to become the true intelligentsia of the working class.

With our socialist consciousness and the revolutionary mettle of the working class, we must urge the working class enthusiastically to take part in the *patriotic emulation movement, fulfil and over-fulfil the state plan for economic and cultural development*. The emulation movement is an important method to draw the majority of the masses into the management of production and the state. Through this movement we can rapidly heighten the sense of being masters and the socialist consciousness of the workers, raise their technical standard, fully develop their positiveness and creativeness and improve the management of production and of the enterprises in every respect. This movement is an important method to accelerate socialist construction. At present, the workers are engaged in an emulation drive to become front-rank workers, teams and brigades; this drive has brought out many emulation heroes and outstanding fighters who have displayed a great sacrificing spirit, heroism and creative labour of the working class; many innovations and initiatives have been introduced to improve organization and technique, rationalize production, raise labour productivity. Our trade union must speed up the emulation drive and transform it into a more boiling and powerful mass movement, aimed mainly at rationalizing production and improving technique. We must see to it that the innovations and inventions be popularized rapidly among the masses and we will urge the great majority of masses of workers to study and follow the examples of front-rank workers and units.

41

A good organization of and leadership over the emulation movement will bring about a high movement of production among factory and office workers and vouch for the success of our plans.

Parallel to the heightening of the socialist consciousness and revolutionary mettle of the workers, our trade unions should *pay due attention to the material and spiritual interests of the working class.* This is also an important factor to accelerate production. Under our regime, the improvement of the material and cultural life of the toiling people is the greatest concern of our Party and state. We have made great effort to raise the living standard of the factory and office workers: to find employment for hundreds of thousands of people, improve the wage system, organize public amenities and social insurance, etc. But we must understand that at present the living standard of our workers as well as of our people is still low and meets with many difficulties caused mainly by the low level of our production. Only by developing production and rapidly raising labour productivity, is it possible to improve rapidly our livelihood. In leading the state, our working class must pay due attention not only to the immediate interests of the whole country but also to its abiding interests, not only to the interests of the working class but also to the common interests of scores of millions of people of the North and of the country at large. To do away with the poverty of our country, we have no other alternative than to rely on our own powers, to build the country frugally and painstakingly and make the necessary accumulation of capital for socialist industrialization. We must see to the improvement of the people's life and the accumulation of funds for economic and industrial development. Our trade union must make the workers realize clearly their immediate and permanent interests, partial and common interests in order to improve their livelihood and develop their spirit of thrift and sacrifice in struggle so as to build up a bright future. On the other hand, it must develop its effectiveness in the mobilization and organization of the masses to improve their livelihood, to contribute to the betterment of the wage system, bonuses, to take part in the elaboration of hygiene regulation and safety in production, protection of labour, amenities and social insurance, improvement of food, clothing, housing, working, entertainment, housekeeping and children's nursing of the workers and to find every way and means to overcome the difficulties encountered by factory and public workers in their livelihood.

Comrades,

In exerting its efforts to build socialism in the North our working class cannot forget that half of our country is not yet liberated. In the South our people, including the workers, are living in a state of burning heat and boiling water. The imperialists and their henchman, Ngo Dinh Diem, are carrying out a most savage fascist policy to turn our South into a U.S. colony and military base and are plotting to rekindle the war and to wreck peace in Indo-China, South-East Asia and the world. But they meet with a strong opposition on the part of our southern compatriots as a whole.

For nearly nine years now, meetings, demonstrations, parades have been held in South Vietnam, involving more than two million people, to protest against the policies of repression, terror, wage cut, dismissal of workers, land grabbing, herding of the population, house eviction, setting up of "prosperity zones" and "agricultural settlements"; to oppose forced recruitment of labourers, pressganging of soldiers, subscriptions of money, fines; to protest against Diem's dictatorship and nepotism and to compel him to resign, etc. In these political struggles the Diem clique have killed hundreds of people by very barbarous means such as disembowelling and beheading. In many localities the inhabitants have armed themselves against terrorist raids launched by the U.S.-Diem clique.

At present, blood is shed everyday on half of our beloved country. We vehemently denounce before world public opinion the unheard-of bloody crimes of the U.S.-Diem clique. We warmly acclaim the heroic struggle of the working class, toiling people and all our campatriots in the South, who are now highlighting their heroic revolutionary tradition, stubbornly fighting against the U.S. imperialists and their henchman, Ngo Dinh Diem, demanding peace, democratic liberties, improvement of the people's livelihood, independence and peaceful reunification of the Fatherland. At the same time we are duty-bound to support by all means the struggle of the working class and toiling people in the South, to stubbornly fight for the rapid peaceful reunification of the country so that North and South will be united. Despite their mad actions in the end the U.S.-Diem clique will meet with a shameful failure. Our beloved Fatherland will be completely reunified.

The U.S. imperialists commit crimes not only in the south of our country but everywhere in the world. In Laos, our neighbour, together with their henchmen they are unleashing a civil war which seriously threatens peace in Indo-China and South-East Asia, we therefore vehemently protest against this scheme of invasion and brazen intervention of the U.S. imperialists. We energetically support the just struggle waged against the U.S. imperialists and their henchmen by the Laotian people to re-establish peace in Laos and take that country to the road of peace, neutrality and national harmony.

Of late, the U.S. imperialists and Belgian colonialists, under the cover of the U.N.O. flag, and their henchmen, have perpetrated a new crime in the Congo, killing Premier Lumumba and two other outstanding leaders of the Congolese people. Our working class and people at large are very indignant and condemn their acts. We energetically support the stubborn struggle of the Congolese people for freedom and complete national independence.

The situation in South Vietnam, Laos and the Congo has laid bare the aggressive and bellicose face of the U.S. imperialists. At present, the U.S. imperialists are the cruellest enemy of our people and the world's people. The Vietnamese working class and people have the duty to spearhead their struggle, together with the world's working class and people, against U.S. imperialism and to energetically denounce and smash all their dark designs.

Our working class is part of the great army of international proletariat. The success achieved by the Vietnamese working class is not taken apart from the support and sympathy of the working class and people of the world, first and foremost of the socialist camp. Therefore, it is an international duty for our working class to constantly strengthen its solidarity with the working class of socialist countries, of countries in Asia and Africa and in the world, to actively struggle for peace and peaceful co-existence, to wholeheartedly support all revolutionary struggle waged by the world's working class and people for peace, national independence, democracy and socialism. A fact of paramount importance for the international communist and workers' movement during the past period was the brilliant success of the Meeting of 81 communist and workers' parties in the world. This Meeting has reviewed the rich experiences gained in the struggle waged by the workers and toiling people in the world over the last years; it has thoroughly analysed the current international situation and has outlined the correct path along which to step up the future revolutionary struggle of the world's working class and people.

Our working class and people are extremely jubilant over the great success scored by the Meeting and pledge themselves to correctly implement the resolutions of the Meeting corresponding to the particular situation of Vietnam.

At present, the world is following with great admiration and esteem the wonder made by the Soviet working class and scientists in the successful launching from a man-made satellite, of an interplanetary station to Venus. This success has opened for mankind the prospect of conquering the cosmos.

With a boundless joy and enthusiasm, we beg to convey our best wishes and congratulations to the Soviet Communist Party, government, working class and scientists.

Comrades,

The tasks lying ahead are very glorious but very heavy. Without a developed and powerful trade-union organization, it is impossible to fulfil these tasks. We must endeavour to develop the trade union more powerfully, consolidate it ideologically and organizationally, raise its position in every branch of social activities so as to transform it into a firm basis for the Party and state. We must thoroughly acquaint the trade union with production and link all its activities to production. The trade union must be brought close to the workers, learn from them and heed their opinions and aspirations. We must strive to overcome bureaucracy in trade unions which consists in standing aloof from the masses and constantly remind T.U. cadres of Lenin's behest that the trade union is not an administrative organization, but a mass organization, an educational organization. The correct method of work of the trade union can only be education and persuasion of the masses and not commandism toward the masses.

In all work, the trade union must follow the mass line, broaden democracy, foster the activists and through them step up T.U. work. The trade union must pay great attention to training and fostering cadres to satisfy the ever increasing requirement of the T.U. movement and to supply good cadres to the Party and state.

T.U. cadres must realize clearly their responsibility, serve the revolutionary work of the working class and toiling people with all their heart and soul and endeavour to temper themselves to become front-rank revolutionary fighters of the working class.

Youth and women's organizations must coordinate closely with the trade unions in the mobilization of young workers and women workers.

State organs are duty-bound to give great assistance to the T.U. in every branch of activity to correctly implement the T.U. law and the Party's and government's policies and regulations relating to the working class, toiling people and trade union.

The Party Central Committee will pay attention to strengthening the leadership of the Party at all levels over the T.U. organizations and help them fulfil their mission toward the working class.

Dear comrades and friends,

The working class in Vietnam has a very glorious revolutionary tradition. Endowed with the traditionally indomitable spirit of the world's people and revolutionary genius of the international working class, our working class has rapidly organized its vanguard party and through it, seized the sole leadership of the Vietnamese revolution for over 30 years.

The glorious success of the August Revolution, the protracted resistance war, the agrarian reform as well as of the economic rehabilitation, transformation and development during these last few years cannot be taken apart from the correct leadership of our working class and Party, it cannot be divorced from the heroic sacrifice and painstaking labour of the working class. We are very proud of this revolutionary tradition of the working class in our country.

Under the leadership of our Party, since its outset, the trade unions have closely united and organized the great majority of workers, urged the working class to implement all the Party's policies and recorded many achievements in all branches of activity.

We are sure that after the present T.U. congress, our working class and T.U. organizations will develop further their glorious tradition and march forward more powerfully.

We are confident that the present T.U. congress will wreak a new change in the working class and T.U. organizations in the North and give our working class a new source of energy and determination and a new upsurge in production and labour.

With this confidence, on behalf of the Party Central Committee, I wish the second T.U. Congress brilliant success.

Some Problems of Cadres and Organization in Socialist Revolution

After the Party has worked out a correct political line, organizational work in general, and cadre work in particular, are decisive factors for success in the revolutionary tasks.

Problems of organization and cadres are particularly difficult and complicated in the conditions of our Party's holding power, when the Party's leadership encompasses all aspects of social life and activity.

In what follows, I shall be dealing chiefly with the problem of cadres, and, in relation to this problem, I shall be discussing only some of the most important aspects. With regard to organization, I shall mainly be discussing fundamental aspects related to the study and solution of the cadre problem.

The Building of a Contingent of Cadres Must Proceed From the Political Line and Tasks

Cadre policy, if it is to be correct, must proceed fully from the requirements of the revolutionary tasks. *The revolution needs a contingent of cadres who are equal to their political tasks, with regard to their number and quality as well as to their composition, a contingent of cadres capable of fulfilling to the highest degree the requirements of the political tasks in each period.*

Complete loyalty to the ideals of socialism and communism, to the interests of the working class and the nation, to the political line of the Party; the severest sense of organization and discipline; close contacts with the masses; and the ability to fulfil the tasks assigned— these are fundamental, *unvarying* requirements in the qualifications of cadres, in whatever period. Nevertheless, from the national democratic stage to the socialist stage, the revolution obviously undergoes *basic changes* in its character and tasks. That is why we cannot stop at general principles when tackling the problem of cadres.

In order to have a correct approach to the problem of cadres in the new stage, we must grasp the theory of socialist revolution in general, the theory of the Party in the conditions of its being in power, the theory of the State, of economic and social life, of the system of collective ownership by the working people, of the new socialist man, etc. We must not only fully grasp the theory of the line, guiding principles and policies, but also the theory of organization, one of the newest and most complicated areas in the building of socialism. Only in this way can we understand thoroughly and concretely the essence, content and requirements of the political tasks set in this stage, and hence examine and solve correctly the problem of cadres.

In the national democratic revolution, which was a long and arduous process comprising many stages and involving many forms of activity, sometimes underground, sometimes legal, sometimes armed struggle, sometimes political struggle, and often with a highly diverse combination of many forms of struggle at the same time, our Party trained batch after batch of cadres who lived up to President Ho Chi Minh's teaching: "Be true to the Party and loyal to the people, fulfil any task, overcome any difficulty, and defeat any enemy." That was possible because our Party was tempered in the national democratic revolution, firmly grasped the theory of the national people's democratic revolution, was armed with a wise revolutionary line and methods and had a thorough knowledge of the content and requirements of the political tasks in each period of the national democratic revolution.

In the socialist revolution, big achievements have been made in cadre policy, but in some spheres we have not done as well as required. Most worthy of mention here is the fact that there has not always been full consistency of theory and practice, of principles and actual deeds. Our cadre work, from recruitment, training, appointment, fostering and promotion to appraisal and evaluation in many cases has not truthfully reflected our basic viewpoint that it is necessary to proceed from the requirements of the political tasks, a viewpoint that has been generally accepted. This is so because the tasks posed by the socialist revolution are something quite new to us, which we have not understood fully, clearly and concretely, either in theory or practice, so that we may have a given starting point when we have to examine and decide on questions of cadres.

To examine and solve questions of cadres is a problem closely associated with the political task. This requires that we base ourselves on the following viewpoint: there exists a very close, dialectical interrelation between cadres and the political line and tasks, between cadres and organization, between cadres and the revolutionary movement of the masses. A cadre's life is lived within the framework of this many-sided relationship. It is actually this relationship that makes a cadre a cadre. In this relationship, the cadre is at the same time cause and effect. Conversely, he is at the same time effect and cause.

1. Relationship Between Cadres
   and the Political Line and Tasks

A wise political line produces good cadres. Cadres are trained and mature under a wise line. On the other hand, they take part in the making and development of the line. They ensure the realization of the line. Without competent cadres, even though we have worked out a line, it will be useless. If cadres are bad, they will damage the line itself. If cadres are good and able, they not only help to carry out the line creatively but also contribute to its development.

The problem of cadres is posed under the premise that the line has been worked out. That is why a wise political line is the precondition for the existence of good cadres. It is quite impossible to have good cadres if the line is wrong. Of course, a wise line alone cannot exclude the possibility of wrongdoing and degradation on the part of cadres because whether a cadre acts rightly or wrongly, is good or bad, depends on many other factors than the line, including his personal attributes. However, a correct line is the basic condition in bringing the revolutionary tasks to success, and as such it produces one batch after another of good cadres and keeps to a minimum the possibility of cadres committing errors in political orientation. To be sure, in a revolutionary movement it is hardly possible to prevent a few bad, opportunist elements from infiltrating into the revolutionary ranks. However, if we have a strong mass movement arising from and developing along a correct line, and if the majority of our cadres stand firmly on this correct line, noxious tendencies not only have little chance of swaying our cadres but also are very likely themselves to be swept aside. But the picture will be quite different if errors are committed in the political line. A wrong line will take the cadres away from a correct direction, throw confusion into their ranks, and push numbers of them into wrongdoing. Of course, in such situations, there are always those who are alert enough to tell right from wrong and are able to defend the truth. But to bring the movement back on to the right path, the revolution must pay what is sometimes a very high price, including in terms of cadres, the most valuable asset of the revolution.

Thus, whether cadres are good or bad depends in the first place on the political line. However, as already stated, cadres in their turn exert a decisive influence on the line itself. Once a line has been worked out, the whole question boils down to how to organize its application. Organization is the *basic measure* to ensure the application of the line. Good or bad organization determines the success or failure of a line. Organization plays an especially big role in the conditions of socialist construction. However, in view of the content, character and scope of the work, we cannot oversimplify the matter by considering the whole question of organization and the work of organizing as a mere question of cadres. Organization has its own, independent role, a role of decisive importance for the cadres themselves. This matter will be further elaborated later on. Here we are discussing the relationship between the line and cadres. Cadres are the people who organize the fulfilment of the line. Thus it is clear that cadres decide the success or failure of a line. By creatively and fruitfully organizing the application of the line, and bringing into play the abundant experience they have accumulated, cadres not only translate the line into reality but also positively contribute to the improvement, development and concretization of the line. And this is an extremely important, *a prime requirement* of any cadre. In the process of socialist industrialization, new problems will crop up one after another. A political line or a policy is not worked out once and for all, especially in the present conditions of our economy and our social life, when everything is growing and moving forward through rapid revolutionary changes. We witness at any given moment, every day and every hour, the emergence of new problems to which the Party must provide correct answers. Any cadre who does not grasp this reality, who is not sensitive to the new, who does not take pains to think, to make efforts to understand the realities, who lacks the ability to think independently and creatively in the process of applying the Party line and policies, is not a good cadre. Sooner or later he will be outstripped by life. Lenin said: "In our struggle we must remember that communists must be able to reason. They may be perfectly familiar with the revolutionary struggle and with the state of the revolutionary movement all over the world: but if we are to extricate ourselves from desperate poverty and want we need culture, integrity and an ability to reason"(1). In the building of a new society, in all spheres of our work, we must fully grasp the concrete problems and tasks posed by life and must decide on concrete solutions and successfully deal with these problems and tasks. To do so, we must exert our mental powers, must be cultured and find the proper methods.

Our Party has laid down the general line on socialist revolution and socialist construction. This general line must be concretized at each step of development, in each branch of activity, in each locality. Obviously, in every domain—industry, agriculture, circulation and distribution of goods, scientific and technological development, culture, education—many questions remain to be clarified. Some of these unclarified questions are actually affecting in a decisive way many aspects of our cadre work. For example, at a given moment, a certain branch of activity might not have decided on a clear direction of development. It has not fully grasped the reality and has not worked out a long-term plan for itself or, if it has, this plan is not yet based on sufficiently solid grounds, and its immediate goals are not yet defined very clearly. As a matter of course, this branch cannot have a firm basis for laying down an all-round and correct plan for the training and fostering of cadres. Nor can the recruitment, appraisal and assignment of cadres have a correct direction.

Once we have defined the political line, orientation and objectives, it is organizational work and cadres that decide. However, saying that *the cadres are the decisive factor amounts, in the final analysis, to saying that cadre policy and cadre work are the decisive factor.* If cadre work is well done and if we have a correct cadre policy, we shall have an adequate contingent of good cadres. A correct cadre policy enables the creation and constant expansion of a contingent of cadres representing the Party's political life, who constantly ensure correct and full application of the tasks laid down by the Party and State, a contingent of cadres strong both collectively and individually; it provides conditions for cadres to give full play to their abilities and contributions, to advance constantly along with the constant development of the revolutionary tasks. This always leads to the most satisfactory results for the revolutionary cause.

There is a big leap forward from the struggle to seize power to being a Party in power. Without understanding the essence of this big leap forward, or the content, nature and unprecedented scope of the revolutionary tasks in the new stage, it is impossible to examine and correctly solve the problem of cadres. A Party in power means a Party leading the people in the management of the country's affairs. It means that Party leadership has been extended to the whole society, encompassing all aspects of life, which are more and more diversified and complicated. This requires that the Party and all its members and cadres—if they are to accomplish their mission as the *vanguard*—deeply understand and correctly apply the laws governing the development of society in general, as well as the laws of the emergence and development of socialist society (this question is even more complicated and difficult in the case of a backward agricultural country directly advancing to socialism without going through the period of capitalist development). The Party and its members and cadres must have a thorough knowledge of all aspects of social activity, master all processes of social development, in order to direct every effort toward the ultimate goal of winning complete, final and thorough success for socialism in the historic struggle to settle the question "who will win?", socialism or capitalism, the socialist path or the capitalist path.

To assume the leadership, it is necessary to clearly understand, firmly grasp and command the extremely complex relations and interrelations between the various spheres: economy, politics, ideology and culture, between science, technology and production, between production and life, between immediate and long-range objectives, between subjective and objective factors in the process of development of society. The Party must organize all spheres of life in accordance with the principles of socialism and create a single, organic system which will enable it to utilize and mobilize all the material and spiritual potential of society with a view to developing economy and culture, and improving the material and moral life of the people at the fastest possible rate.

All these activities actually make up the process of the simultaneous prosecution, on the basis of proletarian dictatorship, of the three revolutions—the revolution in production relations, the technical revolution and the ideological and cultural revolution—aimed at transforming social life from top to bottom. Obviously, these are completely new tasks.

Advancing directly to socialism without going through the period of capitalist development is a road of which experience is still rare in the world. This experience remains to be summed up. Moreover, we must take into full account the characteristics and specific conditions of our country. This requires big efforts from the Party in research and creation on the theoretical plane and the working out, on that basis, of a concrete, really effective programme for social life in order to fight for the triumph of socialism. It requires from our Party, from its members and cadres, high capacity in *practical organization* based on a profound understanding of all aspects of life and social activity of which in many spheres we have very scanty knowledge or were even completely ignorant until recently. Without such a capacity, it is impossible to assume the leadership and to carry out the great socialist tasks. All this is particularly difficult and complicated since the problem is not simply to do away with an old society that has existed for thousands of years but also to build a completely new life that will ensure full development of society as well as of each person.

It is upon these considerations that we must base our thinking concerning the problem of cadres in the socialist revolution. Rather than being an abstract and isolated question, or purely a question of individuals, the problem of cadres must first of all be seen as a *question of the Party, a question of accomplishing the tasks of leadership of the Party in the new stage of history, in the face of new tasks.*

To link the problem of cadres with the requirements of the revolutionary tasks is, in more concrete terms, *to proceed from the political line of the Party.* The general line of the Party in the socialist revolution consists in firmly grasping proletarian dictatorship, simultaneously carrying out the three revolutions of which the technical revolution is the centrepiece, carrying out socialist industrialization with the aim of building large-scale, socialist production, giving priority and rational development to heavy industry on the basis of developing agriculture and light industry, building centrally run industry while developing regional economies, and in combining economic management with national defence. The whole Party line, from the general line to the concrete policies in each sphere of activity, is directed at the fundamental objective of the period of transition, viz. winning definitive victory for socialism in the struggle to determine "who will win?", the socialist path or the capitalist path, in North Viet Nam.

We must proceed from this political line in considering and solving the question of cadres.

This means that the whole of our cadre work and our policy concerning cadres must ensure the successful application of this general line in social life.

This means that it is necessary to have a contingent of cadres capable of ensuring the realization of this political line, who are completely loyal to it, who understand it deeply and are resolved to struggle for its successful realization and for the realization of all the tasks laid down by the Party, and to do this on a principled basis, with the highest determination, with all necessary knowledge and with ability to apply the Party line in a creative manner.

This means that all aspects of our cadre work and cadre policy, from recruitment, training and utilization to appraisal and promotion etc. of cadres must rest on this foundation and take it as the primary criterion.

This means that we must examine the question of cadres in a *concrete manner* and cannot content ourselves with generalities about morality or class stand.

2. Class Stand and Revolutionary Qualities

In the Marxist-Leninist view, the inevitable success of socialism does not stem from the natural disposition of man or from some moral principles, but from objective laws of development of society. The Party line is actually the reflection and application of the laws which have been enunciated in the Marxist-Leninist doctrine. The socialism we are building can be achieved only on the basis of these laws, on the principles of Marxism-Leninism. That is our class stand, the foundation of our concept of morality.

Our class stand and the whole of our morality consist in struggling with self-denial for national independence, for the welfare and happiness of our people, for socialism and communism. *In the past*, this stand and morality consisted in struggling to overthrow the domination of imperialism and the reactionary puppet forces and wresting back power for the people. *At present*, this stand and morality in North Viet Nam is the stand of the working class as master of the State and master of society. This morality is one of collective masters who are struggling to do away with poverty, backwardness, ignorance and disease, create a modern industry, a modern agriculture, and advanced culture and science to ensure continual improvement in the people's material and cultural life, and the building of an independent, free, prosperous and strong socialist fatherland.

All lines and policies of our Party are aimed at this objective. That is why *our class stand, our morality, actually consists in struggling for the successful realization of the line and policies as well as all tasks laid down by the Party.*

As disciples of Marxism-Leninism, the doctrine that advocates reforming the world society and man through revolution in conformity with the laws of historical evolution, we do not talk of morality for morality's sake or in any other sense.

Class stand must also be understood correctly, in a scientific sense. By class we do not mean the aggregation of separate individuals but a social group holding a definite position in the system of social production. What is more, the proletariat fully took shape as a class only after it had changed from a class "of its own" into a class "for its own", that is, after it acquired *class consciousness.* This consciousness is not the simple sum total of individual consciousness but the consciousness of the historic position and mission of the *whole class.* Class stand, therefore, is the *political stand* of the class. It is consciousness of *the overall, fundamental and long-term interests* of the class and a firm determination to defend these interests. With regard to the working class, if it is to realize its historic position and mission, it must be armed with Marxism-Leninism. Marxism-Leninism is the theoretical representation of the workers' movement. It correctly reflects the objective laws of the development of society. It is the ideology of the working class and the genuine and scientific embodiment of the class stand of the working class. In combination with the workers' movement, Marxism-Leninism forms the political Party of the proletariat. The Party is the expression of the class consciousness and class stand of the working class at its highest, most comprehensive and most mature level. Only with a Party armed with the vanguard theory of Marxism-Leninism can the working class become the vanguard class at the helm of the revolution. And only then can the class stand of the working class really take shape. Without knowledge of Marxism-Leninism, of revolutionary science and of the vanguard theory of the proletariat, there can be no class stand of the vanguard class.

Thus, *the stand of the working class is the stand of Marxism-Leninism of which the Party, its political line and activities, are concrete and practical manifestations.* That is why, for a militant of the Party, to struggle with self-abnegation, without fear of sacrifices, to struggle courageously, staunchly, indomitably and untiringly for the successful realization of the Party's political line, is actually the stand of the working class. This is the foundation of our morality. To talk of class stand, of morality, without proceeding from this foundation, is, in effect, to replace Marxism-Leninism and the Party's political line with feudal concepts of morality or with a sort of sentimental petty-bourgeois socialism completely alien to the genuine stand of the working class and genuine proletarian morality. All manifestations of deviation from Marxism-Leninism and the Party political line are contrary to the working-class stand. To struggle uncompromisingly against these manifestations is to embody the stand of the working class. We do not recognize any other criterion as far as stand is concerned.

So, class stand is not only a question of *sentiment* and *aspirations* but also a question of intellectual acquirements. *It is Marxist-Leninist scientific theory.* Only on this basis can the most ardent revolutionary aspirations become realizable. Nor does class stand consist simply of scientific theory. It also embraces the *political science* built on the basis of that theory. What is more, class stand is not only the political line but also *practical revolutionary activities and correct revolutionary methods* aimed at successfully carrying out that political line in real life.

Class stand should not be understood in an intuitive and spontaneous way. The workers themselves, if their movement grows out of sheer spontaneity, cannot have a working-class stand. They can, at best, achieve trade union consciousness and trade unionism—which stops at economic interests of an immediate, partial and professional character. Trade unionism is, in Lenin's words, "the ideological enslavement of the workers by the bourgeoisie."(2)

On the other hand, *we must grasp class stand from a concrete, historical point of view.* Class stand when the working class has seized power and become the masters of society is different from what it was when the working class had not yet seized power and was still in the position of wage earners. With regard to the concrete content of class stand, a completely new, qualitative development has occurred, embodying the greatest leap forward in human history. If, in the past, the task of the working class was to overthrow the yoke of oppression and exploitation—that is, a task of a destructive character—today its task is to build and create a new society which not only abolishes oppression and exploitation but also creates all necessary conditions for bringing the fullest possible material and moral life to the whole of the working class. In order to build such a society, it is necessary not only to possess a full *sense* of being the collective master, but also *to have the methods* and the ability to master society, master nature and master our own personality. This is the basic content of the class stand of the working class. This is also the highest moral requirement of the socialist system.

The Party, the vanguard and the best organized contingent, the highest organization of the working class, is the *conscious* representative of the stand of the working class conceived as collective master. It leads the entire society to put into effect the great historical law of replacing the age-old system of private ownership (from which oppression and exploitation originate) by socialist collective ownership. If the workers cannot spontaneously acquire the revolutionary stand of the proletariat, still less can the peasants, whether they be poor, landless or lower-middle peasants. In comparison with the advance of the peasant from the status of a toiler exploited by landlords to that of a free private farmer, the change from being a private farmer to a collective farmer represents a much more significant leap forward. Obviously, from the viewpoint of historical development, compared with the individual, private farmer, the co-operative farmer is closer to the position of the working class. This represents precisely a new step forward of the worker-peasant alliance in the stage of socialist construction, definitely higher in quality than the previous stage. But the co-operative farmer is still not a worker. On the ideological plane, only the most vanguard representatives of the collective farmer class, the most outstanding co-operative farmers, come close to the stand of the working class. And this can only be the outcome of a process of training and education through the practice of revolution, through collective work in production and through a process of ideological persuasion which thoroughly imbues them with the Party line and policies and makes them fully conscious of the role and tasks of the collective farmer class in the cause of socialist construction, imbued with the working class' sense of collective ownership.

So far, in dealing with the quality of Party members and cadres, we have often failed to make sufficiently clear and to hit right home at the most essential and most necessary points. We have often used abstractions and generalities when speaking of class stand and morality, while remaining unclear or failing to put emphasis on the most important requirements, the most decisive points and criteria which are so essential for a communist, a Party cadre, that without them they hardly deserve the name. It is necessary to point out here that the Party Constitution has adequately and strictly defined all criteria and fundamental requirements for a Party member. All requirements of a Party member in matters of class stand and morality are also clearly stated in the Party Constitution. When we speak of Party cadres, this implies all members of the Party, because every Party member has the duty to exercise Party leadership in his field of work, and, in this sense, a Party member is by definition a cadre. All criteria, requirements and tasks defined in the Party Constitution for each Party member represent the basic and highest principles of a communist's class stand and morality. The problem is that the admission of a new Party member must necessarily meet the criteria provided for in the Party Constitution. Secondly, within the Party, we must constantly base ourselves on the criteria, requirements and tasks of a Party member as defined in the Constitution to educate Party cadres and members and to check up on cadres (here we are referring exclusively to Party cadres) and Party members. Of course, there should be modifications to the Party Constitution in the light of the political tasks in each given period. However, in no period may the Party allow activities that fall outside the provisions of the Constitution. That is why it would be not only nonsense but also plain rejection of the Constitution, if we conceived of the class stand and morality of Party members as anything other than what is stated in the provisions of the Party Constitution.

When looking for strong points as well as weaknesses and defects in the quality of a Party member or cadre, we must first of all examine his level of study and assimilation of Marxism-Leninism, his knowledge and understanding of the Party line and policies, his determination to make efforts and his practical ability to implement this line and these policies as well as his ability to fulfil the tasks assigned and to persuade and organize the masses to join him in implementing the line, policies and all tasks laid down by the Party. In the end, all this must be translated into practical deeds and the extent of the benefits brought to the revolution by these deeds. Certainly we should not base ourselves solely on momentary or inconsequential actions, but must carefully examine a long process, with all the tested evidence. This process is nothing other than the process of implementing the tasks entrusted by the revolution. That is why, whether he fulfils his tasks or not always remains the only trustworthy, objective yardstick in measuring the qualifications of a Party member or cadre, and in making necessary decisions in the various fields of cadre work and policy. In the final analysis, the qualities and abilities of a Party member or cadre, to what degree he is "Red and expert", his class stand and so on, must be judged on that basis. For instance, along with the revolution in production relations, and the ideological and cultural revolution, we must carry out the technical revolution and consider this as the centrepiece. We must build the material and technical foundations of socialism. Thus, the question arises: where does the quality of a Party cadre lie in the building of the material and technical revolution? It lies in his ability to understand the line of socialist industrialization, the line of technical revolution, in the high or low level of his determination to implement these lines, in his ability to accomplish the concrete tasks assigned to him as shown in the practical results he has achieved. Obviously, here the firmest class stand and the highest morality of a cadre consists in making the boldest assault on the technical and scientific battleground, in striving to advance in order to attain a high level of culture and knowledge and in mastering by all means the essence of the necessary techniques and sciences. And all this must be done with the *full awareness* that otherwise there can be no socialism, there can be no victory of the socialist path over the capitalist path, for, "according to the materialistic conception, the determining factor in history, in the last resort, is the production and reproduction of immediate life". (3) Such are class stand and revolutionary quality in this case.

Organization and Cadres

1. Relationship between cadres and organization

We have discussed the relationship between cadres and the political line and tasks. The problem of cadres must also be examined in the context of the close relationship between cadres and organization. By organization we mean not only the organization of the Party, but also of the State, economic and cultural organizations, mass organizations, military organizations, and organizations in all spheres of social life and activity. Organization, in the broadest sense, is the structure for the existence of things and phenomena. Things and phenomena cannot exist without a definite form of combination of the various factors making them up. Organization, therefore, is an attribute of things and phenomena themselves. When we speak of organization in our social life, we are dealing with the relationship and the coordination of the activity of the various parts of a whole, the system of leadership and management in all fields and in all branches, the system of forms and measures for the realization of the decisions from the moment the plans are worked out to the final stage of checking on the results achieved.

We cannot conceive of a cadre outside the organization because the cadre is an element of the organization. The cadre lives in a definite organization, in the apparatus whereby an organization operates. Organization is formed by man. Man is the main component factor of an organization. An organization cannot operate without man. *A product of man, an organization cannot but depend on man, on his qualities and capacities of action. On the other hand, after organization has become a quantity existing in its own right and has struck deep roots in life, organization in its turn has a decisive effect on man.* It determines who will do what, what position and function he should hold in the apparatus of activity. It defines beforehand the direction and objective of man's actions. It directs man and obliges him to act one way instead of another. Organization, in its activity, brings forth in man definite characteristics and qualities. It trains man. The capacities and effectiveness of man's activity depend on organization. Organization increases man's strength manyfold. Organization creates a new quality. Marx wrote: "Just as the combat strength of a cavalry unit or the resistance of an infantry battalion differs in substance from the sum total of the individual strength of each cavalryman or each separate combatant, the sum total of the mechanical strength of each separate worker also differs from the mechanical strength created when they work in co-ordination and at the same time in the same indivisible work . . . . The problem is not only to increase individual productivity, but also to use cooperative methods to create a new production force that operates as a single, collective force."(4)

All this is directly related to the examination and resolution of the problem of cadres. For instance, in looking for the strong points and weaknesses of Party cadres and members, if we confine ourselves to examining their ideological qualities and assessing their ideological standard separately from the question of organization, if we fail to see the influence and impact of organization on cadres, then we are overlooking one main ground for the correct examination and resolution of the cadre problem.

A strong Party branch and a strong Party executive committee give rise to strong Party members and cadres. Wherever the Party branch and committee are rickety, the Party members and cadres find their fighting strength reduced and are prone to degeneration and backsliding. Of course, the reverse in this case is completely true, because in their relations with the organization, Party cadres and members are at the same time the effect and the cause. However, even if this or that individual is the cause of the shakiness of the organization, the question still remains essentially a question of organization. Because those individuals who *are members of the organization*, but have thought and acted contrary to its requirements, have done so because the organization either lacks the necessary guarantees in criteria or the necessary rules for activity and behaviour or is not strong enough to compel the individuals concerned to comply with the norms, rules and decisions of the organization. That is why, in any case, *we must proceed from organization to examine and resolve the question*. We must realize that the question of individuals here is essentially a question of organization and must base our criticism of the ideology of these individuals on the organization; we must base ourselves on the requirements of the organization, on the criteria and principles of the organization and on the ideology itself that is required by the organization when we have to determine the responsibility of individuals. That is the *principled method* of work.

Take the example of the question of internal unity and solidarity among cadres. It is regrettable that lack of solidarity has occurred in a number of places. There are complex causes behind this phenomenon but we must point out at once that if some of these cases have dragged on and become more and more complicated without any definite conclusion being arrived at as to where lie right and wrong, and who is right, who is wrong, it is because we have not examined and resolved the question on a principled basis. In fact, in all such cases, the question will become clear and can be settled rapidly if it is posed on the principle of closely linking ideology and policies with the organization, the principle of comparing the thoughts and actions of the persons concerned with the requirements of the organization. As far as the Party is concerned, the basis for unity within the Party can be nothing other than the Marxist-Leninist outlook on the world, the political line and resolutions of the Party and the Party Constitution—the fundamental law for all Party life, for the building of the Party and all Party activity. The Party forms a single ideological entity. This means that the Party is a monolithic bloc not only in ideology but also in organization, which is a guarantee for its unity of action. If the question of solidarity and the resolution of cases of disunity is not based on these foundations and principles of *Party organization*, and is based instead on considerations of personal relations, there can be no real solidarity. If unity is broken, it is hardly possible to avoid permanent discord and one problem will engender another, paralysing the whole organization, and, as a consequence, each member of the organization will also lose fighting strength.

Man's strength lies in his organization. Only within and through organization and through relationships with other persons and realities can a man show what he is and what he is capable of. Of course, we cannot conceive man as part of a machine. Man is an entity endowed with conscience, will, dynamism and initiative, and each man has his own character and capabilities. That is why it cannot be said that an organization has no room for the role of the individual. If each person is a cipher, the organization itself cannot exist because an organization is actually the combination of many persons. In fact, how can there be the "collective capacity" (Marx) of the organization without the effectiveness of each person? Obviously, there must be strong people if the organization is to be strong, and there must be good people if the organization is to be good. On the other hand, this fundamental point must be made clear: the strength of a person lies in organization and organization creates a new strength which differs completely in quality from the sum of the strength of separate persons. The dialectic in this case consists in the following: *a strong organization ensures the strength of each person and the strength of each person makes the strength of the organization.*

To do cadre work is *to place a cadre in his right place and promote him at the right time, and place him in the most appropriate conditions of organization which will enable him to give full play to his talents and creativity as required by the revolutionary tasks. And this is actually to increase the strength of organization because the strength of organization makes itself felt through the active and creative work of each person and constitutes a collective, organized force.*

In an organization where functions and tasks are not clear, where the distribution of work is irrational, where norms of work and the allocation of responsibility are not well defined, where the relationship and cohesion among the various component parts or their homogeneity are lacking, any person in it will tend to become impotent and inefficient because it is a weak organization. An individual, detached from his organization, is capable of nothing. In an organization which is an organic whole, the strong points of each person will be multiplied while his weak points will be limited and overcome and each person will think and act with all the moral and physical strength of the organization. Organization helps "eliminate the limitations springing from individuals and develop their collective capacities".(5) If the whole body is strong, every organ and every cell will also be strong and vice versa.

That is why we cannot speak of cadres separately from organization. In fact, we are already dealing with organization when speaking of cadres. *We must deal with and resolve the question of cadres on the basis of organization, by proceeding from the character, function, task, structure of organization and the requirements for its activity.* A correct solution to the question of organization is the basis for solving the question of cadres correctly. A judicious political line must be ensured by correct organization, and correct organization is precisely the premise directly deciding a correct solution to the question of cadres. Take the economy for example. If we succeed in building a system of management which really corresponds to the laws governing economic development and to the principles of production, which eliminates methods of management of an administrative character in which money and materials are simply supplied to departments without proper costing, this will be a condition of prime importance in compelling cadres to take into consideration the economic efficiency of production and to make a deep examination of the production structure and process, thereby enhancing their sense of responsibility, their consciousness of being the collective master, and their level and capacity of management. That will be a condition of prime importance in combating bureaucratic practices and the method of casual handling of affairs which exhibits no concern as to whether the plan is fulfilled or not and whether the factory is making profits or is operating at a loss.

Unless organizational work is well done, unless we understand and firmly control an organization, we cannot perform cadre work well. Cadre work is closely linked with organizational work. On the other hand, we should know how to run and control an organization not only with regard to its structure, apparatus, personnel and means, but also deeply understand and firmly grasp its function, task, line, objective and method of work. Only in this way can cadre work be carried out well. In principle, to assume the leadership means to control the organization and he who controls and directs the organization has the decisive voice in questions concerning cadres because he, better than anybody else, understands the cadres and the needs in cadres within the sphere of his responsibility. (Of course, we must comply with concrete regulations in procedural questions concerning proposals and ratifications.)

2. Cadre Work is the First and Foremost Task in Organizational Work

Cadre work is, in its essence, organizational work and it is precisely because of the need for organization, and in view of the necessity to *ensure the highest efficiency of leadership and management that we must do cadre work well, considering it as the first and foremost task of organizational work*. Lenin said: "We shall go our way and try as carefully and as patiently as possible to test and discover real organizers, people with sober and practical minds, people who combine loyalty to socialism with ability without fuss (and in spite of muddle and fuss) to get a large number of people working together steadily and correctly within the framework of the Soviet organization. *Only* such people, after they have been tested a dozen times, by being transferred from the simplest to the more difficult tasks, should be promoted to the responsible posts of leaders of the people's labour, leaders of administration. We have not yet learned to do this, but we shall learn."(6)

Cadre work must be done in meticulous, careful and thorough manner, because men, cadres, are the soul and the motive force of organization. How many cadres and what kinds of cadres are needed for such and such an organization with such and such tasks?

That is the starting point for reaching judicious decisions on cadres. So far, in many cases, we have not acted exactly in this way. Often we make overstatements or understatements, we make inordinate inferences or omissions when assessing a cadre. We use generalities to assess the qualities and capabilities of a cadre and finish up by taking in a man who cannot do the job. In some instances, we do not even proceed from the job and organization to place men, but instead create jobs and organizations out of the need to place men. Such humps are still on our backs.

Only by proceeding from organization to place men can we fully realize the necessity to understand men thoroughly and accurately and set forth the necessary criteria for such men. A Party secretary, a director, a specialist, a production brigade leader, etc., each of these functions represents a definite organization. It is a definite function of a definite organization. We must base ourselves on the *concrete requirement* of each organization, each function, to lay down *concrete criteria* for cadres and proceed to recruit cadres and put them in the right places and also to inquire into these cadres and correctly appraise them. Any organization requires that its cadres have a full sense of *personal responsibility* and make the highest efforts. These requirements must be defined in a concrete manner: what and how many jobs they have to do, what they must know, what regulations they must comply with, whom they are responsible to, what are their responsibilities and power, how they are related to other cadres and organizations, who has the right to appoint and dismiss them, etc. It is through the *practical application* of these regulations that we will supervise and inquire into a cadre, understand his capabilities, his qualities and morality. Lenin said: "To test men and verify what has actually been done—this, this again, this alone is now the main feature of all our activities, of our whole policy."(7)

That is the correct way to understand the work of cadre control. We should not control a man separately from the work that the organization requires from him. Control work, in this sense, is a link of prime importance in organizational work.

3. Collective Method of Work and Individual Responsibility

Each cadre holds a definite position of work in his organization, in the leading and managerial apparatus. Whether each cadre fulfils his responsibility or not naturally influences the common activity of the whole organization, the whole apparatus. If he does his work well, the effectiveness and strength of the whole organization will increase accordingly. Conversely, if he works poorly, the effectiveness and strength of the whole organization suffers. Here, we must point out that the *role of those who head an organization, the leaders, is very great and has a decisive character.* That is why they must meet very high requirements. The leaders must embody loyalty and dedication in the implementation of the line and policies of the Party and State and must have the necessary capabilities and determination to bring the line and policies into effect. They must have rich experience, foresight and aliveness to the new, a creative, imaginative mind to combine collective leadership with the ability to make clearsighted decisions on the basis of a deep knowledge of the tasks assigned and a firm grasp of the situation. With high determination to achieve the set objective, leaders must have the capability to organize and mobilize their collaborators and the masses to follow suit. They must show a high sense of responsibility, great determination and a principled attitude in handling affairs. They must take into account and really respect the opinion of others, and calmly listen to the suggestions of the masses even if they do not agree with them. They must have a generous attitude toward others, and a high sense of self-criticism, must dare to admit their errors and mistakes and have the determination to correct them. These are indispensable qualities in leaders. If they possess these qualities, leaders will enjoy the necessary prestige and trust without which they cannot lead.

The capability and effectiveness of the leadership directly depend on whether or not the leaders can build a *united and like-minded collective* around themselves. In this collective, each cadre must have a profound sense of being the collective master, a high sense of responsibility toward the common cause, and place common interests first. While putting all his mind and energies in service of the common success of the collective organization and clearly realizing his function and role in the common cause, each cadre must accomplish his *personal responsibility* assigned by the organization with his greatest efforts and with self-imposed discipline. Concern for the common objective, the common interest, the common cause, must be manifested first of all in the full execution of his personal responsibility. Whether this personal responsibility is accomplished or not is the first criterion in appraising the contribution of each to the common cause. At the same time, each must *closely co-operate* with others in the working collective. An organization, by definition, is a collective, a working collective in which every member needs the others, the one working with and for the others with the aim of achieving a cause which transcends the capabilities of each separate individual. Co-operation therefore is essential.

Co-operation is effected first of all through the accomplishment by each member of his personal responsibility because the non-accomplishment of the task of one person immediately affects the accomplishment of the tasks of others. In an organization, if every member needs the co-operation of others, it is because of the organic interrelation among the various parts of the work as parts of one and the same whole. Distribution of work implies in itself co-operation, and inversely co-operation implies a distribution of work. The question is to understand this relationship and to put it fully into practice in our work. While accomplishing his task, each must show concern for the others and help them accomplish their tasks. Bound together by a common objective—in the broadest sense, the objective of the entire society and, in the narrower sense, the objective of the organization in which they work—everybody in the collective should be animated by mutual affection, without which there can be no co-operation and joint efforts in the struggle for the triumph of the common cause. We must rejoice at the successes of our comrades as at our own and concern ourselves with the difficulties of our comrades as with our own. We must rejoice at the progress of our friends and comrades as at our own; and we should never be motivated by personal ambition and calculations of rivalry and jealousy. Those are decisive factors for building a *really intimate and united collective*. And such an intimate and united collective is actually the strength of the organization. With such a strength, no task is unrealizable and no difficulty insurmountable. Struggle and mutual love are the *raison d'etre* of man and, in the first place, of revolutionary cadres.

4. Our Strength Lies in our Organization

We cannot speak of cadres without speaking of organization. However, organization is an extremely complex question. Organizing in the most effective way requires a whole science, the science of organization. We cannot organize in any way we fancy. Organization has its own laws. An organization is created to ensure the realization of the political line and tasks. Accordingly, any organization must conform with the political line and respond to the requirements of the realization of the political tasks. Any organization must also suit the objects to be organized and the areas in which the organization wants to exert its influence. Different spheres of activity require different forms of organization. For instance, in productive activity, the objects of organization are the working people and the means and objects of labour, whereas in fighting, the objects of organization are the combatants, weapons and armaments, and the objective is to defeat an organized and armed enemy engaged in a life-and-death struggle with us. Each sphere of activity has its specific laws. Obviously, economic laws differ from the laws of war. Accordingly, the organization and methods of organization in different spheres of activity cannot but differ among themselves. The forms of organization also vary with the period, depending on the level and extent of development of the objects of organization. Things and social and economic processes are developing unceasingly and the role of organization consists in vigorously promoting this development. Therefore, organization must be very dynamic and flexible at the same time. An organization can give full scope to its strength only when it fully corresponds with its objects and the laws of development of its objects. When it does not, organization may seriously hamper the development of its objects. An organization may be either highly revolutionary or highly conservative. It is most revolutionary when it fully corresponds with the needs of life. It is most conservative when it develops a tendency to inertia while life is constantly changing and moving forward. *The big industrial organization has a highly revolutionary character whereas the handicraft organization has a highly conservative character.*

At present, our organization in many spheres still belongs to the second category. We may say that in some areas our organization is not only backward but also obsolete. That is the cause of our inertia. Obviously, in such cases, there must be a whole revolution in organization from the structure of the apparatus, the mode of activity, the internal relations and the style of work, to the disposition of cadres. There have been suggestions in some quarters that it is time to resolutely and boldly replace a number of cadres who not only fall short in their tasks but are also seriously hampering the functioning of the whole machine. This is absolutely necessary. We need to replace them with cadres with a flair for organization who are not only loyal and dedicated but also capable of grasping and creatively applying the line, policies and tasks laid down by the Party and the State, and capable of getting the whole machine moving. However, in any case, we should always bear in mind that in the final analysis and from a basic and overall point of view, *our strength lies in organization,* and all the effectiveness of our activity stems from organization. In a broader sense, the steadiness and unshakable strength of our regime as a whole are not due to one or two persons of special talent but to our organization, to the whole politico-economic and social structure based on the principles of socialism which we must build at all costs.

This, evidently, is an extremely complicated and difficult task since we are advancing from a backward agricultural society, a system of small production. Everything has to be created virtually from scratch; modern industry, modern agriculture, advanced culture and science. Everything has to be built up: a new system, a new economy and a new man. But in what way and in what forms, with what measures and through what processes to reach our objective in the shortest possible period, and to make up for the lag caused by centuries of inertia? That is the sum total of the difficulties we face in our organizational work.

It is made all the more difficult by our lack of capacity in practical organizational work, a serious shortcoming left over from history. It must also be pointed out here that the *difficulty stems first of all from our failure to see the importance of organization.* Organization makes strength. Yet, we have not seen the strength of organization. The small producer, the handicraftsman, cannot see the strength of organization because the conditions of their productive activity and their livelihood are inherently conditions of non-organization and constantly bring about states of non-organization. Only workers in large-scale industry can see the strength of organization because the strength of organization actually derives from large-scale industry. The centuries-old influence of Confucianism also prevents us from seeing the strength of organization. Confucianism has left in us the vestiges of a kind of egoistic, individualistic morality, an ugly product of the feudalist system of ownership and the caste system. Everything in this "moral code" is completely contrary to our revolutionary outlook on life, to the needs of our great organizational work aimed at building socialism. Only Marxism-Leninism, the revolutionary science of the proletariat, the class whose strength lies in its organization, can see the strength of organization, the strength of the organized working class and working people.

We should ponder over and draw the necessary lessons from the following words of Lenin: "Give us an organization of revolutionaries, and we will overturn Russia."(8) He also said: "In its struggle for power, the proletariat has no other weapon but organization."(9) Once, Lenin put it in an even more imperative way, stressing that the whole task is to "organize, organize and organize."(10) After power has passed into the hands of the revolution, Lenin pointed out that "the most important and most difficult aspect of the socialist revolution is the tasks of organization."(11)

5. It is Necessary to Make Ideology
   and Organization into One

We should get rid of our inveterate habit of talking of ideology alone (and in many cases we do not understand correctly what ideology actually means) and seldom speaking of organization. To carry out revolution we must have a revolutionary ideology and also a revolutionary organization. Organization ensures the realization of ideology. Organization ensures that words are matched by deeds. If we speak of ideology without speaking of organization, that is mere empty theorising and empty morality without any practical effect. That is the inherent defect of petty-bourgeois intellectuals and Confucian scholars. Practising means organizing. If we want to practise anything, we must have an organization and must *make ideology one with organization.* It is actually out of the needs of action, of the needs of revolutionary practice, that we must have a revolutionary ideology. No revolutionary movement can take place without being prepared and promoted by ideological campaigns. The deeper the revolutionary changes we want to effect, the deeper and more extensive the ideological campaigns we must undertake. Without revolutionary theory and revolutionary ideology, there can be no revolutionary actions. However, theory and ideology alone are absolutely insufficient. As Karl Marx pointed out, "Ideology is essentially *incapable of achieving anything.* If an ideology is to be materialized there must be men using practical forces." In other words, if an ideology is to be put into practice, there must be organization. Men must be organized with definite means and act strictly in accordance with this ideology. The question of cadres is posed in the light of the need to carry out the line and policies of the Party, the needs of revolutionary practice. That is why, when we speak of cadres we already mean organization. Only with a very practical mind, a sense of realism, and a revolutionary will can we see the importance of organization and the strength of organization, hence the importance of the problem of cadres, what is required from cadres, in terms of ideology, ardour, will and energy, capacity and creativeness.

6. Building a System of Correct Relations
   Between the Party, the State and the Masses

Our foremost task in the field of organizational activity is to create, on a nation-wide scale as well as in every locality, every branch and every grassroots unit, all the way up to the highest level and down again, a system of correct relations between the Party, the State and the masses. These relations must reflect the *essence of the new regime* and must be employed as the biggest and most *powerful combined force* for the vigorous promotion of the process of creating a socialist system in all spheres of the economy and culture, and building and developing social relations in all fields, and relations between man and man. Such a correct system of relations will ensure in the firmest way the all-round and absolute leadership of the Party over social life and the development of society, ensure the highest capacity and the greatest effectiveness of the role of the State as the organ of economic and cultural management, ensure to the highest degree the genuine right of the people of being collective masters and the most success for the efforts of the masses in the creation of history.

The question of cadres is posed on this basis, within the framework and in the light of the needs of that system of relations. The Party could not lead society and the people to build socialism without the State and without the medium of the State. The working people cannot become masters of society and successfully prosecute their cause without the leadership of the Party—the representative of the most correct thinking and line of collective mastery in conformity with the laws of development of society. The people play their role as masters of society under the leadership of the Party and through the medium of the State which was founded and is managed by the people themselves. The leadership of the Party and the rights of the people as collective masters of society find a concentrated expression in the State and State activity—all this can only be realized through the medium of the State. The State would cease to be a proletarian State if it did not reflect the power of the working people and if its activity were not based on the Marxist-Leninist line of the political Party of the working class.

As the political Party leading the State, it goes without saying that the Party organization, the apparatus of the Party and most of the Party members and cadres must be assigned to and strike deep roots in all spheres of activity of the State and society, without exception. The life of the Party essentially resides in the entire activity of the State, over the whole range of political, military, economic, cultural and social activity. The Party is the nucleus lying at the heart of social life which sets in motion the whole apparatus of the regime, and drives the entire society forward.

We can thus see how many more cadres of all kinds are needed and how much is required of cadres. There are so many new areas where cadres must be active and establish themselves as capable, competent masters: industry, agriculture, trade, culture, science, education, military work, law, etc. This we must realize because otherwise we cannot understand the lines and policies of the Party, contribute to the working out and development of these lines and policies, or organize their achievement—in a word, we cannot exercise Party leadership.

On the other hand, by leadership we mean that the Party exercises its leadership *through the State and by means of the State.* It is necessary to transform the line, policies and resolutions of the Party into policies and activities of the State. The State is the highest, broadest and most concentrated organization for the exercise of the right of the people as the collective masters of society. The Party exercises its leadership over the State. It does not replace the State in ruling. We have the dictatorship of the proletarian State, not the dictatorship of the Party. The proletarian State is essentially the exercise of the working people's right as collective masters of society under the leadership of the working class and through the Marxist-Leninist political Party. The Party's exercise of its leadership of the State means that all lines and policies of the Party must be transformed into policies, plans and resolutions of the State and must be reflected and carried out in a State form and by the organizational means and forms of State activity. They must be transformed into *State affairs.* And this is not simple. "With the transition of all power—this time not only political and, not even mainly political, but economic power, that is, power that affects the deepest foundations of everyday human existence—to a new class, and, moreover, to a class which for the first time in the history of humanity is the leader of the overwhelming majority of the population, of the whole mass of the working and exploited people—our tasks become more complicated."(12)

The apparatus of the proletarian State is not only a ruling

machine. It is also an organ of economic management, a machine for running social production on the basis of a correct reflection of socialist economic laws and appropriate solutions to the objective requirements of production. It is precisely from this starting point that we should determine the structure, scale, tasks, power and mode of activity of the State organs for economic leadership (such as the Ministry of Industry, Ministry of Agriculture, Ministry of Trade, etc.). This we have not clearly realized and strictly observed, hence the bureaucratic and purely administrative forms of handling affairs in organizational work and in the mode of activity of many State organs having responsibility for economic leadership.

As an organ of economic management and a production machine, the State is central to economic activity, functioning as the owner of the main means of production and a producer who organizes and directs social production. On the basis of a firm knowledge of objective economic laws and the principles of socialist economy, we must learn to manage according to State methods and must conform with the regulations and norms of the State in economic management as well as in the management of society in general. The State is law. We must manage society and economy by means of State laws. Only through the State, the systems, regulations and norms of the State, through the system of economic laws and the whole system of State laws can the line, policies and tasks worked out by the Party penetrate into social life and become a reality. Formerly the Party line and policies penetrated the masses and were implemented through propaganda and agitation work with regard to each person or each group. Today, besides these methods which we must apply even more effectively, broadly and adequately, we must also use large-scale organizational measures involving millions and tens of millions of citizens. This can be done only through State laws which reflect the interests and will of the working people. The whole system of State legislation and economic legislaton *represents the line and policies of the Party and also the interests and will of the labouring people manifested in the form of the State. They are powerful and very effective organizational instruments of the State in carrying out the line, policies and tasks worked out by the Party on the basis of a powerful dictatorship of the proletariat.* Yet, our cadres are for the most part still ignorant of this truth or have not yet acquainted themselves with it. Some even look upon these laws as a burden or an obstacle. They try by all means to free themselves from the burden of them. And what is the result? Autocratism and arbitrariness on the one hand and anarchy on the other. In general, this is an attitude of defiance of State laws. This also means that they have infringed upon the rights of the people as collective masters and upon Party leadership which find their concentrated expression in the State. To avoid this state of affairs, ideological education alone is not enough. We must also strengthen State laws and perfect the regulations concerning organization, systems, discipline, etc., so as to make it impossible for anyone placed within the limits of these laws to do otherwise than obey them. The strength of these organizational relations dominates everyone. It is the same strength that ensures the fullest freedom of action of the people because it represents the common interests of society and the aspiration of each citizen in the new society in which he has his share in the right to be the collective master.

We must work in strict accordance with the regulations and norms of the State. On the other hand, not for a moment should we forget that our State is a *proletarian State, a people's State, and that the only master of our society is the people.* The State cannot be a patron standing above the people. On the contrary, it is actually the people composed of the working class, the collective farmers and the socialist intellectuals which form their own State functioning under the leadership of the Party with the aim of building a new society. The building of a new society is the cause of the broad masses of the people themselves.

That is why it is our task to carry out permanent education to raise the political and cultural standards of the masses. On the other hand, we must found a system of most appropriate organizational relations and methods of work in order to draw the broad masses of the people into the management of the State and the economy and of all social affairs. Only by means of large-scale, meticulous, persistent and creative organizational work, only through constant study, thinking out, experimentation, control and repeated changes in the various forms of organization and management of the State organs and the various economic, mass and social organizations in conformity with the requirements of the laws of social existence and development can we found a system of correct and viable relations. And only then can our daily watchwords such as "a co-op is a home, and the co-op members are its owners", or "workers must take part in the management of factories" and, in a broader sense, the right of the masses as the collective masters be translated into a living reality. Otherwise these remain slogans and statements.

To combine the unified activity of the State under the leadership of the Party with the broad initiative and creative actions of the popular masses is the law of development of our regime. We must proceed from this law and this principle in tackling the question of cadres and setting requirements for cadres as well as in tackling the question of organization and setting requirements for the organization.

For a Communist Party in power, for communists managing the State, one of the biggest and most frightful dangers is to stand aloof from the masses and deprive the people of their right as the collective masters. The strength of the Communist Party, of the communists, always lies in their close relations with the masses. In the conditions of a Communist Party already holding power, this must be understood all the more deeply and carried into effect in all organizational measures and methods of activity.

Cadres build up a movement and in return the movement gives birth to cadres. That is a law in the question of cadres. The whole method and organization of our activity, the whole system of our State and economic management must ensure the fullest observance of the right of the working people as the collective masters and on this basis to ensure the capability to mobilize the major sources of strength of the masses, and the whole of their power and potential, in the creation of material and moral values in order to give rise to the broadest, most powerful, best organized and most effective movement for socialist construction. Cadres must mingle with the masses in this movement, march in the van to set an example for the masses, persuade and organize them, understand their feelings and aspirations, and concern themselves with their everyday moral and material life. They must show modesty and simplicity, listen to the opinions of the masses, gather the masses' experiences and knowledge to complement their own experiences and knowledge. They must constantly place themselves under the control of the masses. In this way, cadres are trained, selected and tempered, and mature along with the movement. And the movement will not cease to give rise to new cadres, able organizers springing from the masses, from the workers, collective farmers and intellectuals—people who, by their self-denying work and their creativity, have made the most notable contributions to the socialist ideal. These are *new men* of socialism whose most prominent characteristic is their consciousness of being the collective masters and their ability to assume this role, their new attitude toward work, their high sense of organization and discipline. Closely linked with their collectives in the struggle for the common cause, they constantly foster and develop their fine moral qualities and their intellectual powers in accordance with the requirements of a man who is the master of society, master of nature and master of himself.

Deeply imbued with the sense of collectiveness, they understand that their own material well-being and moral happiness and their own future lie in the common welfare and future of all, in the development and in the advance of the whole collective and the whole society. Having identified themselves with the whole society, imbued with the spirit of "each for all and all for each", they know what is good for the collective, society and themselves, and what is bad for the interests of the collective, society and their own interests and, consequently, place all their energies and talents at the service of the collective and society. They resolutely defend the interests of the collective and society, and thereby win the esteem and admiration of all. Such persons have emerged and are emerging more and more in our society. They are first of all the heroes, heroines and model combatants, and individuals with outstanding records in the emulation movement for resistance to U.S. aggression, for national salvation, and in the movement of productive labour to build socialism. Never will the source of supply of cadres dry up, provided we take care to discover, encourage, foster and promote them.

Let Us Endeavour to Train and Foster Cadres

Generally speaking, cadres are products of a movement. They mature in the organization, in the life and activity of the organization, in the process of work and struggle to bring to reality the political line and tasks. On the other hand, in order to give rise to a movement and to ensure its more and more vigorous development, we must have cadres. To ensure that our organizations can operate, and operate fruitfully, we must have cadres and good ones at that. That is why the foremost task of all revolutionary movements and all revolutionary organizations is *to endeavour to train and foster cadres* in a systematic manner. At the same time, cadres must endeavour to *train themselves* and *raise their capabilities.* This task is now posed before us in all its urgency.

To adequately meet the need for cadres which is very great and covers many spheres, not only at present but also in the long term—a need arising from future stages of development in the economic, cultural, political and social fields, stages which, it can be predicted, will come at a leaping pace and on very broad scale—we must, on the one hand, make the best use of, and endeavour to foster the existing contingent of cadres. On the other hand, we must urgently train batch after batch of cadres through the regular methods such as schools and classes, according to elaborate programmes which correspond to (and go one step ahead of) the plans for long-range development of the economy and culture. The building of socialism and the development of economy and culture are, by their nature, planned work. All activities must be carried out on the basis of, and according to, accurate and scientific norms. That is why the path of training cadres in a regular, large-scale, basic and systematic manner is of decisive importance.

1. Quickly Fostering and Raising the Standard
   of Leading and Managing Cadres, and Training New Ones

We must take care to foster and quickly raise the standard of leading and managing cadres and at the same time organize on an ever-larger scale, training in a basic and systematic way young cadres who are likely later to assume leading and managing responsibilities. It is necessary to arrange and re-organize in a rational way the network of schools to train and foster theoretical and political cadres, cadres for organization and management, for cultural activities and technological services, and to clearly define the objectives and goals of the the training and development in each type of school and class. In particular, we must pay attention to building and perfecting the system of schools to train and foster leading and managing cadres for the various branches of economy, production and commercial units, as well as scientific and technological branches. There must be a plan to select the objects of our training and expand classes for the training of managing cadres coming from the ranks of technical workers who have shown an aptitude for management, from young demobilized army officers and political cadres of the army, from front-rank workers and co-operative farmers, from all those who have been well tested and have recorded outstanding achievements in production and fighting. Besides full-time schools and classes, it is necessary to develop vigorously such forms of study as on-the-job or correspondence courses. Only in these ways can we satisfy the urgent and increasing demands of training.

We must show great concern for the unceasing improvement of training, both in content and quality. With regard to the leading and managing cadres of the various branches and spheres of activity, they must be firmly armed with Marxism-Leninism and the line and policies of the Party, with knowledge in organization and management, with the necessary professional knowledge as well as scientific and technological knowledge. Without a profound knowledge of the Marxist-Leninist theory and the line and policies of the Party, a cadre cannot grasp the laws governing social and economic development which are the basis of all leading and managerial activities. He will not be able to analyse events as required by the class and scientific viewpoints. Nor will he be able to discover the essence, the linchpin, of the various events and developments, innumerable in their manifestations, of economic and social life.

Nor will he be able correctly to determine what tasks should be attended to intensively in a given period, nor find the way to carry out economic and political tasks correctly and fruitfully. In a word, without a firm knowledge of Marxist-Leninist science (especially of dialectical materialist methodology, historical materialism, and economics), without a firm grasp of the Party line and policies, we will be left in the dark groping, will easily lose our political bearings and will lack foresight, initiative and creativity in our work.

However, it is quite insufficient for leading and managing cadres merely to have a firm grasp of Marxism-Leninism and the Party line and policies. They must also have great expertise in the areas under their charge, know their work perfectly and also know the up-to-date technological and scientific developments and the latest developments in organizational and managerial work related to their branches of activity. Lenin said: "Anybody who studies real life and has practical experience knows that management necessarily implies competency, that a knowledge of all the conditions of production down to the last detail and of the latest technology of your branch of production is required: you must have had a certain scientific training."(13) This is a necessity not only for managing cadres and leading cadres of each branch but also for leading cadres in general. Obviously, the realities of life, the level of the masses and the necessity to do our work better will no longer permit survival of the old habit of making a few political and ideological remarks and releasing interminable, banal political instructions, allegedly to encourage the masses.

We must absolutely set definite cultural standards for Party executives at all levels. In the leading organs of the Party, including the Party committees, we must in the long run also provide for an appropriate proportion of committee members who are able scientific and technological cadres and experts who also have a firm political stand and rich experience in political struggle. In addition, one thing of prime importance is that Party cadres, and leading cadres at various levels and in various Party organizations, should raise the scientific standard of their leadership by working in close co-operation with scientists and experts and making use of their knowledge and experience. Lenin said: "The Communist who has failed to prove his ability to bring together and guide the work of specialists in a spirit of modesty, going to the heart of the matter and studying it in detail, is a potential menace."(14)

2. Training a Contingent of Scientific and Technological Cadres: a Task of Especial Importance

The task of training a contingent of scientific and technical cadres is of particular importance. Socialism and science and technology are organically linked. We often say that socialist industrialization is the central task of the period of transition. We often speak of the necessity to build the material and technical foundations of socialism. We often stress that the technical revolution is the key to socialist industrialization. But if we do not have—in addition to the fundamental political premises—a numerous and able contigent of scientific and technical cadres we can never attain our objectives. Advancing to socialism without going through the period of capitalist development means that in this respect, too, we are inheriting virtually a complete nought from the past. That is why a very heavy task incumbent on us is to train a large and powerful contingent of scientific and technical cadres *sprung from the working class and peasantry, from the ranks of revolutionaries.*

This task requires big and ever bigger efforts from the entire national education system, from the general schools to the higher and vocational institutions, from the institutes of social sciences, natural sciences and all branches of science and technology, from all economic and cultural branches, from the trade unions and the Ho Chi Minh Working Youth Union, from the entire people and the whole State machine. We will spare no effort or outlay in this domain, which plays the decisive role with regard to economic progress in our time, and to the process of our advance forward. Our country is endowed with abundant natural riches, and socialism contains immense sources of strength enabling us to tap and make the fullest use of these riches in service of the welfare and happy life of our people. The biggest scientific and technological revolution in the history of mankind is unfolding excitingly in the world. We must take every opportunity to make use of its gains in order to quickly complete the building of socialism in our country. Technology can be imported but the question is that there must be men to use that technology. That is why we must have a big contingent of scientific and technical cadres completely loyal and dedicated to the socialist cause, eager to move into work on the scientific and technological front, for the sake of the prosperity of the country and the happiness of the people, deeply imbued with the Marxist-Leninist outlook on the world and scientific methodology, with an adequate knowledge of the realities of our country and a firm grasp of the theoretical foundations of the relevant branches of modern science and technology. These cadres must be able to apply this knowledge in an independent and creative manner to the solution of scientific and technical problems posed by the realities of production and life in our country and know how to make the best use of the traditional experience of our people, in order quickly to catch up with advanced world standards.

It is necessary to build an educational system in which all the higher educational institutions and vocational schools, and all branches of the economy and research institutes, share the responsibility for and work in close co-ordination in the training of experts in conformity with the needs of economic development and with the trend of scientific and technological progress. We must proceed urgently to a reform of education in the light of the needs of a quickly developing modern science and technology and make the best preparations for the young generation to carry out productive labour and undertake creative labour in the different domains of science and technology necessary for the national economy.

We must achieve a balanced and homogeneous improvement of the level of the different branches in the whole system of training in the light of the needs of the building and development of the economy and culture, not only in the immediate future but also for a long time to come. The rational utilization of scientific and technical cadres has in itself the effect of training. All branches and levels of leadership and all organizations engaged in scientific and technological activities should review the situation in this sphere and take resolute steps to correct irrationalities without delay. A very fruitful way of training cadres on-the-job is to assign them appropriate work, give them all the help needed, and create conditions for them to accomplish their work, supply them with adequate study materials and widely develop all forms of part-work-part-study. It is necessary on the one hand to combine correctly the unified management of science and technology, and organize the various forms of collective work and socialist co-operation that will make it possible to concentrate the efforts of scientific and technical cadres on resolving definite tasks and, on the other hand, to care for, discover, encourage, support and develop to the maximum all creative power of the collectives of scientific and technical workers and of each scientific and technical cadre. This has an important significance for the continuous raising of the standards and capabilities of scientific and technical cadres.

3. Cadres Must Constantly Train
   and Temper Themselves

Training and tempering oneself is for any leading and managing cadre or scientific and technical cadre an indispensable condition for the consistent raising of his qualities and standards.

Cadres in general, and, in the first place, Party members and cadres, are the most advanced representatives of the masses with regard to political and ideological stand, scientific knowledge, understanding of social obligations, and the capacity to find ways and means to resolve these tasks, as well as with regard to the sense of being the collective master, the spirit of putting public interest above personal interests and a sound, modest, and healthy way of life. Each cadre, first of all, each Communist, must be an example to the masses with regard to the unfailing loyalty to Marxism-Leninism, to the socialist and communist ideal. He must show the highest sense of organization and discipline, a great deal of revolutionary enthusiasm and ardour for work, clearsightedness in action and the firmest will in daily endeavours for the success of the revolutionary cause. We cannot conceive of a cadre who falls short of mass levels in revolutionary consciousness, in level of knowledge and in capacity to resolve questions posed by the revolutionary tasks, in revolutionary ardour and zeal in work. There is no doubt that today the level of the masses is definitely higher than in the past and has the most favourable conditions to grow and mature quickly in all fields.

All of this requires from each cadre sustained and major efforts, a strict sense of responsibility in learning and training in order to raise himself constantly to the level of his tasks. His responsibility consists first of all in *learning* and he must understand this word in its fullest and deepest sense. It is necessary to read books and newspapers, to acquire therefrom the knowledge accumulated by mankind. Lenin said: "One can become a Communist only after having enriched one's mind through the acquisition of all the treasures of knowledge created by mankind . . . only on the basis of modern knowledge can that society (Communist society—L.D.) be created . . . and without this knowledge, Communism remains but an aspiration."(15) It must be said that quite a few of our cadres are still lazy, very lazy in the matter of reading books, and some do not even read Party newspapers. That is absolutely unpardonable for a Party member and cadre. Of course, reading books is not synonymous with being a bookworm. However, we cannot use opposition to being a bookworm as an excuse for laziness in learning. The point is to know how to read books in order not to become a bookworm but to acquire knowledge, to enrich our minds with science in all practical matters.

We must learn not only through books and newspapers, but also in practical life, in our own work, in the summing up of the experiences of our work, through frequent self-criticism and criticism. The ultimate goal of learning through books is to solve questions arising from life and work. *Summing up experiences and self-criticism and criticism* are methods of study of paramount importance. A cadre must create for himself the habit of thinking independently and the capacity to analyse, in the process of endeavouring to carry out his tasks, the class significance, the socio-economic effect of each measure being applied. He must proceed from his own experience to review each step he has taken and hence to draw accurate and scientific conclusions that will help him to illuminate the path ahead, give the fullest scope to what is right and severely and sincerely to make self-criticism of the wrong without fearing to mend his errors and persist in his efforts. Never should he be complacent. It is difficult for any cadre who lacks such qualities and qualifications to mature and to be equal to his tasks.

We must combine learning through books with learning from the practice of life, work, the experiences of the collective, the experiences of one's organization and of kindred organizations, the experiences of the leaders and of the masses, the experiences of our country and of others, the lessons of success and also the lessons of failure. *Theory constantly linked with practice and practice enlightened by theory, our minds active at all times, and our thinking always linked with action, this is our method of learning.* This is the main method for improving our theoretical thinking and our capacities for practice. In both these areas our deficiency is still evident, limiting our creative powers and preventing us from achieving the highest results in our work.

The leading and managerial tasks of the Party and State are very heavy and will become more and more so. With our full sense of responsibility to the people, we never hide our weaknesses, shortcomings and even the errors sometimes committed in our work. The fact is that "the art of administration does not descend from heaven, it is not inspired by the Holy Ghost. And the fact that a class is a leading class does not make it at once capable of administering . . . . We, therefore, say that the victorious class must be mature."(16) It is precisely for that reason that we have realized all the importance of the task of learning. "Learn, learn more, learn forever." Every cadre, whatever his position, whether he is an old hand or a newcomer, must study hard. The higher his position and the heavier his responsibility, the harder he must study because some defect or error resulting from his incapacity could lead to great damage. Veteran cadres must study still harder in order to meet new requirements. New and younger cadres naturally must show the greatest zeal and perseverance in learning. They must show genuine modesty and should never be complacent or consider themselves as knowing more than others. They must show determination to scale the highest peaks in all domains of knowledge necessary for our cause of creating a new society.

Learning has always been for all Party members and cadres, a criterion of Party character. For cadres in general and for every citizen without exception, learning is a duty already laid down by the National Assembly. It is necessary to bring about a stirring, widespread and permanent movement for learning. The goal of learning should not be limited to raising our level of knowledge. Rather it is to achieve the best results in our productive labour, our work and our struggle. We must try by all means to bring about a stirring movement to attain high peaks in culture and knowledge in our productive labour, our work and our struggle, *with the determination to make culture and knowledge our weapon and our strength in the struggle to become masters of society, masters of culture and masters of ourselves.* This is an important manifestation of the fighting stand of the class engaged in building a system of collective mastery and creating a really civilized society.

We should never forget that learning and the whole system of education *must combine the need of raising our consciousness and knowledge with that of raising our communist qualities and morality,* and that "Communist morality is based on the struggle for the consolidation and completion of communism. That is also the basis of communist training, education and teaching."(17) We are learning for the sake of this great cause. We must learn in such a way that all the knowledge we accumulate will help in the formation, strengthening and constant raising of our proletarian ideology, our Marxist-Leninist outlook on the world and our Communist outlook on life, in such a way that the communist ideal and the scientific knowledge of communism really become the personal beliefs of everyone, the motive force and the compass for all our daily activities.

In the conditions of a Party holding State power, and of the implementation of the socialist law of distribution according to work done, it is natural that in the life of cadres there arises the question of position and remuneration which should be solved by the Party and State policies in a rational way, and in keeping with the principle of giving incentives to labour and talent and with each step forward of socialism. However, a Communist would deny himself that noble name if he let such questions prevail over and even replace his noble ideal and qualities, the ideal for which we have of our own free will placed ourselves under the Party banner and have sworn to fight all our life in defiance of all hardships and sacrifices, the ideal for which we have so many times risked our lives and for which our people have consistently and loyally followed the Party, trusted and loved us, the ideal for the realization of which our people have shed and are shedding so much sweat and blood even though its complete realization is still a long way off and many privations and hardships are ahead. We *must link learning with struggle*, struggle against ourselves and struggle for the realization of our revolutionary tasks, so that the noble socialist and communist ideal completely prevails in our minds, in our lives and in all our daily activities, and also in the life of the entire society, so that individualism has no more room in our minds and actions or in social life as a whole.

The sense of organization and discipline is absolutely necessary in revolutionary struggle. That is why one of the foremost qualities which a cadre must constantly foster is the sense of organization and discipline. This is the most important virtue manifesting *the ideology of the proletariat of being the collective masters*, which is basically opposed to individualism and bourgeois and petty-bourgeois liberalism.

Not only in theory but also through the whole experience of proletarian dictatorship in the world, the following famous proposition of Lenin has proved its extraordinary vitality: "The essence of proletarian dictatorship is not in force alone, or even mainly in force. Its chief feature is the organization and discipline of the advanced contingent of the working people, of their vanguard, of their sole leader, the proletariat."(18) The enemy can knock down the revolutionaries when their ranks are confused, when they are "like an orchestra in which the drum and the trumpet do not play in tune." But if they are a monolithic army in which millions keep the same pace and act as one man, the revolution is invincible, proletarian dictatorship is invincible.

Even the slightest slackening of discipline suffices to create a fissure for the enemy to thrust his hands into. On the contrary, if we can maintain the sense of organization and discipline and the unity of mind of the proletariat and the vanguard leading brigade of proletarian dictatorship we can already to some extent cool the counter-revolutionary hysteria of the class enemy in their criminal plots. And, when proletarian dictatorship needs violence for repression, it is also this sense of organization and discipline that constitutes the basis, the main source of strength, to ensure the triumph of revolutionary violence over counter-revolutionary violence.

We need organization and discipline not only to defend proletarian dictatorship against all plots and acts of revival and subversion of the counter-revolutionary forces inside and outside the country, but also to ensure that proletarian dictatorship really becomes a power of the people. The people give us ample powers to work in their interests. But, if after having been vested with powers, we do not bind ourselves by very stringent rules in organization, discipline and also in law, if we do not severely place ourselves within these ties, then we are very apt to do wrong things harmful to the interests of the people.

The absolute necessity for us to be an organized and disciplined body stems from the very nature and objective of the struggle of proletarian dictatorship aimed at reforming the old society and building a new one. This is the prime condition for the building of the socialist economy. Socialism is the abolition of the capitalist regime and the system of private ownership in general, the source of inorganization in production leading to sharp contradictions and conflicts in the whole of social life. This regime and system are being replaced by the collective, socialist, system of ownership of the means of production which makes possible and requires organized, centralized and unified production on a nation-wide scale by millions of persons according to a calculated plan and by means of large-scale mechanized industry.

However, the greatest difficulty for socialism, for the building of socialism, actually lies in the organizational field, in the task of establishing a new labour discipline and a new social discipline. This difficulty is all the greater and all the more intractable if we are advancing from small-scale production. In this case, proletarian dictatorship must go through a period of protracted and arduous struggle between the organizational and disciplinary character of the proletariat on the one hand and the very dangerous power of spontaneous development of the state of inorganization and anarchy of the petty-bourgeoisie on the other. This state of things pervades all domains of social life: in economy, in style of work, in ideology and in the general attitude of people, in their customs and habits . . . .

We have steered small-scale production onto the path of collectivization. The system of small private ownership has been replaced by collective ownership which forms, together with the system of all-people ownership, the unified socialist economic structure. That is a success of historic significance. That is a very fundamental victory of the organizational and disciplinary character of the proletariat over the liberal, scattered, inorganized and anarchist character of the petty-bourgeoisie. However, this is only an *initial step* and barely an initial step. The organizational path is a long path to create new forms of social discipline. It takes decades. In fact, only large-scale mechanized industry can truly create and ensure an organizational and disciplinary character in a really full and lasting way. However, big mechanized industry is precisely what we are striving to create in order to equip all sections of the national economy and to provide the foundation for socialist production relations.

We have always believed that only when this objective is reached can the socialist transformation of small production be considered really completed.

It is because our economy still bears the marked characteristics of small production in all respects: technology, organization of production and methods of production, that there is still ground for the state of dispersion, liberalism, spontaneous development, inorganization and anarchy, to flourish. The struggle against this state of things, which runs completely counter to socialism, must be carried on with the greatest firmness and perseverance. Otherwise, socialism cannot triumph.

The political and ideological education and the organization and control work undertaken by the Party and the various mass organizations, especially the trade unions and the Youth Union, as well as the legal work of the state, must be closely combined in order to consolidate and strengthen the organizational and disciplinary character of our society, especially within the Party organizations, within the ranks of cadres, in the State organs and managerial organs. Our proletarian dictatorship, first of all the vanguard leading contingent of the dictatorship, i.e. our Party itself, must prove its strength by its organizational and disciplinary character. This is *one of the fundamental conditions* to ensure success for the great cause of socialist construction.

A new period of the revolution in our country has begun.

The great victory of our sacred resistance to U.S. aggression, for national salvation has created unprecedentedly favourable conditions for the building of socialism in the North as well as for the completion of the national people's democratic revolution in the South. This is the most glorious period in our national history. Many new possibilities have emerged and are emerging, making it possible for us to take still greater strides forward on the road toward building a unified Viet Nam in independence, freedom, peace and prosperity.

The victories recorded by our people are extremely great. Extremely bright prospects are open to us. However we *should by no means rest on our laurels* and forget that the *road to our ultimate goal remains very long, very complex and full of hardships.* Our Party and people are facing new battles that require concentrated and major efforts to give a powerful stimulus to the building of a new economy, a new regime and a new man so that the socialist North can develop to the highest degree its historic influence on the revolutionary cause of the whole country in the new stage. The victories of historic significance recorded in the past period of struggle prove that our people, our nation, under the leadership of our Party, armed with an independent, sovereign, correct and creative line, are fully capable of solving the questions posed by the present era in the life of our nation. This is a firm basis for our confidence in final victory in the process of our struggle for the radiant future of our country and for the high peaks of human civilization.

"To build socialism, it is necessary to have socialist men." That teaching of President Ho Chi Minh, now more than ever, must be understood in its fullest meaning and strictly observed, first of all among Party cadres and members. In the new struggle, in our capacity as the collective masters, we must give full play to the revolutionary heroism and intelligence which has been so magnificently displayed in the anti-U.S. war of resistance, for national salvation. Let every one of us devote all his energies and talents to the revolution in the new period in order to bring prosperity to our country and happiness to our people!

Let all our Party cadres and members strive still harder, make still greater and continuous efforts in order to be worthy of their duties, worthy of our glorious Party and our glorious nation.

Le Duan on the
Vietnamese Revolution

The New Stage
of our Revolution
and the Tasks
of the Trade Unions

Our revolution has entered a new stage in very favourable conditions but the battle for complete independence and freedom throughout the country remains very difficult and complex. This calls for a vigorous all-round growth of the North, and consequently for the latter's quicker and stronger advance toward socialism. That is the natural requirement born of the law of internal development of the socialist revolution itself in North Viet Nam. The Party's Central Committee's 22nd Plenum defined *the North's general tasks in the new stage* as follows: unite the whole people, fight for the safeguarding of peace, actively carry out socialist industrialization, vigorously impel the three revolutions,(1) build the North and take it speedily, vigorously and steadily to socialism; closely coordinate economy and national defence, heighten vigilance, stand ready to foil every scheme of the U.S. and its agents; do our best to discharge our duty in the revolutionary struggle for the completion of independence and democracy in South Viet Nam and for ultimate national reunification, fulfil our internationalist obligation toward the Lao and Khmer revolutions.

The North's task in the two years 1974 and 1975 is: to rapidly complete the healing of the wounds of war, actively rehabilitate

---

Speech at the third Viet Nam Trade Union Congress (February 11-14, 1974).

99

and develop the economy, promote culture, continue to lay the material and technical foundations of socialism, consolidate socialist relations of production, strengthen the socialist system in every respect, restore to normal the economy and the life of the masses, consolidate national defence, do our utmost to discharge our duty toward the heroic South.

The above task is part of the initial steps to socialist industrialization aimed at providing the necessary facilities for the North's construction to be carried out on an ever greater scale and at an ever quicker rate. Its purpose is also to strengthen the forces of revolution in the entire land and provide a firm basis for the fight to preserve peace and achieve complete independence and democracy in South Viet Nam.

The more vigorously the shaping of a new society is prosecuted, the heavier the responsibility of the working class and the tasks of trade unions become. *In this connection, a clear realization as to what stage we are in on our way to socialism is necessary; we should have a clear view of what has been done and what has not been done and remains to be done in the immediate and more remote future.*

The greatest achievement of the North's socialist revolution has been the elimination of oppression and exploitation, the liquidation of the exploiting classes as such, and the replacement of small-scale and scattered production by co-operation. The class of individual farmers ground down for thousands of years by poverty and ignorance has been replaced by a new class—the collective peasantry—although the latter's quality remains to be improved. A socialist intelligentsia consisting of an overwhelming majority of people of worker and peasant stock trained under the new regime has emerged, taken shape and has rapidly grown up. Our working class, motive force of our nation's history for the last fifty years, has been growing qualitatively and quantitatively. Under the leadership of the working class whose representative is our Party, the working people of the North have become masters of our society and State and of their own fate. It is the biggest leap forward in our nation's history and a source of inexhaustible strength for the great rear-base, bastion of the revolution in the country as a whole. It is the greatest motive force contributing to the process of wiping out poverty and backwardness and of building a strong and prosperous socialist country.

On the basis of such a basic change, our economy and culture have made initial advances. During the war years, when combat and assistance to the South had to be attended to, the North's economic potential continued to be built and increased, understandably in a way suitable to the war situation, and under the serious limitations imposed by the war.

Though they were the target of the enemy's most furious, relentless and concentrated strikes, transport and communications were kept going. Millions of workers were mobilized to do or help the fighting; yet production in the rear went on and even made progress in many respects. In some areas, intensive farming and labour productivity recorded gains. In industry, a number of branches continued to manufacture a considerable quantity of products in service of production and combat and to meet the people's needs. Education, culture and public health were not checked by the war in their vigorous advance. The training of technicians and skilled workers not only did not slow down but was even accelerated, in anticipation of large-scale post-war construction.

In the context of a mainly agricultural economy, of weak productive forces and of a host of handicaps caused by a protracted war—the most savage, most brutal and greatest war in size and in genocidal violence ever waged by the most affluent and powerful imperialism against a nation of medium size and population—an adequate supply of prime necessities, education and medical care was ensured for the people, and no great disturbances were recorded in the distribution of goods, their prices and the living standard of the masses, who were made safe from hunger and cold, the usual companions of a fierce and long-drawn-out war, as has been seen in many countries.

What is one to think of all this? One may describe it as a tremendous feat. Thanks to the superiority of the new relations of production, the North's undeveloped economy stood the bitter test of war and played its part in the signal success of the resistance against U.S. aggression, for national salvation. No other social system could have survived in such conditions, let alone accomplished what we did in those gruelling years.

In 1973 alone, the first year of economic rehabilitation, important parts of the direct aftermath of the war were remedied. Production and the people's living conditions are being stabilized, many aspects of production have surpassed the levels of 1965; economic management has made progress. These are but initial achievements; however, they prove the great vitality of our regime and reflect the strong will of the working class and people in the North who are entering a new stage of the revolution; they at the same time testify to the correctness of our Party's line.

When referring to our working class and people's successes and achievements, we never forget the substantial, precious and many-sided contribution to them of the fraternal socialist countries, first of all the Soviet Union and China, of the world's working class and working people, and of all countries and peoples who love indepencence, freedom, justice and peace.

I avail myself of the presence of trade union representatives from various countries in this hall to request them to convey to our fellow class members in the whole world, fresh expressions of our heartfelt gratitude for their support and assistance, imbued with the spirit of proletarian internationalism.

An Urgent Requirement:
To Step up Socialist Industrialization

A full realization of the great significance of our achievements is necessary but it is equally imperative to be perfectly clear about what stage our socialist construction is now in and what key problems need solving at this juncture to get to socialism. More than anyone else, trade union cadres and all politically conscious workers must ask themselves that question, must ponder over it. There must be full realization that the *working class as the ruling class, as the leading class of the State, is the vanguard class in the transformation of the old society and in the moulding of a new society.* As a result, the conditions of trade union work have radically changed. If one of trade unionism's principal functions is to uphold the interests of the working class, *its supreme and most basic interest once that class has taken power is to successfully build socialism.* The trade unions must drive this home to all their members, to all toilers, in order to instil in them the sense of responsibility, as collective master, for all happenings in our society, a personal interest in, and the habit of pondering over, every important and burning issue which may arise in the course of the shaping of a new society.

It is obvious that we have recorded great achievements, but there is still much room for dissatisfaction in many respects, most particularly in our economic situation. We must not be complacent, and we are still far from having any grounds for complacency, about what we have accomplished. It could have been more if it had not been for our mistakes and shortcomings. We will be even less complacent if we check our results against the noble objectives of socialism.

Looked at from this angle, the North's economy faces great difficulties and problems requiring radical solutions. There is a lot to be done immediately and urgently. Otherwise it will be impossible even to inch forward on the road to socialism. Otherwise even what are called the initial fruits of socialism will be in jeopardy.

We do not hesitate to speak of our difficulties. If we want to advance, we must realize them all in order to surmount them; we must be aware of all our problems, of all our tasks. As a matter of fact, building socialism is never and nowhere an easy job. Even in normal conditions, that is, when material prerequisites have been prepared by developed capitalism, free from war and aggression, such an undertaking is by no means plain sailing, let alone in our special situation where the stage of capitalist development must be by-passed, and the economy has been heavily damaged by the war of aggression and destruction.

With the highest level possible of military deployment against our country, with millions of tons of bombs and shells, the U.S. imperialists destroyed nearly all the economic structures our people had built at the cost of a tremendous amount of energy. Without the war, the North would have been in much better shape economically. The war has rolled back our originally underdeveloped economy, which had just made a step forward, to where it was more than ten years ago. Apart from material damage estimated at many billion *dong*, other after-effects will take a rather long time to overcome.

When recalling these problems we do not entertain any feeling of regret. No, we never feel any regret over the price of independence and freedom. For our nation, our class, and for each of us, independence and freedom are priceless. Our view about it has been expressed by President Ho Chi Minh: "Hanoi, Haiphong and other cities may be flattened, but this prospect will not cow us into submission. Nothing is more precious than independence and freedom. When the battle is won, we shall rebuild our country into a better, bigger and more beautiful one."

Nearly a century of colonial domination has caused our people to realize clearly what independence and freedom really mean to them. Socialism, this truth of our times, has brought out in bolder relief the fact that independence and freedom are invaluable. Now that peace has been restored in the North, we must seize the opportunity and give a big boost to our construction, thereby raising our economic and national defence potential and making our country sufficiently strong to preserve peace, and force our adversary to fully and strictly implement the Paris Agreement, which is the dearest wish of our entire people. If the enemy should fail to learn the lesson, which is still fresh, and starts a new war of destruction against the North, we must be instantly ready to make every sacrifice, and "with hammer or plough in one hand, and rifle in the other," to confront and crush the aggressor. In construction and combat alike, our only motive is to defend independence and freedom.

Our present most important daily task here in the North is to build. It is precisely because of this that we must know every aspect of our present economic situation well, be aware of all our difficulties and of their causes, if they are to be overcome.

The great, varied and ever increasing requirements which are placed on our economy, which is poor and unbalanced in nature, and whose problems have been compounded by our mistakes and shortcomings in leadership, guidance and management, only highlight its imbalance and fundamental weaknesses.

Our social labour force is considerable but it is not made full use of, and its productivity is still very low. The state apparatus, particularly administrative bodies, non-productive organs, have swollen excessively in recent years. Salaries and similar expenditures have outstripped the possibilities of the economy. Moreover, a population explosion (a ten-million rise from 1954 to 1973) has worsened the lack of equilibrium between the multiple needs of life and our present financial and economic resources. Agricultural production is still unstable and very uneven, unable to meet the people's needs in foodstuffs, in raw materials for industry, in export products. In industry most of the important factories were destroyed during the war and while a large number of them have been rehabilitated, production has not been brought back to normal. Life has been restored only to a small degree of normalcy, the supply of food still falls short of plans, many consumer goods are still not available. Due to a low level of production, a population explosion, a low national income which does not meet adequately the needs of consumption, we cannot yet ensure a balance between imports and exports. In short, the outstanding feature of the North's present economic situation is that social labour and economic potential are not made the most of, while social production is still very low, domestic capital accumulation absent, and the life of the masses still hard.

The root cause of such a situation lies in the fact that there are mistakes, shortcomings and immaturity in our economic leadership, guidance and management. There have certainly been serious mistakes which we must severely criticise and resolutely make good.

However, to get to the root of the problem, we must ask ourselves this question: if we had made no mistakes at all, how good would the situation have been? Naturally, it would have been better, and, in some respects and in some places, far better. But our poverty and backwardness would not have been basically done away with. For, starting from a very low level, the North has been engaged in socialist construction for less the 20 years—12 of which were taken up by the war and only eight of which were really devoted to construction—and, as pointed out above, our severe losses have substantially impeded our progress.

Then, what is the crux of the matter now? It is the fact that we are still in an abnormal, unnatural position. We are building socialism, but a small-scale, basically agricultural economy still prevails. There are new relations of production, but we cannot yet say that we have a socialist mode of production. So we may say we do have and at the same time do not have full socialism. *There lies the paradox of our development.* All things considered, *the crux of the matter is that we have not been able to lay the material and technical foundations of socialism.* While these are lacking, nothing else can survive and develop normally, naturally. Thus, many difficulties are inevitable. As we all know, capitalism in its manufacturing stage could not be said to be viable because, as Marx explained, "it had not acquired a material framework independent of the worker himself." Only when machines were invented could it secure such a framework. "Capitalism could in the end stand on its feet only thanks to the economic force of things."(2) Capitalism could not survive in the context of handicrafts, let alone socialism.

Therefore we are faced with a grave choice: either rapidly create the "material framework" of socialism or keep whatever new things have been engendered by socialism in a permanent state of debility and instability. Either move quickly forward, or reverse back to individual production, bankruptcy and destitution.

There is only one course of action to choose: *give a strong impulse to socialist industrialization, advance quickly to large-scale socialist production.* This was the basic objective of the resolutions of the 19th, 20th and particularly the 22nd sessions of the Party Central Committee. These dealt with many facets of economic construction and development, of economic leadership and management. But all aspects were geared in the discussions to the implementation of the central task, i.e., to develop socialist industrialization and rapidly take the North to large-scale socialist production. They were all geared to the satisfaction of the central requirement, i.e., to vigorously expand the forces of production and concurrently to consolidate and constantly perfect socialist relations of production.

To develop the forces of production, we must rely on the new relations of production, which must be readjusted and consolidated, and whose superiority must be brought into play. Any farming or handicraft co-operative which works badly or whose members have "one foot in and the other out" must be promptly and resolutely set right, otherwise its production and productivity cannot be raised. On the other hand we must regard the all-out development of the forces of production as the basic method to consolidate and perfect the new relations of production. Clearly, the new relations of production have not been consolidated (in the state-owned sector or in the collective sector, but chiefly in the collective sector). This is due to many causes. So a series of measures must be undertaken simultaneously. But all things considered, the development of the forces of production remains the most decisive means to consolidate and perfect the new relations of production. And to this effect, socialist industrialization must be impelled forward, and the whole economy must be shifted to large-scale socialist production.

The Revolution to Take Small Production to Large-Scale Socialist Production

There cannot be, there will never be, socialism in a society based on small production. Even capitalism could emerge only from large-scale production, let alone socialism which is a socio-economic structure higher than capitalism, for on the basis of the large-scale production created by the latter, socialism will develop a social production of much larger scale after overthrowing capitalism and removing the antagonistic contradictions inherent in large-scale capitalist production. The triumph of socialism over capitalism can only be regarded as definitive when it is able to give birth to a social productivity higher than that of capitalism; such productivity is the outcome of highly and widely mechanized production, capable of making full use of the newest achievements of modern science and techniques.

Large-scale production is a system of social production based on the socialist ownership of the means of production existing in the form of ownership by the entire people and collective ownership, and with large-scale industry as its foundation. It is a production embracing many branches, many sectors, many different economic undertakings operating along the line of specialization and co-operation and expanding in a balanced and harmonious fashion into an organic entity of a national economy under the centralized and unified leadership of the State of proletarian dictatorship. In large-scale socialist production every link, from production to circulation and distribution, even distribution to each individual, even a handicraft enterprise or a family sideline, is a cog in the common machinery of the social division of work in service of the national economy. In economic activity as a whole, each private individual's labour is not taken separately and opposed to social labour. It is labour with a social character aimed at directly meeting *first and foremost* the common needs of society, and, on this basis, meeting the needs of every person, every family, every community.

Large-scale production is the negation of small production with its scattered and petty character, with its rudimentary tools, with its small output of each product, with each producer "turning out enough for his own use," at best with a small surplus which he can barter at a small local market. In mankind's history, small production has been replaced by large-scale capitalist production. Thus, according to the general law, the task of socialism is no longer to expand small production into large-scale production, but to bring about a basic change in large-scale capitalist production, according to the principles of socialism. It is also to bring into play the superiority of socialist relations of production and reorganize and greatly improve the existing large-scale production and enable it to satisfy to the maximum society's ever-growing material and cultural needs, on the basis of ever higher techniques.

However, such is not our path. By-passing the stage of capitalist development and advancing straight to socialism implies that with us, it is not capitalism but socialism that is responsible for expanding small production into large-scale production. And, naturally, what we have to create should be large-scale socialist production, that is to say a large-scale production which is much higher than large-scale capitalist production not only in its socio-economic nature but also in its size and degree of development. *So the burden placed by history on the shoulders of our working class is a double one.* We have to create a large-scale production with an efficiency not only superior to that of small individual production but also to that of large-scale capitalist production. Otherwise there will be no ultimate and total victory of socialism.

"Socialism begins where large-scale production begins", Lenin said. "Only these material conditions, the material conditions of large-scale machine industry serving tens of millions of people, only these are the basis of socialism, and to learn to deal with this in a petty-bourgeois, peasant country is difficult, but possible."(3) The task of enlarging small production into large-scale socialist production is a complete novelty indeed. With the realities of life helping us to acquire a clearer and clearer idea of this, and with the Party's correct line, we believe that this extremely complex and tough task can still be brought to fruition.

To turn our country from a backward agricultural land with a system of mainly small-scale production into one with large-scale socialist production, there is for us no other alternative than *socialist industrialization,* which the Party's Third Congress defined as our central task for the whole transitional stage in our country. The process of building large-scale socialist production in our country is that of transforming the relations of production coupled with the technical revolution, with the turning of handicraft labour into mechanized labour. It is also that of a new division of labour, of expanding new branches of activity, of greater specialization and closer co-operation. It is also a process of building a national, sovereign economy and of concurrently broadening economic relations with the outside world, first of all with the countries of the socialist system. The path to large-scale socialist production, the shortest way to socialism, is to wield with a firm hand the dictatorship of the proletariat and to carry out three simultaneous revolutions: a revolution in the relations of production, a technical revolution, and an ideological and cultural revolution. They are three facets, closely connected and interacting, of the same process, with the technical revolution occupying the key position.

To advance to large-scale socialist production, it is not possible to develop industry one-sidedly, it is not possible to build heavy industry one-sidedly. Industry cannot grow, short of prerequisites supplied by agriculture like foodstuffs, raw materials, manpower, markets—hence the necessity of a balanced expansion of agriculture and industry.

It is not possible to build heavy industry one-sidedly, to develop industry in the absence of a balanced growth of agriculture. But it is wrong to recommend leaning on agriculture alone to advance to large-scale production. It is tantamount to failure to grasp, or to deny, the role of industry. It is a virtual negation of the historical role of the working class. As a matter of fact, agriculture cannot on its own achieve large-scale production. When we say agriculture is the basis for industrial development, we mean that such an agriculture must be one which has started to record high yields and a high percentage of marketable products. Short of this, it cannot serve as a basis for industrial expansion. And to attain such a rate, agriculture needs aid from industry *right from the start*; industry must exert an immediate beneficial influence on agriculture.

Thus we should not wait until a developed modern industry comes into being to launch large-scale agricultural production nor should we try to advance to large-scale production from agriculture. In our country the process must be: priority rational development of heavy industry on the basis of the development of agriculture and light industry, building the centrally-run economy coupled with expansion of the regional economy, and co-ordination of economy and national defence. It is the only suitable line for the specific conditions of our country. It shows consideration for the leading role of industry, and for the law of priority development of heavy industry, a fundamental law from which any departure makes it basically impossible to create large-scale production. It will help us avoid unnecessary strains in our economic and social life, bound to be caused by the one-sided development of heavy industry. It will help us solve two sharp contradictions in our industrialization: *first*, the contradiction between the need for rapid and substantial capital accumulation and the context of a poor and backward economy; *second*, the contradiction between the necessity of capital accumulation and the necessity of improving the masses' living conditions, since our job is not capitalist industrialization but socialist industrialization, since our aim is large-scale socialist production, and since we carry out our undertakings with the revolutionary enthusiasm of the working masses who are the collective masters of the country concerned with the steady betterment of their own welfare instead of being exploited by capitalism. These two contradictions were exacerbated by the necessity to reserve a considerable amount of manpower and resources to wage a nationwide war. At present, though peace has been brought back to the North, the task of strengthening national defence, defending it and assisting the South still retains its full importance.

Organically co-ordinating industrial and agricultural development on the basis of priority rational development of heavy industry—and this right from the beginning and all through the process of industrialization. It is essentially the path of the *worker-peasant alliance, with the working class as leader.* By this path, the working class leads the peasantry to socialism in the shortest time and without having to suffer the pangs of capitalist development. By this path, our country will be able to wipe out a centuries-old state of backwardness and stagnation within a few decades.

The North's agriculture went through an early co-operativization, prompted by the need to reorganize labour, to make a more rational use of land, to have the necessary forces to carry out hydraulic works and also to benefit from the latest achievements of agricultural science. Such a course of action was possible thanks to the revolutionary zeal of our peasantry who right from the birth of our Party have been loyal followers of the working class. If in national democratic revolution the foundation of the worker-peasant alliance was the realization of the slogan "national independence and land to the tiller," the slogan in the present socialist revolution is agricultural co-operation and socialist industrialization. Without the former, the worker-peasant alliance is inconceivable. And a co-operativized agriculture can only be viable if based on large-scale industrial production. This is a specific feature of North Viet Nam according to which we can carry out agricultural co-operation before mechanization has been effected, and this course of action has proved to be suitable. It is however time to speed up socialist industrialization if the new relations in agriculture are to be consolidated, the worker-peasant alliance is to be strengthened and the leading role of the working class is to be confirmed.

Expanding small production into large-scale socialist production is the greatest, most far-reaching and most radical revolution. It is a most difficult and complex revolution whose success will have a decisive impact on the whole socialist cause in the North. *This is fundamentally a revolution which changes small production into large-scale socialist production.* It will radically transform the economic foundations of our society, in terms not only of the relations of production but also of the forces of production, and not only in the field of production but also of distribution. It will provide the entire economic life and activity of the North with a modern, socialist basis.

In the process, *the working class* will keep pace with the incessant growth of industry and so will its economic, social and political standing and leading role. *The worker-peasant alliance* will be further consolidated and expanded in the course of the development of agriculture into large-scale socialist production and of the growth and coming of age of collective relations of production and of the collective peasantry. Thus *the foundations of the dictatorship of the proletariat* will become more solid. Parallel with the vigorous development of the technical revolution, of culture and science, during the advance toward large-scale production, the socialist intelligentsia will grow quickly in numbers. As an extremely important motive force of the advance from small production to large-scale production, *the alliance of the workers, collective peasants and socialist intellectuals will be further strengthened*. This will be a firm social basis for our State and for the political and spiritual like-mindedness of our society. The revolution designed to take small production to large-scale production will not only be the process of creating the socialist mode of production, of consolidating and expanding the economic foundation of our politico-social life, but also that of discarding die-hard conservatism, lack of concentration, casualness and indiscipline inherent for thousands of generations in small production. In short, it is an all-sided revolution.

The motive force which speeded up the emergence of large-scale capitalist production was the unquenchable lust for profit of the capitalists, the desire to exploit, exploit more, exploit always. That of large-scale socialist production is diametrically opposite. It is the eagerness for revolution, more revolution and uninterrupted revolution. It is the will to emancipate labour, to win the right to collective mastery for the toilers. It is the dictatorship of the proletariat with three revolutions: revolution in the relations of production, technical revolution, and ideological and cultural revolution, in which the technical revolution holds the key position. It is the self-imposed, selfless, heroic and creative labour of the working class, collective peasantry, socialist intellectuals, and of all workers by hand and brain, led by the Party of the working class, following the objective laws of development of society. If we carry out these three revolutions strictly step by step in every production base, in every branch of activity, in every locality and throughout the country, we shall rapidly create the motive forces required to bring about large-scale socialist production.

Launching an Impetuous Revolutionary Movement Among Workers and Employees

Our working class in North Viet Nam has become the ruling class of the country. As for the trade unions, they are no longer a tool for struggling against oppression and exploitation, but are assuming the role of an extremely important link in the system of the dictatorship of the proletariat. One cannot imagine the working people's regime of collective mastery without the existence of the trade unions with their extensive rights guaranteed by laws of the State. Lenin said: "The trade unions must collaborate closely and constantly with the government, all the political and economic activities of which are guided by the class-conscious vanguard of the working class—the Communist Party. Being a school of communism in general, the trade unions must, in particular, be a school for training the whole mass of workers, and eventually all

113

working people, in the art of managing socialist industry (and gradually also agriculture)."(4)

The trade unions actively participate in the political life of the country, in the all-sided development of our society; and, especially, they should draw all the workers and employees into the work of building and developing the economy and of promoting culture. Expressing the sense of the ruling working class of being masters, the trade unions should have a general view of *the whole* of industrial activity, of economic activity embodied in concentrated form in the State plan. Each worker or toiler should be made to realize clearly the basic objectives of the State plan, and understand his duty as well as his real interest in the successful fulfilment of the State plan.

In order to carry out their tasks, the trade unions have extensive rights. We already have the Trade Union Law. Recently in the Rules on the organization and activities of the Government Council there have been laid down the broad principles of the relations between the State and the trade unions. On the basis of these principles, there should soon be documents having legal force which stipulate concretely the responsibilities and rights of the trade unions to participate in the management of the economy and the State. The trade unions have the right to take part in the drawing up of these documents as well as of all other laws and regulations of the State concerning labour productivity, working conditions and the life of workers and employees.

The bases of union activities are the trade union organizations in the enterprises. Therefore, *to strengthen the role of the trade unions in the enterprises* is the most important direction in the work of improving union work. It should be done in such a way that the unions in the enterprises can work with full capacity as representatives of the workers and employees' interests in these enterprises, in any field dealing with their production, their labour, their material and cultural life. It is necessary to discover and make full use of various measures suitable for workers and employees to take part in the management of enterprises, in discussing and deciding on production plans, in realizing plans for application of new techniques, labour plans, wages and bonuses, plans to build workers' housing, and other undertakings concerning the collective social and cultural welfare of the enterprises. There should be fixed and ensured for the trade unions the right of organizing the mass control by workers and employees of the various aspects of the realization of production plans, the implementation of managerial systems, the protection of socialist property as well as the implementation of labour rules and regulations. In towns and industrial areas, the trade unions may also organize the control and supervision of the implementation of policies on food distribution, and of prices of consumer goods. The above-mentioned control activities aim at finding out for the Party and Government acts contrary to the lines and policies laid down, helping the managerial organs to overcome shortcomings, contributing to the consolidation of socialist relations of production, of the socialist State system.

By nature, the relationship between the trade unions and the State in general, and between the trade unions in the enterprises and the directors of the enterprises in particular, *is a harmonious one.* Because both are organizations of the ruling working class, both have a common goal: to develop society and economy, to constantly raise living standards and broaden the rights of the working people as collective masters. On this basis, the directors of enterprises—in their capacity as representatives of the State, with great rights and responsibilities in the whole development of the enterprises—for the sake of fulfilling their own tasks, need to win the close collaboration of the trade unions, to respect trade union rights, which will soon be expounded very concretely in the Rules on the rights and responsibilities of unions in the enterprises, to be worked out by the trade unions and ratified by the State. For their part the leading bodies of the enterprise unions have the task of using trade union rights first and foremost to reach the goals set for the enterprises by the State by increasing productive and economic effectiveness, and successfully achieving the norms of the plans of the enterprises.

The enterprise unions should *give priority to production problems*, and together with the enterprise managers find out and make full use of all reserve sources, all potential capacities in all fields, especially in the field of labour organization, to develop production and fully ensure the fulfilment of the plans of the enterprise. It is necessary to introduce widely *collective contracts*, signed between the enterprise director, who is the State representative, on the one hand, and the trade union on the other, which is the representative of workers and employees, in order to strive together to ensure the realization of the production plans. These collective contracts need to clearly stipulate the tasks and objectives to be attained in production, the principal measures ensuring the realization of the objectives, the work to be done in order to improve the living standards of the workers and employees, and to expand collective welfare in the enterprise. The collective contracts must become programs for daily action, concrete rules of the enterprise, which must be strictly observed and fully carried out by all, from the director downwards.

The signing and implementation of collective contracts should be regarded as the content for the education of the masses in the sense of *linking their personal interests closely with the interests of the enterprise and the State.* The thorough and full implementation of collective contracts should be made a focus of attention and greatest concern of the leading organs of the enterprise, all mass organizations and all cadres, workers and employees of the enterprise. The signing of collective contracts, the implementation of these contracts and the control of the implementation of contracts by the masses organized by the trade union are an important and most effective formula to intensify the sense of responsibility of the enterprise director and of each worker, inculcate the conception of being collective master, unify the rights and obligations of the trade union in the enterprise, and concretely carry out in the framework of the enterprise the relations of cooperation between the State and the trade unions.

The present primary task of the trade unions is to launch among the workers and employees a surging revolutionary movement of emulation to work and produce, to raise labour productivity and strictly practise thrift and carry out successfully the resolution of the 22nd session of the Party's Central Committee. Lenin said: "Following its seizure of political power, the principal and fundamental interest of the proletariat lies in securing an enormous increase in the production forces of society and in the output of manufactured goods."(5) This teaching by Lenin must penetrate deeply into our understanding and conceptions, into all trade union activities and into each toiler's daily work. In order to carry out industrialization and build up large-scale socialist production, we should follow this teaching. This task can only be accomplished by painstakingly, persistently and valiantly engaging in work.

To say "the trade union is a school of socialism and communism" means first of all that it must educate the working people in the socialist and communist ideology. But it is by no means an ordinary school. The educational work described here can only be done successfully in the course of and on the basis of a movement for productive labour of a mass and revolutionary character with a view to successfully building socialism. The central point of this educational work is to foster in every worker *a really new and correct attitude towards work*. Such an attitude has begun appearing among the masses of workers, leading to substantial achievements in the emulation movement in the past years. In the course of the destructive war in the past, many enterprises, warehouses and communication lines were heavily damaged, but the workers and employees with determination stuck to their positions in production and work, fulfilling at all costs their production tasks and defending their production bases. Living up to the watchword "hammer in one hand, gun in the other," and "to fight when the enemy comes, to resume production when the enemy leaves", at many places workers fought back at the enemy and carried out production simultaneously; there were places which were attacked by the enemy day and night over a long period, but the workers resolutely maintained production and valiantly fought back at the enemy to limit to the lowest level losses in lives and equipment. That was a bright embodiment of the new attitude towards labour, of the virtue of devotion to independence, freedom and socialism of the working class. One year elapsed, and this tradition was constantly upheld and developed. As a result many enterprises overfulfilled their 1973 plan, healed an important part of the wounds of war and speedily restored and developed production.

However, the socialist attitude toward labour is not yet found in every worker. Many people have not yet become fully conscious that they are the ruling class, the masters of society. The trade unions have the task of awakening these people. We should set out to uproot the sense of being a hired labourer, the old habit of looking on labour with the eyes of a slave, of taking on the least burden possible and of taking as much as one can from society and the State.

Labour was and is always the source of life of society. Slave society existed on the surplus labour of the slaves; feudal society on the land-rent contributed by the peasants; and capitalist society, on the surplus value created by the proletariat. *Socialism is the replacement of hired labour with labour for oneself, for the society of which one is master. This is the greatest change in the history of mankind.* Socialism is a society of free workers, in which personal interests merge with the interests of society, the interests of each worker and his family merge with the interests of the production collective and of the State. Only when the society is prosperous, can each member be well-off. What is beneficial to society also benefits each member. And what is harmful to society is also detrimental to each member. Society takes care of the life of each person and consequently every person must do his best for the benefit of society. Working for society means working for oneself. Working for the collective is the highest interest and the loftiest obligation, the very foundation of the new sentiments and ethics, the basis for the building of a new society and a new man, the source of a spiritually and materially abundant life, the motive force of the development of socialism. The trade unions must make each worker by hand and brain, each State employee, fully possessed of that sense, so that he may display all his ardour in his work. Public opinion must be mobilized in strong condemnation of parasites and lazy persons who live off the resources of others. The administration at all levels should by all means give jobs to able-bodied working men and, at the same time, should give high consideration to the *obligation to work* of each citizen as promulgated by the State. Any person reaching working age and having the capacity to work should work. The person of working age who is not yet provided with legitimate work should be placed under the manpower authority of the State. With regard to the idle and jobless elements, indulging in trouble making, we must compel them to work or punish them severely. The principle "work much, earn much; work less, earn less; and no work, no earnings", a *basic law* of socialism, must be strictly carried out.

When speaking of labour, we also mean *labour productivity*. At the present time, labour productivity is still too low. In some branches, labour productivity is even lower than in 1965. In the meantime our machines operate at only half their capacity. Materials are short in some places, whereas in other places they are left unused, or have even been damaged or lost. That is a serious waste. Industrialization is a fundamental way of creating the material foundations for speedily increasing social labour productivity. But, in order to achieve industrialization, it is necessary to increase to the maximum labour productivity on the basis of the present material and technical conditions. Attention should be attached to mechanization, to renewing partly or wholly the process of production, to improving, modernizing or supplementing equipment, machinery and instruments, while giving consideration to a better utilization of raw materials and processed materials in the most economical and effective way. The attitude of wait-and-see, of relying solely on machinery, must be criticized. In working, if machines are not available, we must make full use of hand tools and renovated ones. In the conditions of limited mechanization, importance must be attached to *technical innovations, to the rationalization of production and to the improvement of the organization of production and labour* which should be considered as specially important factors for increasing labour productivity. Without mentioning the necessity of making still greater efforts, I would like to stress only the necessity of making fuller use of the production capacity of existing machines, of organizing work well, of good management, of using in the most rational way and with a high sense of economy the materials at our disposal, of making every worker strictly fulfil the fixed working days and hours. Only by so doing can we increase labour productivity and produce more material wealth for society.

Labour discipline constitutes a basic manifestation of the new attitude towards labour, a very important factor in increasing labour productivity. The trade unions must pay especial attention to educating the workers and employees in this sense. We must carry out an energetic and radical struggle to eliminate all manifestations of indiscipline, of disorganization, of slackness, of negligence in work. But ideological educational activity must be carried out in conformity with the fixed quotas, norms, standards and processes. Every task must necessarily be carried out according to the set norms. Norms set before the war and abolished during the war must be restored right away. Old and unsuitable norms must be changed. The trade unions must contribute their efforts together with the managerial organs to the setting of norms where norms have not yet been set for certain kinds of work. On the basis of such norms, we can broadly apply payment on a piece-work basis. The trade unions must work together with the managerial organs to work out better norms in order to contribute effectively to the consolidation of labour discipline, stimulate the working people to work well and increase their productivity.

Raising the professional qualifications of the workers has great significance with regard to increasing labour productivity. In the past years, our contingent of workers and technical cadres has gone through a speedy development, but the quality is still poor as compared with the requirements of production and construction. The average technical level of the workers in many production units is still low compared with the demands of the concrete tasks. That is one of the reasons why the productive capacity of the machines still remains low; a great number of machines have been damaged, the quality of products is poor. So labour productivity simply cannot increase.

The trade unions, together with the organs of economic management, must take charge of the technical and cultural education of the workers, must broadly develop different forms of technical guidance and training in production teams, organize after-hours technical courses, vocational schools, complementary education and correspondence courses for the workers. Special attention must be paid to the training of highly-qualified workers such as production team leaders and foremen, to the popularization and application of advanced experiences in production, to innovations aimed at the rationalization and improvement of production and technique.

To carry out large-scale production, we need instruction and knowledge to master modern science and technique. If we lack education, we cannot build socialism. The workers also need instruction and knowledge to develop their initiative and their creative capability in organization. To become masters, we must, *firstly*, have a correct, socialist ideology; *secondly*, have education and knowledge, fully grasp science and technique, thoroughly understand the process of modern production in its technical as well as organizational aspects. The new man is not a man who only has a correct ideology, high revolutionary ardour, a socialist attitude toward labour, but also a man with a high educational level, first of all know-how in production and management.

We are now badly in need of more and more able cadres of working-class stock. Being "a school of management", the trade unions must actually be the biggest source of supply of management cadres for the industrial branch, for the national economy as a whole, and for the State machinery as well. President Ho Chi Minh taught us: "In order to achieve the aim of 'speeding up production and practising thrift,' trade union cadres must firmly grasp the Party's policies, take a correct mass line, exercise a democratic leadership, share the weal and woe of the workers, form a bloc with the workers and set a good example to them. If they don't form a bloc with the workers, they are bureaucratic-minded people. Whether the workers are good or bad in production, are united and enthusiastic or not in production—this is the touchstone for establishing whether trade union cadres are good or not."(6) Trade union cadres are revolutionary militants who live and thoroughly understand the life of the workers, the feelings, aspirations, needs and thoughts of the masses, and are fully trusted by them. Trade union cadres are at the same time good organizers with a wide and deep knowledge of economics, technology and the production process. Only in this way can the trade unions take part in management in the name of the workers.

A very important tast of the trade unions at present is, together with the State, to care for *the stabilization and gradual improvement of the lives of workers and employees*. After years of a fierce war, this is an urgent task aimed at alleviating the difficulties, maintaining and replenishing labour capacity, creating conditions to ensure enthusiastic labour in production and construction, while solving adequately the problems left behind by the war. At present the State's economy and finances are very limited. As loans and aid for consumption are not permissible, the State, along with the people, will have to overcome the difficulties met in daily life. In this respect, the trade unions' responsibility is therefore all the greater.

When conditions do not allow notable improvement, the settlement of the problems of daily life must be focused on key points, on the most pressing needs, such as housing, food, education, medical treatment, assistance to war-stricken families. Special attention must be paid to the solution of women workers and employees' difficulties. Regarding food supply for instance, it must be conducted according to the present quotas, priority being specially reserved to those who are directly engaged in production. The arbitrary cutting or reducing of producers' food quotas shall be strictly prohibited. In the present conditions regular supply, equitable distribution, well-organized collective dining rooms, complete elimination of corruption and waste in circulation and distribution, this alone will help eliminate numbers of difficulties in the worker's life. The managing boards and the trade unions, the local party committees and administrative authorities will seek ways and means to give the workers and employees better meals. In places where conditions permit we must promote a movement of producing foodstuffs to improve our daily meals. We must try to solve the problems of manpower and building materials to speed up the building of houses and schools for the working people's children. At the same time, the families of war dead and war invalids, demobilized servicemen, and people wounded or disabled in the war, must be cared for.

Given the present economy of North Viet Nam, the trade unions must help the workers and employees to understand thoroughly the relationship between consumption and the needs of accumulation. It is quite clear that we are making an initial, small step on our way to socialism, starting from a poor, backward economy severely devastated by war. The numerous difficulties we are encountering in our daily life at present are unavoidable. To change this state of things, there is no other way than to do our best to build our country with a high sense of thrift, ensure the accumulation of capital for industrialization, and steadily advance toward large-scale socialist production.

Capitalism accumulates its capital first by reducing to misery and ruthlessly exploiting the working people. Our line of socialist industrialization helps us to quickly accumulate capital while gradually raising the people's standard of living, a fact which reflects right from the beginning the superiority of socialist relations of production. To raise the people's standard of living constantly is a requirement of the basic economic law of socialism which reflects the lofty goal of socialist production. But that goal cannot be attained without the means for it. That is why the first requirement of the basic economic law of socialism is to increasingly develop production with ever higher technique on the basis of the working people's right to be the collective master. As the goal and result of the development of production, the improvement of the people's standards will consequently become a motive force impelling production forward. But living standards can never surpass production capacity. If one consumes all one produces, this means there is no accumulation at all for industrialization, for extended reproduction; in this way one cannot raise living conditions in a fundamental and steady manner. Therefore, in the first stage of industrialization, in order to correctly solve the relation between accumulation and consumption, we *cannot help giving priority to accumulation.* Thus there must necessarily be sacrifices, hardships in the immediate future for the sake of a bright morrow. The trade unions should help their members and all workers and employees to become fully conscious of this matter. Everyone should deeply understand that only by working, toiling very hard with high productivity, can we ensure both the enlargement of accumulation and the constant improvement of living standards. This is the sole measure which can create a practical possibility of associating immediate interests with long-term interests.

To Raise High the Banner
of Socialism, Independence and Democracy

We are living in the most glorious period of our national history, and at the same time facing heavy historical responsibilities.

The anti-U.S. resistance for national salvation has ended in a great victory. But the revolutionary objectives in South Viet Nam have not yet been reached, our country has not yet been reunified. Therefore our people still have to carry out simultaneously two strategic tasks: to build socialism in the North and to struggle for the completion of the national democratic revolution in South Viet Nam, and to proceed to the peaceful reunification of the country.

The Vietnamese working class, the leading class of the Vietnamese revolution, constitutes a part of the international working class, a class standing in the very centre of our era. The Vietnamese revolution constitutes a part of the world revolution, and is directly linked to the three great currents of the proletarian revolution in the present era, that is: the building of socialism and communism in the world socialist system; the struggle of the working class and labouring people in the capitalist and imperialist countries; and the national liberation movement and the upsurge of the forces fighting for national independence with a view to leading their countries straight to the path of non-capitalist development. The revolutionary cause of our people is a concrete embodiment of the lofty objectives of mankind in the present era: national independence and socialism. It is because our people have stood on the common offensive position of the world revolution, and made full use of the combined strength of various revolutionary trends of the era, that they have acquired that supremacy in the balance of forces which has enabled them to defeat the U.S. imperialist aggressors and their henchmen. On the other hand, the victory of our people's anti-U.S. resistance for national salvation has further consolidated the position of socialism in the world, strongly stimulated the struggle of the peoples of the countries in the Third World against old and new colonialism, and influenced the revolutionary struggle of the working class and labouring people in developed capitalist countries; at the same time, together with these revolutionary currents, it has made deeper and sharper the general crisis in the imperialist system. It is quite obvious that today the positions of imperialism headed by U.S. imperialism are being weakened, and that the offensive position of revolutionary forces in the world and the possibility of preserving peace are stronger than ever before.

Identifying class interests with national interests, and national interests with international interests, the Vietnamese working class is constantly raising high the banner of socialism, independence and democracy, determined to lead the entire people ahead to complete the revolutionary cause in the new stage. We will undoubtedly implement the Testament of President Ho Chi Minh in the building of a peaceful, reunified, independent, democratic and prosperous Viet Nam, contributing an active part to the common struggle of the working class and people all over the world for peace, national independence, democracy and socialism.

At the present time, the revolutionary struggle in South Viet Nam is a struggle to achieve national independence and at the same time an extremely sharp class struggle. The U.S. imperialists are still obstinately maintaining their neo-colonialism. Their agents, the clique of fascist, militarist, bureaucratic and comprador capitalists are now frenziedly countering the aspirations to peace, independence, democracy and national concord of our people. Under the banner of the National Front for Liberation of South Viet Nam and the Provisional Revolutionary Government, our South Vietnamese compatriots are determined to push ahead their struggle to defend and secure strict implementation of the Paris Agreement, developing the victories already recorded with a view to completing the national democratic revolution in South Viet Nam and proceeding to the peaceful reunification of the Fatherland.

Through the delegation of the South Viet Nam Federation of Trade Unions for Liberation, the toiling people in the North would like to convey to their blood brothers and sisters in the South their most affectionate feelings and pledge to them that under all circumstances the socialist North is resolved to fulfil its duty of being the rear-base for the revolution in the whole country. We are acting upon the teaching of President Ho Chi Minh—"Let the people of the North redouble their efforts in emulation"—to rapidly rehabilitate and develop the economy, promote culture, boost socialist industrialization, strengthen economic and national defence potential in order to make North Viet Nam a mainstay for the revolutionary struggle of our Southern compatriots.

The common revolutionary cause of our country is facing extremely bright prospects. No reactionary forces whatsoever can subdue us. Our people will win. Our compatriots in both South and North will certainly be reunited under the same roof.

We have the right to be proud of the extremely heroic tradition of the working class of our country, in struggle as well as in labour. The working class of our country has also the right to be proud of its vanguard Party founded and educated by President Ho Chi Minh, the great leader of the class and the nation, a Party which is thoroughly revolutionary and entirely faithful to Marxism-Leninism.

Being a vast organization linking the Party with the working class, the trade unions, with the important resolutions adopted at this National Congress, will surely fulfil their responsibilities in the education, mobilization and organization of the broad masses of workers and employees so as to successfully carry out the political and economic tasks set by the Party.

Role and Tasks
of the Vietnamese Woman
in the New
Revolutionary Stage

*The Vietnamese Woman, One of the Most Beautiful Images
of the Vietnamese People*

Our people have just gone through extremely critical yet very
glorious months and years which will be vividly remembered in the
history of our nation. For nearly 20 years, after the great victory of
the resistance to the French colonialists, our people have waged
another life-and-death struggle against U.S. imperialism, the chief-
tain of imperialism, the number one enemy of mankind. In this
confrontation, in the spirit of "nothing is more precious than
independence and freedom", the entire Vietnamese people, from
the front to the rear, in both the South and the North, without
distinction as to age and sex, have risen up as one man, ready to
accept all hardships and sacrifices, and have devoted all their forces
and capacities to the cause of national liberation and defence of the
Fatherland. We have foiled the biggest and most brutal war of
aggression ever conducted in the history of the U.S. imperialists,
compelling them to withdraw their troops and recognize the
independence, sovereignty, unity and territorial integrity of our
country. We have preserved and increased the forces of the North
in all respects under a rain of millions of enemy bombs and shells,

---

Speech at the Vietnamese Women's Fourth Congress (March 4-7,
1974).

and continued to take the North steadily forward on the path of socialism. Our struggle has made a worthy contribution to the common struggle of the world working class and peoples for peace, national independence, democracy and socialism.

To this great cause, the Vietnamese women have made a considerable contribution; worthy of admiration and pride. Ardent patriotism and undauntedness have for thousands of years been a prominent tradition of Vietnamese women, ever since our ancestors began founding our nation. This precious tradition, nurtured and promoted by our Party and our beloved Ho Chi Minh, found its fullest and most brilliant expression in the period of anti-U.S. struggle for national salvation.

As the saying goes, "When the aggressors come even women should take up arms." That is perfectly true! To defend our Fatherland against the U.S. imperialists, the Vietnamese women took up arms to directly participate in the fighting and have become dauntless combatants, heroines, valiant fighters and outstanding military commanders.

In the epic tableau of the people's war in the North, our women are ever present, intrepid and undaunted daughters of the country who stoutheartedly fought to the end to defend the country and their dear ones. Numerous militia-women units, all-women anti-aircraft platoons more than once brought down U.S. aircraft, captured U.S. pilots, set U.S. warships afire, bravely protecting their native villages. Tens of thousands of girls, trudging day and night on all the roads of the country and defying enemy fire, de-activated time-bombs, repaired bridges and roads and kept communications open in the service of the front. Hosts of wives and mothers imbued with love of their country and their homes encouraged and exhorted their husbands and sons to go to the front. How many others gave their dearest ones to the Fatherland! With the "three responsibilities" movement, a surging revolutionary movement responding in time to the imperative demands of the resistance, our women shouldered the very important and heavy task of building and consolidating the great socialist rear. Constantly supplying the front with material means and moral encouragement, braving bombs and shells, scorning the inclemencies of the weather, our women stuck to the fields and the factories to ensure production in all circumstances, upholding the tradition of heroism and industriousness of the Vietnamese women. Each grain of paddy sent to the front is imbued with the "three responsibilities" spirit of our women in the rear, with their profound feelings of affection, their sweat and even their blood. The might of the socialist North, the revolutionary base of the entire country, is, in large measure, drawn from the strength of our women rising up to be masters of society, of the country.

Our Party and State highly appreciate the efforts and achievements of our women in the national democratic revolution as well as in socialist revolution, in production as well as in fighting. The patriotism, valiant fighting spirit, devotion, self-sacrifice, self-abnegation, resourcefulness and creativeness of the heroines Nguyen Thi Suot, Nguyen Thi Hanh, Vu Thi Nham, Dao Thi Hao, Nguyen Thi Song, La Thi Tam and many other women are brilliant manifestations of Vietnamese revolutionary heroism. The heroic, undaunted, loyal and capable Vietnamese women are one of the finest images of the Vietnamese of our generation.

National Liberation, Liberation of the Working Class and Emancipation of Women

In the old society, women were those who suffered most, and who were most oppressed. Therefore they were highly responsive to the revolution, and constitute a great force of the people. No revolutionary campaign can succeed without the participation of women. The socialist revolution, the most profound, thorough and all-sided revolution in the history of mankind, is all the more unimaginable without the active participation of women. Lenin once said, "If women are not drawn into public service, into the militia, into political life, if women are not torn out of their stupefying house and kitchen environment, it will be *impossible* to guarantee real freedom, it will be *impossible* to build even democracy, let alone socialism."(1)

The emancipation of women must be associated with national liberation and the liberation of the working class. If the nation and the working class are not liberated, the women will not be liberated. Yet, if the women are not emancipated and do not yet share the role of masters of the country, the nation as well as the working class are not really liberated. A society cannot be considered civilized and advanced if women are still dependent and do not enjoy freedom. The extent to which women are masters of society is a yardstick of the development and progress of a society, because women were those who endured the greatest injustice in the old society. As President Ho Chi Minh has put it, "If the women are not emancipated, socialism is only half established." But it is only socialist revolution and the cause of socialist construction that can create all necessary conditions, economic and social, material and spiritual, for the total emancipation of women and the achievement of equality between men and women in every field, provide women with a decent position in society, bring into full play their ability and energy to serve society, and at the same time ensure them a happy family life. That is why, more than anybody else, women cherish revolution and socialism.

As an integral part of the revolutionary movement, the emancipation of women can only be carried out step by step along with the common victories of the revolution. The glorious victory of the August 1945 Revolution, the great victories of the two heroic wars of resistance against imperialist aggressors, the great achievement of the land reform, of socialist transformation and initial socialist construction constitute big leaps forward for the Vietnamese revolution and at the same time big leaps forward in women's life, fundamentally changing women's position in society. Freed from all social injustices and the bonds of feudalism, the Vietnamese women of today, from the status of slaves most heavily oppressed and downtrodden, have become the collective masters of society and the State.

These great changes in practical life have been recognized by law in the democratic republican regime. The constitution of our country, as well as many laws of the State, specify equal rights in every respect for women, confirm women's rights in all spheres of social activity as well as in marriage and in the family. The Party, the State, the women's and youth organizations and the trade unions give due consideration to the work of raising the political consciousness, and the scientific and technical levels of women, help them with their family problems and constantly promote the role of women in production and in the management of the State. The force and capacity of women which our Party, Government and regime seek actively to encourage, foster and promote, have become a big source of strength, and an extremely important guarantee for the successful fulfilment of every revolutionary task. The achievements and progress of the women's movement in the past few years represent a great success of our Party in mass mobilization and also an outstanding achievement of the Viet Nam Women's Union.

However, we cannot be content with the achievements recorded so far in the mobilization of women. Although women in our country have made greater advances than ever before and become masters of society and of the State, they have not brought into play all their capacities, since they still meet with many difficulties in terms of working conditions, educational and vocational standards and family burdens. The labour force of women is very abundant, but it is not reasonably distributed and employed. The root cause of this situation lies in the fact that our country has for many years been engaged in war against imperialism, especially U.S. imperialism and hence has had neither conditions nor time to concentrate its efforts on developing its economy and large-scale socialist production to serve as a basis for the new regime and make it possible to step up the emancipation of women. The other important cause is that in our society there still exist not quite correct conceptions concerning the relationship between family and society, the responsibilities of a woman toward society and her family, and those of society toward every family, every woman, every mother and every wife. Among the people, and even among the cadres, there are still remnants of backward feudalistic ideas such as paying more consideration to men than women, not duly respecting and protecting the legitimate rights of women, not setting out to free women from "family slavery", and, worse still, the committing of brutal and inhuman acts on women. Such a situation prevents the implementation, even in the present socio-economic conditions, of the policies, rules and regulations aimed at raising the role and position of women in society. It requires us to work even harder in many respects to fully realize equality between men and women and emancipate the women.

So, what does the question of women's emancipation and the achievement of equality between men and women imply in the present stage of the socialist revolution in North Viet Nam? It is clear that after the decisive victories of socialist transformation and the establishment of new relations of production, the principal content of the struggle for the emancipation of women is mainly a struggle against economic poverty, against the backward and wrong conceptions of the old society with regard to women. It is mainly to achieve an ever wider participation by women in the management of society and production in line with their characteristics and capacities. It is to reduce the burden of housework by means of rational reorganization of their life; it is to work actively to raise women's political, educational, scientific and technical standards. Thus, in the socialist revolution, to emancipate women is *in essence to ensure their fullest participation as collective masters in all three respects: to be masters of society, to be masters of nature and to be masters of themselves.* This is the content of the struggle for the emancipation of the women in the period of transition to socialism.

It is only in the socialist regime that everyone is master; this is a wholly new regime in history, which can emancipate not only the whole of society but also every family, bringing about a new life both for society and for each family, and harmoniously combining the interests and well-being of society with those of every family. Furthermore, not only does the regime of collective mastery promote women to the rank of masters of society and of the State, it also creates conditions for them to master nature and themselves, and to make ever greater progress. Therefore, to establish a socialist regime of collective mastery conforms most closely to the interests and aspirations of women, and is a basic means of their thorough emancipation. Of course, this lofty cause can only be the product of the successful achievement of the three revolutions (the revolution in relations of production, the technical revolution, and the ideological and cultural revolution) of the transformation of small, backward production into large-scale socialist production. As Lenin has pointed out: "The real emancipation of women, real communism, will begin only where and when an all-out struggle begins (led by the proletariat wielding the state power) against this petty-housekeeping, or rather when its *wholesale* transformation into a large-scale socialist economy begins."(2)

In this revolutionary cause, a cause dear to the hearts of women themselves, they ought to strive to set forth, move vigorously forward, trample underfoot all difficulties and obstacles, doing away with their inferiority complex and self-resignation. With all their strength and intelligence, let the Vietnamese women rise up as a dynamic force to speed up the process of building a new regime, a new economy and a new man so as to render our society truly fine and superior, and bring splendour to the Fatherland and happiness to every family. This is both a heavy responsibility and a great honour of the women's movement in the present new stage.

To Fulfil the Duty of a Citizen
and the Function of a Mother in the Socialist Regime

In order to successfully fulfil such a noble historic mission, the especially important task of the women's movement in the North is *"to build a new socialist woman"*. What do we mean by a new woman? One who carries out well her duty as a socialist citizen. One who fulfils satisfactorily her noble function as a mother toward her children, and as a wife in the family. As a matter of fact, in every society a woman is a citizen, mother and wife. But there is a basic and striking difference between a slave citizen, a hired worker in a regime of private ownership and a socialist citizen who is collective master and master of the State; between a feudal or capitalist family and a socialist one; between a mother and wife in the old society and a mother and wife in the new one. In our regime, not only women's participation in public affairs (economic management, State management) but even their childbirth, the bringing up and education of their children, and housework, all assume a *profoundly social character*, are closely related to the general progress of society and constitute an integral part of the cause of transforming the old society and building a new one.

At present, following the great victory of our resistance war against U.S. aggression, for national salvation, the Vietnamese revolution has entered a new stage in which the *general task of the North* was laid down by the 22nd Plenum of the Party's Central Committee as follows: to unite the entire people, strive to carry out socialist industrialization, speed up the three revolutions, build up, and quickly, strongly and steadily take North Viet Nam to socialism; combine economy closely with national defence, remain vigilant, stand ready to smash all maneuvers of the U.S. imperialists and their henchmen, strive to fulfil one's duty in the revolutionary struggle for the completion of independence and democracy in South Viet Nam, advance toward peaceful reunification of the Fatherland, and fulfil the internationalist obligations towards the Lao and Khmer revolutions.

In the two years 1974-1975, the task of the North is: to rapidly complete the healing of the wounds of war, strive to rehabilitate and develop the economy, promote culture, continue to build the material and technical foundations of socialism, consolidate the socialist relations of production and socialist regime in every respect, stabilize the economic situation and the people's life, strengthen national defence, and strive to fulfil its duty towards the heroic South.

To carry out well her duty as a Vietnamese citizen who loves her country and socialism, each women must do her utmost to contribute to the successful fulfilment of this general task.

Nowadays, the female labour force accounts for more than 60 per cent of the total labour force in agriculture, 42 per cent of the total number of workers and employees, 52 per cent of handicraft workers, nearly 60 per cent in commerce, nearly 60 per cent in the public health service, 52 per cent in education, etc. With their participation in all branches of our national economy, with their industriousness and their capacity to endure inclement weather conditions, Vietnamese women may actually become the mainstay of the movement for labour, production and the practice of thrift in socialist construction. Just as we spared no sacrifices and devoted our lives to the independence and freedom of our Fatherland, we now stand ready to dedicate all our strength and intelligence to the cause of national construction. Just as Vietnamese women were capable of writing splendid pages in the history of our nation's struggle against foreign invasion, they are now all the more capable, with their self-conscious and creative labour, of making worthy contributions to enhancing the strength of our country, eliminating poverty and backwardness, wiping out all negative and unhealthy manifestations which are at variance with the nature of our regime and the lines and policies of our Party and State.

In our society, when speaking of work we should emphasize work accompanied by technique, organization and discipline, for in our system it should be work with high productivity, turning out as much material wealth as possible for ourselves as well as for society, for the present generation as well as for generations to come. Work without technique or without high productivity is rudimentary work at variance with the nature of our socialist labour. Therefore, more than anybody else, Vietnamese women should strive to study, constantly raise their professional standards, master science and technique, set an example in the observance of labour discipline, criticize the "hired labour" attitude, idleness, laziness and sluggishness. How many heroines and model workers there are in various economic and cultural branches who have upheld the new style in labour and have provided eloquent testimony to the great capabilities of women workers. The question is how to mobilize, above all how to organize and direct them.

Being good citizens in our society and a big force in the population, women should assume a worthy position in the management of society and the State. At present, in our National Assembly, 30 per cent of the deputies are women and in the people's councils the rate is 40 per cent. There are 50 vice-chairwomen and women members in provincial administrative committees, more than 3,000 chairwomen, vice-chairwomen of district and village administrative committees; 130 managers or deputy managers of factories, 1,200 college lecturers, nearly 7,000 presidents or vice-presidents of agricultural cooperatives. This is big step forward on the part of women and in realizing women's role as masters of society. In the days to come, we must create favourable conditions for the women to participate more effectively in the management of the economy and the State.

Our Party and State hope that this Congress will concentrate its discussions on discovering all measures to arouse an effervescent revolutionary upsurge among women, and, together with the trade unions and the Youth Union, strongly step up the movement for production and thrift, for the socialist cause, for the kith-and-kin South and for the reunification of the country.

The woman is a citizen, a worker in society, and at the same time a wife and a mother. Only if we see all these aspects can we correctly solve the tasks of women's problems, correctly solve the tasks of women's emancipation and thoroughly understand the women's movement. When we speak of a wife and mother, we speak of a family. The question of women's emancipation is closely associated with the building of a new, socialist family.

The family is a natural cell of society, a form of existence of human life. Without the family there cannot be reproduction of man himself and society cannot survive and develop.

As a social product the family has developed together with the evolution of society. The socio-economic conditions in a determined period of development of history are the factors which decide the character and structure of the family. In exploiting societies, the family was based on private interests; it therefore gave rise in the feudal family to the principle "the husband calls the tune", and in capitalist marriage to the principle "hand over the money first". These inhuman principles brought untold suffering and humiliation to women. In socialist society, which does away with the regime of private ownership, of oppression and exploitation, the family is built on equal relations and genuine love. The family is no longer an economic unit as in former societies of small-scale, individual production. As an element closely reflecting the relations of socialist sentiment and virtue, the socialist family fulfils an indispensable social function in the life and development of the new society.

Hitherto, a number of us have not paid sufficient attention to the study of the problem of the family. Thus they have not seen clearly the relation between the family and society, the rights as well as the function of the family in the socialist regime. It seems that there are comrades who still think that as a revolutionary one should not speak of the family; that if we speak of the family, it means that we speak of individual interests, of private affairs which run counter to collective morality.

This is not so. A revolutionary does not make light of the family. He is not a "no-family" person as the anti-communists used to allege. On the contrary, being a patriot, a person who cherishes the high ideology of socialism, a fighter who heartily struggles for the happiness of the people, he pays great attention to the family. With regard to this question, our basic point of view is: the interests and happiness of the family totally depend on the interests and happiness of society. And the happiness of society is manifested in the happiness of each member of society, of each family.

In fact, there can be no family happiness if there is still class exploitation, if people are still suffering and if the whole society has not yet achieved complete well-being. For this reason, in their resolute struggle to liberate the nation and the class, the revolutionary and the patriotic citizen know how to put the common interests before and above all. For the sake of common interests, they are ready to sacrifice all private interests. And what is the whole significance of this struggle full of sacrifices? It aims at realizing a free and happy society free from want and care. Once the society is happy, naturally the family is happy, too.

The socialist revolution brings happiness to all families. Together with the building of socialism, the material and moral life of the family is secured and enhanced in quality with every passing day. On the other hand, a well-organized, cheerful and happy family life is a very important condition for the peace of mind and enthusiasm of the working people in serving society. Organizing family living conditions well, in conformity with the norms of the new life, constitutes an important condition of the building of a new society, of social progress in the fields of economy, culture and morality. President Ho Chi Minh has said: "It's correct to pay great attention to the family, because many families added together make up a society; a good society makes families better, and good families make a good society."

Constantly developing production, to satisfy the ever-growing material and cultural needs of the people, is the requirement of the basic economic law of socialism. In many respects, these needs were met according to family unit. That is why the Party, Government and mass organizations must take care of the life of each family, of the clothing, food, lodging, education and rearing of children. When we solve the problems relating to the people's life, we must pay attention to the family unit with its diverse requirements. We must see to it that families have the best services, the most convenient for their needs. What is to be done for a family, for the needs of family life? This question should naturally come forward when thinking of the economy, production and living conditions. This matter should be raised in cooperatives, at district and provincial levels, and in the State plan in general. Only when we have a deep sense of serving the people, knowing well the living conditions of each family, how it fares for food and lodging, etc., can we really answer the questions "What should be done for a family?", "What should one do to serve the people better?" Society as a whole takes care of each family and builds it into a happy and well-off unit so that it is able to put greater efforts into building a new society. Everyone must care for the life and happiness of the family, not with any selfish narrow-mindedness, but with a sense of being collective master of society. Not only does he care for his own family but he also pays attention to all other families in society. Efforts should be exerted to arrange family life rationally and in accordance with the general situation in the country so as to create conditions for each family member to fulfil to the utmost his duty to society.

In the socialist system, the conjugal relationship is based on genuine love. The wife and the husband do not depend on each other economically, their marriage is based on love. This love is not a fleeting thing, but a lasting sentiment constantly consolidated by mutual respect and shared ideals. The mutual respect of wife and husband means that they take into due consideration each other's habits and opinions and show constant concern and care for each other. Their true mutual love and respect will help them live in harmony and together settle their family's affairs, take good care of their children, help each other to make progress in all fields, and encourage each other to fulfil their social obligations. A Vietnamese proverb says: "A husband and a wife who live happily together can scoop dry the Eastern Sea." Such a family is a happy family and when all families are happy, the whole society will have an abundance of happiness.

I would like to talk especially about *the great social significance of the role of the mother in the family.* The mother gives birth to children, brings them up, maintains the existence of the race, ensures society's life and development. Of course the father's role cannot be neglected. However, "the father's giving life to a child cannot match a mother's care." This Vietnamese saying is a particular feature of Vietnamese culture. In contrast to the feudal culture which humiliated the women, regarded women as "difficult to educate" and demanded that the "wife obey the husband's orders," the people's culture holds that "if they live in harmony, wife and husband can scoop dry the Eastern Sea," and raises the mother to a respected position: "the father's giving life to a child cannot match a mother's care," "care" here meaning bringing up and educating. Our new culture, the socialist culture, has inherited and developed this noble tradition of humanism of the national and popular culture.

The mother gives birth to the child, she has gone through many difficulties during her pregnancy and delivery, she brings up her child with her own milk and devotes her essential strength to the child. Besides the great obligation to the Fatherland and the revolution, what is more sacred than motherly love? Is there any sacrifice and devotion which can match that of the mother for her child? "We must educate our children from infancy"—the child's acquaintance with human culture is first of all through the mother. Every second, every minute, the mother hands down to her child her own feelings, her own thoughts and her own experiences of life. Each word, each smile, each expression on her face, sad or joyful, leaves a deep imprint in the child's mind which he keeps throughout his life. To teach him how to talk, how to smile, to sing him to sleep with meaningful songs, to give him good advice, etc.—it is precisely in this way that the mother contributes to safeguarding and handing down the national culture from generation to generation.

There is no assessment of the mother's contribution that is more correct and comprehensive than the following one by President Ho Chi Minh: "Our people are very grateful to the mothers in both zones, South and North, who have given birth to and fostered many generations of heroes in our country." The Viet Nam Fatherland owes its heroic sons and daughters to the contributions of heroic, undaunted, faithful and responsible mothers. For many centuries, the Vietnamese mothers have handed down to us the mettle of the Trung Sisters and Lady Trieu, the tradition of industrious labour and love of country and of home. We can rightly be proud of our Vietnamese mothers.

We understand the mother's function with all its noble social significance. The child in the socialist regime is the offspring of his mother and father and at the same time of the society as a whole. To give birth to a child, to foster him and educate him is a special function of the mother. However, it is also the responsitility and obligation of the whole of society, because, in our society, no one lives isolated from the community of working people and broad social co-operation. On the contrary, in the old society, giving birth to a child and bringing him up was regarded as a duty of the mother alone, of each family. That is why mothers in the oppressed and exploited classes, who endured untold suffering as hired labourers, felt yet greater humiliation in giving birth to and bringing up their children.

The mother in our regime no longer suffers from these social evils. Women now enjoy a new life, they have become the collective masters of society, enjoying due social respect. The whole society cares for women in childbirth and in the bringing up of children. Society has to take this responsibility for the sake of its own existence and common happiness, for the interests of social progress and the future of mankind.

The mother who brings up healthy and good children is, in fact, discharging a noble function for the happiness of society and for her own happiness. The glorious contribution of the mother and father is to supply worthy sons to society: good citizens, strong, serious and resourceful workers. For the interests of the society and for the happiness of future generations, the State must seek measures to care for the material and spiritual life of mothers and children.

To build up the new man is a task of prime importance of the socialist revolution. The new man is the product of the entire socialist revolution and socialist construction. However, the new man must be formed and trained right from the start, from the first suckling, from the first care given him by the family and society, from the first affection, advice and recommendations of his mother and father. Many traits of the mind and character of a man are formed very early, in embryonic form, in childhood under the direct influence of the family. Many social influences have an impact on the child through the family environment. Only serious parents can bring up their children to be serious adults. The example of the parents alone constitutes a very great educational strength. Therefore, the mother, together with the father, has an important role and responsibility to play in the formation of a new man. The family should be an expression of all that is new, beautiful, progressive, emerging, in our society; it should meet everything that the new society requires from each person.

The Protection of Mothers and Children is our Central Preoccupation

To form a new, socialist woman is the common task of our Party, our State and our people's mass organizations. All of us must make it our duty to find effective measures enabling women to tackle successfully their three tasks as citizens, mothers and wives. This is also the basic task of the Women's Union—the organization representing the interests and aspirations of the Vietnamese women.

First and foremost, *we should mobilize, organize and manage the female work force in the best and most rational way*, in order to bring into full play women's great abilities on the fronts of labour, production, and economic rehabilitation and development. On the one hand, the mass organizations—in the first place, the Women's Union—must step up political propaganda and education, raise the women's socialist consciousness, arouse their sense of collective ownership and of self-reliance, so that they may understand thoroughly the close relationship between the building of socialism and the emancipation of women. They must have a clear sense of their responsibility to the Fatherland, society and the family. On this basis, they are asked to take the most active part in the emulation drive for labour and production, to economize and to build socialism. On the other hand, the organs of economic management will do their best to help the women acquire and improve their scientific and technical knowledge, and raise their professional capacities. They will pay particular attention to ensuring that women get the right jobs. Irrational assignment harmful to women's physiological constitution must be firmly redressed. All public services of the State, from the centre down to the grassroots, all production and working units, are to be particularly concerned with the amelioration of women's working conditions, the improvement of the tools they use in order to alleviate the intensity of women's labour. The Women's Union must contribute ideas to the State and the trade unions in deciding the directives, policies and regulations related to women's work such as training and fostering women cadres, using and protecting women's labour, etc., and, together with State organs and trade unions, control and supervise the implementation of these directives, policies and regulations.

While it mobilizes women to participate in the emulation drive for labour and production in general, the Women's Union should study to work out and launch emulation drives of the women in each branch, each locality, in the countryside, cities, enterprises and offices, concentrating on very concrete tasks adapted to women's capabilities, such as the emulation drive in livestock breeding, in seedling planting with new techniques, the women's movement in education and culture, in training and competition among skilled workers, the women's movement against dishonesty in commerce, for the protection of public property, etc. Through its guidance and organization of such concrete activities at the grassroots, the Union carries out political education well and pushes the women's movement forward.

To strongly promote women's role and ability as collective masters, the Party, the State and the mass organizations should pay more attention to *the task of training and fostering women cadres* so as to have many capable women cadres with important responsibilities in the leadership and management of various branches at various levels. We must sharply criticize those cadres who are unwilling to assign women to important posts, on the grounds that women sometimes run into difficulties with regard to their health and families. Sometimes women have been appointed to leading bodies in a formal, perfunctory manner. They are denied rational participation in the work and the necessary assistance for the effective discharge of their tasks. For their part, women must strive to study and unceasingly acquire more and more knowledge in every respect. They must have the courage to assume fresh responsibilities, to fight any sign of narrow-mindedness, envy and selfishness. More than anyone else, women themselves must unite, love one another, give each other mutual assistance to make common progress and give full play to their revolutionary capacities. The Women's Union will attend closely to the conditions of women cadres in the various public services, State-run or collective economic establishments, contacting them in this or that way, with a view to assisting and stimulating them to forge ahead, to do their best to work and study, and carry out well the tasks assigned to them. At the same time, women must be given all facilities to make use of, and develop, their abilities to do mobilization work amongst people of their sex.

A task of particular importance to enable our women to adequately meet their obligations as citizens, mothers and wives, consists in *caring for their health and living conditions*—especially for the kinsfolk of families of war dead and invalids and armymen, or those in the worst-hit areas and mountain regions. This is an imperative task for our Party, State and mass organizations, and in particular the Women's Union. It is incumbent on us to exert ourselves to the utmost and, by relying on existing possibilities, coordinate State activities with the positive contributions of the people and of the women themselves, to help them overcome difficulties in their everyday life, from living conditions and child care to study and working conditions. The State must complete all policies and regulations relating to the lives of our women; the State organs and the trade unions should build and efficiently run nurseries, kindergartens, canteens, medical stations, maternity homes, public bathrooms and wells, and enlarge the network of distribution of consumer goods and home service groups in cities and townships. The Party committees and administrative bodies at all levels, and the mass organizations, should take the most practical and concrete measures to help our women surmount immediate problems in family life, and gradually alleviate the burdens of housework, especially shopping and cooking. Those are the most practical tasks to achieve the emancipation of women, ensure their right to collective mastery and equality between men and women.

We have been conscious of the function of the mother as well as of her role and obligations in the socialist regime. Therefore, our entire society, our Party and State, our mass organizations must care for the mothers so that each of them may fulfil with honour her lofty function. *The work of the Women's Union on behalf of mothers thus figures among the tasks that must be given first priority.*

We must pay great attention to the health of our women and help them bring up their children properly. The Women's Union should cooperate closely with the public health services to initiate them into a hygienic mode of life, guide them in practicing gynecological hygiene, pre-natal care, family planning and scientific child-rearing and persuade them to renounce backward habits in everyday life and child-rearing, so that lying-in women are properly delivered, and are able to bring up their children satisfactorily and remain in good health to carry on with their work. The Women's Union must take the initiative in this work, discuss with the trade unions, the Committee for the Protection of Mothers and Children and other State organs, to work out the most effective plans to enlarge the network of nurseries and kindergartens in the countryside as well as in the towns, and qualitatively improve the service of these establishments, so that mothers and families can confidently send their children to the nurseries and kindergartens. We must organize nurseries and kindergartens in such ways as to conform to the concrete conditions of work in various production bases and offices, in order to create the most favourable conditions for the mothers to send their children to those establishments. The Union must exhort the women to contribute actively to building nurseries and kindergartens and launch "build good nurseries and kindergartens" drives.

In the socialist system, we attach much importance to family education and social education. Every child of ours must be brought up properly in the family and given adequate education in society, from nurseries, kindergartens to infant classes, from primary and secondary schools to universities, from the Ho Chi Minh Young Pioneers' organization to the Ho Chi Minh Working Youth Union. The conditions of our children should be determined through class cooperation between family and society; however, nobody can be in a better position to understand, approach, help and educate our little ones than their parents.

The Women's Union, together with medical, educational and cultural organs, etc., is to guide mothers in bringing up and educating their children so that they fully understand the social meaning of this task, are fully conscious of their responsibility as mothers, and acquire the necessary scientific knowledge in the matter, launching "Loving Mother Excelling in Rearing and Educating Children" drives. It is desirable to organize in grassroots units discussions dealing with the bringing up of children by their mothers, and collaboration between families, nurseries, kindergartens, schools and mass organizations in the education of our little ones.

The education of children, the guidance of the mothers in the bringing-up of their offspring, is a task of great importance. The Women's Union must sum up experiences in its work among mothers with a view to further improving work in this field of activity in the coming period.

Thus, *the activity of the Women's Union* is very tightly associated with the vigorous efforts of our women as a whole to meet their obligations as citizens and mothers, with the formation of new, socialist women.

Every activity of the Union is designed to stir up a surging revolutionary movement among women. To effectively arouse and continuously impel forward the women's movement, the leading bodies of the Union at all levels must always grasp the spirit of the general revolutionary tasks in the entire country, as well as the immediate important tasks of the North in the new stage, perfectly assimilate the policies of our Party, understand the major decisions of our Party and Government relating to economic and State management in different periods, closely follow the activities of economic, cultural, scientific and technical branches, thereby laying down precise and correct tasks, adopting appropriate forms and methods of agitation appropriate to women of different ages, of different callings and in different regions.

The Women's Union should permanently work in close cooperation with the trade unions, the Ho Chi Minh Working Youth Union, and the State offices and mass organizations to mobilize the women's movement, and to care for the conditions and interests of women. For their part, the trade unions, the Ho Chi Minh Working Youth Union and the State organs must offer to the Women's Union their unstinted cooperation in work among women and consider such cooperation as their obligation.

The Party Committees at all levels are expected to guide agitation work among women, to lead the administrative bodies and mass organizations in fully applying the Party's policies and line on mobilizing the women, thus creating favourable conditions for the Women's Union to successfully rally, educate and organize the Vietnamese women to play their part in the glorious struggle for the common revolutionary cause of the nation and the people and for the emancipation of women.

Let the Women of Both North and South
Viet Nam Unite and Strive to Fulfil the
Common Revolutionary Cause in
the Whole Country

While the Northern part of our country is entering a new stage and our Congress is discussing the tasks of the women in the building of socialism, our minds always turn toward the South, the beloved half of the country which is still continuing the struggle to achieve the cause of national liberation.

In the past 30 years, gunfire has not ceased even for a single day in the South. The French colonialists defeated, the U.S. imperialists rushed in, step by step intervened, then committed armed aggression, staged a permanent "pacification", a large-scale massacre, a genocidal war which has left a very heavy aftermath for our people and in the course of which the South Vietnamese women have endured untold suffering and mourning.

The U.S. imperialists and their lackeys have turned the South into a huge prison; innocent people, women and children are herded into concentration camps with all kinds of harsh repression; patriots are searched, arrested and killed; hundreds of them are subjected to slow death in the "tiger cages" and the concentration camps; women especially suffer all kinds of brutal tortures. They pressganged the youth and vast numbers of men to take up rifles to fight as U.S. mercenaries in opposition to the fatherland, to kill their compatriots, leaving behind countless widows and orphans. U.S. bombs and bullets and noxious chemicals have not only ravaged rice fields and orchards but also destroyed foetuses in the wombs of mothers, and caused sterility in many women. U.S. culture trampled on women's dignity, poisoned the children's minds, destroyed the fine tradition of the nation's culture, pushed a part of South Vietnamese society into a life of frantic debauchery and disrupted hundreds of thousands of families.

But the yoke of domination by the U.S. and its lackeys, which provokes the deep hatred of our Southern compatriots, and their dream of conquering and turning the South into a new-type U.S. colony, can never extinguish the ardent patriotism of the South Vietnamese people and women of all strata. It finally collapsed in face of the powerful offensive of those who had stood up together with the entire country to wage the great and successful August Revolution and carry out the anti-French Resistance war to victory.

Seething with hatred of the enemy who had occupied their country and destroyed their families, the South Vietnamese women rose in a resolute struggle against the enemy, valiantly holding high the banner of independence and freedom over the past 20 years, and, together with all our compatriots and combatants, have written glorious pages in the history of the Fatherland's "Brass Wall". The unflinching and ingenious struggle of the "long-haired army" (3) on the three fronts of political, military and agitational propaganda among puppet soldiers has brought into relief the marvellous strength and nature of the patriotic fight in the South.

Throughout the period of development of the South Vietnamese revolution, women formed the greatest popular force who actively volunteered in the hard, persistent and very resolute struggle against the very brutal measures and "pacification" schemes of the U.S. and its puppets. Especially, our women made up the main force in a series of successful uprisings that marked the growth of the revolution in each stage. These were the concerted uprisings carried out in the vast rural areas in the years 1959-1960 which basically defeated a typical strategy of U.S. neo-colonialism; the three-pronged attack (4) of the political army that smashed completely the system of strategic hamlets, thus creating conditions for the South Viet Nam armed forces and people to defeat the U.S. "special war" strategy and topple the fascist Ngo Dinh Diem dictatorship; and the simultaneous uprisings in the rural areas and in a number of cities and provinces in the general offensive of 1968 which dealt telling blows at the U.S. "local war" strategy, and the big uprising that struck at the rural pacification plan of the U.S. and its puppets, thus making an important contribution to winning a great victory in the strategic offensive of 1972, devastatingly crushing the U.S. "Vietnamization of the war" program.

The outstanding combative image of our Southern sisters is that of tens of thousands of women in the women's army who, defying enemy weapons and repressive actions, have stoutheartedly marched forward, combining persuasion with violence, opposing terror and massacre, steadfastly sticking to their native land, determined "not to yield an inch", holding firm to their every hamlet, their every orchard. It is the image of mammoth uprisings to shatter the scheme of strategic hamlets, of hosts of women's detachments pushing forward to brave tanks and cannon, repelling U.S.-puppet sweeps, of all-women guerilla units and artillery platoons ingeniously countering enemy aircraft and warships, opposing smaller to bigger forces, lesser to larger quantities. It is the image of columns of supply carriers made up of women, those "brass-legged and iron-shouldered transport fighters" who, though often going without food, never left the frontline, and always ensured the timely delivery of goods and ammunition to the front; of those women cadres who day and night stuck to the land and the population in the enemy rear, present at every hot spot to win over every inhabitant, every hamlet, every village; of thousands of women detainees who, despite cruel tortures, remained unwavering in their rock-like belief and kept their revolutionary dignity intact in confrontation with the enemy right inside the U.S.-Saigon prisons. It is the image of innumerable patriotic mothers who wholeheartedly protected and cared for combatants and wounded, or saved every bowl of rice for their armed forces to be adequately fed to fight the aggressors; of how many other mothers and sisters of ours serving on all the battlefields across South Viet Nam. All this reflects well the resplendent image of Vietnamese women who are fully worthy of the honourable qualities of "heroism, undauntedness, loyalty and ability to shoulder great responsibilities".

Our people boundlessly admire the self-sacrificing, arduous and supremely valiant behaviour of the South Vietnamese women, the heroic examples of Nguyen Thi Ut Tich, Nguyen Thi Hong Gam, Tran Thi Tam, Ta Thi Kieu, Nguyen Thi Phuc, Y Buong, and of so many other heroines and war dead, those fighters with or without a name who have contributed so meritoriously to the brilliant record of our women.

The conclusion of the Paris Agreement is a great victory of our people. Struggling for the full implementation of this Accord is the most advantageous way to end the disasters caused by the cruel U.S. war of aggression to the South Vietnamese population and women.

But for more than a year past, the U.S. imperialists and the Saigon junta have systematically torpedoed the Agreement. To their towering crimes of the recent past, the U.S. and its henchmen have been adding fresh felonies!

The U.S. maintains its military involvement in South Viet Nam, using the bloody hands of the Saigon bureaucratic militarist clique to continue the war in the illusory hope of doing away with the achievements of the revolution, perpetuating the partition of our country and imposing U.S. neo-colonialism. The traitorous Nguyen Van Thieu clique, aided and abetted by the U.S., is intensifying land-grabbing operations against the liberated zone, feverishly stepping up "pacification" raids, and conducting downright terror, slaughter and looting in the areas under its control, trampling underfoot every legitimate aspiration of all sections of the population.

Faced with this obdurate and arrogant attitude of the U.S. and its puppets, our people in the South cannot remain passively inactive. Joining the torrential movement of the population, the South Vietnamese women in Saigon-held areas are closing their ranks and vigorously opposing all Saigon policies and measures of repression, exploitation and money-squeezing, demanding democratic liberties and the right to return to their land to earn their living; repelling and foiling "pacification" moves; rising up to abolish coercion and wrest back their right to be masters, to win back every relative, every family, every hamlet; determined not to let their husbands and sons be hurled into desperate operations, not to let their native places be obliterated. The women in cities and towns, unable to live suffocated in misery any longer, are joining other sections of the population in the struggle for improvement of living conditions, for rice, relief payments, tax cuts and a solution to unemployment, against terror and looting, determined not to let the U.S.-Thieu regime drag on the war to their detriment. In the liberated zone, the women, forming a considerable force, are bringing into play their role of masters, earnestly taking part in production and fighting, defending and building the revolutionary power, building a plentiful and good life with a view to consolidating the liberated zone into the mainstay of the South Viet Nam revolution.

Under the leadership of the NFL and the PRG, we are certain that the South Vietnamese women will develop their glorious revolutionary tradition, and will always merit the name of valiant shock-brigade in upholding the banner of independence and freedom. The South Vietnamese women will devote all their spirit and strength to uniting with the entire South Vietnamese people and combatants, so as to foil all sinister designs of the U.S. imperialists and their henchmen, demand the implementation of the Paris Agreement and achieve by all means peace, democracy, the improvement of the people's lives, bring the South Vietnamese revolution to complete victory, thereby ending misery, suffering and erasing all shame and hatred.

The lofty objective of our entire people is successful socialist construction in the North, and the struggle for the completion of the national democratic revolution in the South, in advance towards the peaceful reunification of the country. Socialism, national independence and democracy represented the invincible strength of our people in the recent anti-U.S. struggle for national salvation. They are also the inexhaustible and invincible source of strength to guarantee our advance towards the complete victory of our people's revolution throughout the whole country.

Viet Nam is one! The Vietnamese nation is one! North and South are under the same roof! The entire country is singleminded! The women of both North and South Viet Nam are united in their struggle, and with the assistance of the Lao and Cambodian women and women all over the world, will certainly fulfil together throughout the entire nation the behest contained in President Ho Chi Minh's Testament, that is, "to build a peaceful, reunified, independent, democratic and prosperous Viet Nam, thereby contributing worthily to the world revolution."

Looking back at the revolutionary path traversed since the founding of our Party, especially since the August Revolution, we are extremely proud of the outstanding maturity of the women's movement.

At present, our revolution is entering a new stage. Our Party's Central Committee is confident that the Viet Nam Women's Union and all women, with their abundant strength and glorious revolutionary tradition, will strive to make the North stronger in every respect and to fulfil its tasks toward the revolution in South Viet Nam.

Problems of Revolutionary Strategy

In the light of Marxism-Leninism, our Party from the beginning had a clear and complete conception of the necessary path of development of the Vietnamese revolution. Its *Political Theses* of 1930 pointed out that the Vietnamese revolution must go through two stages: first, the national democratic revolution; then, bypassing the stage of capitalist development, a direct passage to the socialist revolution. The ultimate aim of the Party remains the realization of communism. Guided by this program, the Party has worked out a concrete line for each period and has led the people through successive stages—each beset with difficulties, hardships and complexities—to the present glorious triumph.

Once the French colonialists had conquered our country, we lost our independence, freedom, right to live, and even our national culture with its heritage of thousands of years. It would be necessary to drive out the imperialist aggressors, liberate the nation, win back independence and freedom for the fatherland, provide the people with a decent standard of living, and restore their cultural and spiritual values. These were the deepest aspirations of all Vietnamese patriots.

But these national aspirations were thwarted by the imperialist aggressors in alliance with the feudal class. This collusion between imperialism and feudalism is the characteristic feature of colonial regimes. It is why the contradiction between our people and aggres-

Written on the occasion of the 40th Anniversary of the establishment of the Indochinese Communist Party (1970).

sive imperialism is tied up with the people's opposition to the feudal regime, the prop of imperialist rule and exploitation. The anti-imperialist struggle cannot be separated from the anti-feudal struggle. Thus, the national liberation revolution must necessarily have a democratic content. At all times, a genuine national movement must have a definite democratic context, for any class wishing to regain national sovereignty or to "become a nation by itself" must satisfy certain democratic claims of the popular masses, the force which secures the victory of the national movement.

Since our country is agricultural, with 90 per cent of its population composed of peasants, imperialism relies on feudalism to exploit our people. That is why to liberate our nation, it is essential to liberate the peasants. In our situation, democracy means essentially democracy for the peasants. They desire an independent nation in which all who farm can have land and be free from the oppression of imperialism and feudalism. Oppression and exploitation by the landlords can be overcome only if imperialism, the defender and protector of feudalism and therefore the worst enemy of our nation and peasantry, is defeated. The freedom of the peasants from the tyranny of the feudal landlords and the granting of land are the basic goals of the democratic revolution; it also meets the demands for national liberation, for "the national problem in the colonial countries is in essence a peasant problem."

Emphasizing the national and democratic program with its two strategic slogans, "National Independence" and "Land to the Tillers," our Party has succeeded in organizing large masses of the peasantry around the leadership of the working class, as well as mobilizing other popular strata in the people's anti-feudal and anti-imperialist struggle. By basing our revolutionary course on an analysis of concrete class relations, it has been possible to divide the ranks of our imperialist and feudal enemies. We have related this strategy to the concrete objectives suited to each period in order to concentrate our revolutionary strength on the most dangerous enemy at the moment. In all periods, the concrete objectives and political tasks set forth by the Party have been fundamentally national and democratic in orientation, closely bound up with the anti-imperialist and anti-feudal struggle.

During the war of resistance against the French colonialists after the August Revolution, the thrust of the revolution was directed essentially against the imperialist aggressors and their agents. Yet at the same time, the Party carried out the tasks of the agrarian revolution. When the war of resistance entered a most decisive stage in 1953, the Party mobilized the masses for a drastic reduction of land rent and for the initiation of land reform—an implementation of the slogan, "Land to the Tillers." As a result, the spirit and force of resistance of millions of peasants were intensified, reinforcing the worker-peasant alliance and strengthening the people's power and the National United Front. The fighting ability of the people's army improved tremendously and further encouraged all activities of the resistance. This drive decisively contributed to the great victory at Dien Bien Phu. The implementation of land reform during the war of resistance was a well-planned and creative policy of our Party.

At the present, the invincible strength of the revolution in South Vietnam is due to the fact that the people of the South, whose ten million peasants are the bulk of the population, have been given genuine national and democratic rights by the revolution. The revolution in the South has imaginatively combined the national and democratic objectives in the struggle against the neo-colonialism of the American imperialists. Neo-colonialism is characterized by the fact that it is not brought about through direct administration by the imperialists, but through a servile indigenous regime representing the interests of the feudal landlords and the comprador bourgeoisie under a "national democratic" guise. In these circumstances, the revolution must vigorously attack the puppet regime to smash the imperialist prop of neo-colonialism. By overthrowing the Ngo Dinh Diem administration,(1) the people of the South dealt a severe blow at American neo-colonialism and precipitated a period of continual crisis for the puppet regime.

Refusing to accept defeat and stubbornly persisting in their policy, the American imperialists began to send massive numbers of American troops to South Vietnam in 1965 in the hope of salvaging the situation. But the Vietnamese people, far from retreating, resolutely pushed forward and directed the thrust of the people's war against the American aggressors while continuing the relentless attack on the puppet army and administration. Determined to fight both the Americans and their puppets until "the Americans quit and the puppets topple," the people of the South, encouraged by their victories, are sure to achieve their immediate and fundamental objective at all costs. This objective is an independent, democratic, peaceful, neutral and prosperous South Vietnam—the precondition for the peaceful reunification of their country.

While struggling together with our Southern countrymen to bring the national democratic revolution to completion, our people in the North, under the leadership of the Party, set about building a socialist society after the victory of the war of resistance against the French colonialists in 1954. This objective is a strict implementation of the first program of the Party. It is in conformity with the irresistible trend of national liberation movements of our time—the transition from the national democratic revolution directly to the socialist revolution, bypassing the stage of capitalist development. This is the only way to guarantee complete victory for the cause of national liberation, genuine independence, and uninterrupted progress and prosperity for people previously kept under backward conditions by imperialism and colonialism.

The socialist revolution which has been going on for the last ten years has reaped only initial results so far. But, these results are extremely important. They are fundamentally changing the face of the North in all fields—political, economic, social and cultural—and are turning the North into an ever stronger base for the completion of the national democratic revolution throughout the country. By building socialism, completely frustrating the American imperialist war of destruction, and fulfilling the role of a great rear area for the epic fighting front of national salvation in the struggle against the American aggressors our people are providing a vivid illustration of the greatest truth of our time: in the present era, national independence, democracy and socialism are inseparable.

Over 100 years ago, Marxism came into being with a rousing battle cry: "Workers of all countries, unite!" Later in the era of imperialism, when capitalism had not only become an intolerable yoke on the proletariat and the toiling people of the "mother countries," but had also clamped the fetters of servitude on the colonial peoples, Lenin called out: "Workers of all countries and oppressed peoples, unite!" This strategically significant slogan points out that in the present era the revolution to overthrow capitalism and establish socialism can only succeed through an alliance of the proletariat in all countries and the colonial peoples in a common struggle against imperialism. The battle for national liberation, independence, and democracy fought by the people of colonial and dependent countries can only end in total victory if it becomes part and parcel of the world proletarian revolution in the advance toward socialism—the necessary trend of development of society in the present era. As President Ho Chi Minh asserted: "Only socialism, only communism, can free the oppressed nations and the toiling peoples of the world from servitude."

Since the capitalist system is deteriorating, the problems of national independence and democracy do not rest solely with the people of colonial and dependent countries; they are also the responsibility of the communist and workers parties of developed countries in their struggle for socialism and communism. At present, the monopoly capitalists controlling these countries are forfeiting their national sovereignty and selling out to the American imperialists, the international capitalist organizations, and the supra-national military blocs. Meanwhile, they are intensifying the exploitation and oppression of the working class and laboring people in their own countries and are curtailing, even in many instances denying, all democratic liberties, though they are but bourgeois democratic liberties. For these reasons, the communists must now seize hold of the national democratic banner and march forward as Stalin had insisted they do.

The transition from the national democratic revolution directly to socialism, bypassing the stage of capitalist development, is the strategic line of our Party proven wholly correct by the realities of the Vietnamese revolution over the past 40 years, and by the world revolution as well. The victory of the Vietnamese revolution is a victory for Marxism-Leninism creatively applied to the conditions of a colonial and semi-feudal country.

Because of its correct line, our Party has succeeded in rallying around it all patriotic classes and strata, and building a strong and large revolutionary army fighting for the liberation of the nation and the people.

The first crucial problem of the revolution is correctly and fully to assert the *leading role of the working class.* Because of its economic, political and historical position, the working class has become the representative of social progress in our time—the only class capable of leading the toiling peoples so that they may control their own future. Although it is relatively new and small in number, the Vietnamese proletariat is a resolute revolutionary class. In existence before the formation of a Vietnamese national bourgeoisie, it had hardly developed when it absorbed the revolutionary tradition of Marxism-Leninism and quickly became a conscious political force unified throughout the North, Center and South of the country.(2) Because the proletariat originated from the pauperized peasantry, favorable conditions were created for the setting up of a firm worker-peasant alliance. Furthermore, the Vietnamese working class entered the political arena at a time when the repercussions of the Russian Socialist Revolution spread throughout the world and when the Chinese proletariat, after the treason of the bourgeoisie, had stepped forward to lead the national democratic revolution. This historical background added to the political prestige of the Vietnamese proletariat. It gave the workers the necessary strength and moral ascendency which helped them win the preeminent position in the Vietnamese revolution, taking over its leadership after the failure of the Yen Bai Insurrection.(3)

President Ho Chi Minh declared: "The *working class* is the most courageous and revolutionary class which firmly and fearlessly stands up to the imperialists and colonialists. Armed with a vanguard revolutionary doctrine and the experience of the international proletarian movement, our working class has proven to be the most deserving and trustworthy leader of the Vietnamese people." Our Party's correct political course through all periods of the Vietnamese revolution has guided it from one victory to another because it holds firm to the standpoint of the working class and has a thorough grasp of Marxist-Leninist theory, the revolutionary doctrine of the working class.

Besides the proletariat which is the leading class, the peasantry is the most active opponent of imperialism and feudalism. The peasants make up the majority of our population and are the greatest force in the national democratic revolution. By following the lead of the working class, the peasants develop their great revolutionary potential to the utmost. The *worker-peasant alliance* is the basic condition insuring victory for the revolution. Since this alliance is a strategic principle of Marxism-Leninism—a universal necessity for all revolutions led by the proletariat—it is a problem which assumes particular importance in a country such as ours. Under the colonial and semi-feudal regime, our proletariat, though small in size, displayed a strength out of proportion to its numbers. Besides following a correct revolutionary course, it had won over an extremely reliable, natural ally—a powerful peasantry which expressed great revolutionary enthusiasm. Immediately after its formation, our Party was able to establish itself as the leader of the revolution, for it had succeeded early in building a worker-peasant alliance. The political prestige of our Party and its leadership of the revolution are absolute and indisputable because they stem from the invincible strength of the Party's grassroot support, the worker-peasant masses.

In the present era, a movement for social emancipation and national liberation can only be truly revolutionary when its core is made up of workers and peasants, when it matures as a result of this alliance, and when it is lead by the working class. If revolution is the work of the masses, then in the conditions prevailing in our country a truly revolutionary movement must be one whose main force includes workers and peasants. This alliance provides a firm foundation for the party of the working class to broaden the ranks of the revolution to include other classes and strata with national and democratic aspirations. There can be no National United Front without the worker-peasant alliance. The people's democratic state born of the August Revolution reflects a broad national union, but it is first and foremost a worker-peasant power under the leadership of the working class. Thus, the people's democratic state could set about discharging the responsibilities of the dictatorship of the proletariat immediately after the basic completion of the national democratic revolution in the North without having to go through another political revolution. Without the worker-peasant alliance, one cannot bypass the stage of capitalist development and proceed directly to the socialist revolution. Similarly, the revolutionary army, which is a very important instrument of violence in our national democratic revolution, can only be a worker-peasant army under the direct and absolute leadership of our Party, the party of the working class.

The unity of the Party as vanguard of the working class and the worker-peasant alliance means everything. Of the factors insuring victory for the Vietnamese Revolution, one must give priority to the *leadership of the party of the working class and the role played by the worker-peasant alliance.*

Unlike the peasantry in other countries, the Vietnamese peasants never followed the lead of the national bourgeoisie, which was weak economically and flabby politically. Their revolutionary fervor and aspirations went far beyond bourgeois limitations. Although the peasantry is highly revolutionary, it cannot lead the revolution, for it does not represent any distinctive mode of production and has neither an independent political position nor an ideology of its own. In our national democratic revolution, it can only join with and be guided by the working class. It is even unable to carry out the agrarian revolution by itself. In a bourgeois democratic revolution of the old type, the land problem could only be solved in accordance with the political aspirations and interests of the bourgeoisie. Throughout the new democratic revolution, the agrarian revolution must be carried out under the leadership of the proletariat according to its standpoint and line. Only then can both the peasants' immediate and long-range interests be satisfied. Only by uniting with the working class will the peasantry become an immense force. Similarly, the strength of the working class is greatly increased through an alliance with the peasantry. Furthermore, the peasants' power can only be fully realized in alliance with and under the guidance of the working class.

Our Party's political line reflects the stand and viewpoint of the working class and has fulfilled the peasants' eager aspirations and vital interests. Because of this, over the past 40 years, the peasant masses have faithfully followed the lead of the party of the working class, making the worker-peasant alliance firmer and stronger. The Vietnamese revolution proves that a revolutionary movement which adheres to the working class line of Marxism-Leninism and has a worker-peasant alliance as its main force is bound to triumph, no matter how powerful its enemies and how numerous the trials and dangers it may have to face.

Throughout all periods of the national democratic revolution, our Party, on the basis of a firm worker-peasant alliance, has brought together all patriotic and progressive popular strata and has united all the nationalities and religious communities within the country that could be rallied. It has won over all forces opposed to the common enemy of the nation and has brought into existence a broad *National United Front*, which, by neutralizing many forces, was able to direct the thrust of the revolution against the imperialist aggressors and their agents. The success of the revolution is a result of the correct Front policy pursued by our Party.

Experience has shown that in carrying out the Front policy one must guard against and oppose both the Rightist and "Leftist" tendencies. The Front is a unity of opposites which includes various classes cooperating with each other on the basis of a definite common program of struggle. That is why one cannot conceive of a classless Front. On the basis of a principled line, one should view and solve all problems related to the Front policy from a class standpoint. There are classes with essentially similar interests and classes whose interests converge only to a certain extent. Each class, for the sake of its own and the common interests, joins forces with other classes within the Front. Moreover, the common interest itself is viewed by each class from its own angle. On account of the historical position of the proletariat, its class interest and the common national interest are the same. But for the other classes, their respective interests and the common national interest converge in some respects and diverge in others. For this reason, there must necessarily be a struggle between the viewpoints of the various members of the Front who represent different classes, even though the Front must strive to maintain and strengthen unity. One-sided unity unaccompanied by struggle leads in practice to the disruption of unity and the collapse of the Front. If one knows how to conduct a principled struggle based on the implementation of a common political program, then, instead of breaking up unity and weakening the Front, one will have done the only thing that could strengthen unity and consolidate the Front.

As the leader of the revolution with a political line that fully represents the common national interest, our Party has naturally been recognized as the leader of the Front. The interest of the revolution and the nation require that one should constantly enhance and consolidate the leading role of the Party within the Front by firmly maintaining and opposing all tendencies to downgrade and dissolve the Party in the Front. The key to the firm maintenance of the Party's leadership for a strong Front is the constant reinforcement of the worker-peasant alliance. Without this alliance as its firm foundation, there can be no genuine national democratic Front, let alone a broadening of its base.

The petty bourgeoisie in our former colonial country shows great revolutionary enthusiasm. In particular the various strata of intellectuals and students are fervently patriotic and eager to safeguard the nation's fine cultural traditions and to restore the noble spiritual values of Vietnam which have been degraded by the imperialists and their feudal allies. They are historically conscious and aware of the trend of events. Awakened and stimulated by the revolutionary upsurge of the workers and peasants, they have increasingly joined the revolutionary ranks and have played an important role in the people's struggle, especially in the towns and cities.

The national bourgeoisie, restricted by the imperialists, is also patriotic in some respects. It has made some contribution to the national liberation struggle. Present day capitalism, utterly out-moded historically, has displayed its odious reactionary features right on our soil in the form of old and new colonialism. Socialism is without a doubt the inevitable trend of social development. Because of the historical advance of socialism, the powerful revolu-tionary movement of the masses, and the great achievements of the revolution, a certain number of intellectuals of national bourgeois origins—even some national bourgeois, their children in particular—have become conscious of the trend of the times and gradually have shown a fundamental shift in their stand by going over to the side of the workers and peasants and following the road of national independence and democracy of the new era.

Relying on the basic force of workers and peasants and in each period making an accurate analysis of the changes in class relations to single out the most dangerous enemy to defeat, our Party has applied extremely flexible tactics, successfully broadened the National United Front, and consistently drawn new forces into the Front organizations or into various forms of joint action aimed at securing an immediate concrete objective for the revolution. While carrying out the Front policy, our Party has never failed *to take the utmost advantage of the contradictions within the ranks of the enemy, dividing and isolating them to the greatest extent.* This strategy weakens their position and influence, increases the strength of the revolution to the highest degree and paves the way for its advance. Therefore, the problem of utilizing the internal conflicts of the enemy is strategically significant in the proletarian revolution.

The inevitable collapse of capitalism and its replacement by socialism will result from the struggle waged by the proletariat to topple it, and also from internal contradictions within capitalist production and conflicts in the ranks of the bourgeoisie which undermine this system.

The Leninist strategy of world revolution in the era of imperialism was based on three fundamental contradictions: between the proletariat and capital, between the oppressed nations and imperialism, and among the imperialists themselves. After the Russian Socialist Revolution, a fourth fundamental antagonism appeared—between the socialist and capitalist systems. The development of these contradictions as a whole creates the relation of forces between revolution and counter-revolution on a world scale.

Communists never harbor any illusions and never wait passively for the contradictions within the enemy's ranks to work themselves out. Moreover, we are aware that in the face of action by the people, the hostile forces attempt to settle their differences in the hopes of "closing their ranks" against the revolution. But, Lenin pointed to a more fundamental truth: "Capitalist property disintegrated them, transformed them from allies into savage beasts."(4)

Far from pinning our hopes on antagonisms within the ranks of the enemy, we are fully aware that the development of these contradictions and the extent to which they may be capitalized upon are in the last analysis determined by the strength of the revolution. The experience of all genuine popular revolutions shows that the stronger the revolutionary forces become and the higher the revolutionary tide rises, the more the enemy's ranks are torn by contradictions and are likely to split. Ultimately, the time comes when these conflicts have grown so exacerbated as to render impossible all compromise between the various enemy factions. This constitutes one of the unmistakable signs of the maturity of the revolutionary situation. The revolution then breaks out and the enemy's rule is overthrown in decisive battles.

The revolution in our country has always had a powerful imperialist enemy and on many occasions has had to cope with several enemies at one time. In such circumstances, our Party has applied creatively Lenin's shrewd observation: "The more powerful enemy can be conquered only by exerting the utmost effort, and by *necessarily*, thoroughly, carefully, attentively and skilfully taking advantage of any, even the smallest, 'rift' among the enemies . . . by taking advantage of every, even the smallest, opportunity of gaining a mass ally, even though this ally be temporary, vacillating, unstable, unreliable and conditional."(5)

By taking advantage of the enemy's internal contradictions to divide and isolate them, our Party, while adhering firmly to principles, has used various tactics in a very flexible and clever way. Before the August Revolution, our Party took opportune advantage of the mortal conflict between the Japanese and the French to advance the anti-Japanese resistance for national salvation. After the Japanese surrender, it seized the opportunity and led the people in a victorious general insurrection. After the

August Revolution, when the revolutionary power was still weak, we faced serious dangers created by internal and external enemies. Indeed, the situation could be likened to a "thousand-pound weight hanging by a hair." Under the leadership of President Ho Chi Minh, our Party pursued an extremely clear-sighted political line, rigorous in principle and flexible in tactics, which guided the nation through countless and seemingly insuperable difficulties. We would reach a temporary compromise with Chiang Kai-shek to be free to cope with the French colonialists, only to do the same with the French in order to drive out Chiang Kai-shek's troops and wipe out the reactionaries and their agents. Thus, we gained time to consolidate our forces and prepare for nationwide resistance to the inevitable French colonialist aggression. Those extremely perspicacious moves will go down in the history of our revolution as magnificent examples of the Leninist tactic of exploiting contradictions within the enemy's ranks by granting concessions, while holding firm to principles.

The fusion of boundless loyalty to the revolutionary cause, strong determination to liberate the nation and the people, and firm reliance on the strength of the masses—in combination with our special political knowledge and skill—resulted in a creative and effective application of the strategic principle of capitalizing upon the enemy's internal contradictions so as continually to advance the revolution to new positions.

On The Vietnam People's Army

Editor's Note:

In writing about Vietnam, most authors and journalists created the clear impression that the direction of the war was the sole responsibility of General Vo Nguyen Giap, Deputy Prime Minister, Minister of Defense, and Commander in Chief of the Vietnam People's Army (VPA). This is a grave theoretical error:

First: Like in any people's war of modern times (China, Cuba, Angola, Mozambique, Guinea-Bissau) and in any people's army, it is "politics which commands the guns". A military decision is reached only after a careful assessment of the political (national, international), economic, and cultural factors in a precise situation.

Second: in the case of Vietnam: All day-to-day political-military decisions were collectively made by the Bo Chinh Tri Trung Uong Dang (Political Bureau, Central Committee of the Party) of which General Vo Nguyen Giap is a member and the Quan Uy Trung Uong Dang (the military commission of the Central Committee). The chairman of this commission is Mr. Le Duc Tho who negotiated the 1973 Paris Agreement. General Vo Nguyen Giap is also a member of this commission. At every unit of the VPA, a chinh uy (political commissar) shares the responsibility with the tu lenh (commander).

It is clear then that Mr. Le Duan, in his capacity as First Secretary of the Central Committee of the Party, the "first among equals", participates in all military decisions with his colleagues in the Party

167

and in the government. The technical implementation of the military decisions made by the Party and the government (the senior members of which are also members of the Central Committee) falls on the VPA's Commander in Chief, General Vo Nguyen Giap, and the VPA's Chief of Staff, General Van Tien Dung (also a member of the Political Bureau of the Central Committee). In other words, there is complete unity and close coordination between the Party and the government, with the Party in the leading position (see chart).

The following excerpts come from: *Ban Ve Chien Tranh Nhan Dan va Luc Luong Vu Trang Nhan Dan* (Discussions on the People's War and on People's Army). Published in Hanoi in 1966 by the Nha Xuat Ban Quan Doi Nhan Dan (Vietnam People's Army Publishing House). It is a collection of thoughts on the subject by Ho Chi Minh, Le Duan, Truong Chinh (Chairman, National Assembly), Vo Nguyen Giap, Nguyen Chi Thanh (a general who died in July 1967 at the age of 53), Van Tien Dung and Song Hao (Director of the VPA's political department). Most of the excerpts are from articles in the Party's magazine *Su That* (Truth). The translations are mine.

(T.V.D.)

In wars, only when the enemy is defeated can victory be achieved. To do so, it is important to organize the Chinh Quy (regular army). The guerillas and the provincial armies cannot do this . . . . Without the Chinh Quy, it is not possible to conduct mobile, annihilating operations . . . . A war of defense, of simple reactions against the enemy's moves, will result in failures, losing in the end the very defensive posture. Only by taking initiative, by offensive against the enemy can one organize the defense. Without the Chinh Quy, it is impossible to be in command of a military situation.

Report to a military conference in Nam Bo
(Southern Vietnam), 1949.

The consolidation of the Party's leadership in the regular army and in the Dan Quan (People's militia), the full implementation of the party's leadership in the regular army and in the people's militia are the decisive factors for the success or failure of a national revolution.

Report to a military conference in Nam Bo 1949.

In order to have an army capable of defeating the French and all foreign aggressors, we must maintain strict discipline, develop correct strategy and practice widespread democracy.

Report to a military conference in Nam Bo 1949.

In the southern part of Vietnam, we do not have high mountains and deep forests. Our army must rely on the forests of people in struggle. We must follow the "Circle" strategy, to enable ourselves to win. Unlike areas with wide space and high mountains which allow the army to advance and retreat easily, in southern Vietnam, the realities force us to use the "Circle" strategy [to rely on the organized masses to encircle the enemy. ed.]

Report to a military conference in Nam Bo 1949.

The present balance of power does not necessarily lean on the side which produces more steel. In Vietnam, we have not yet produced steel, but we defeated the French troops and forced France to stop the war. Power does not necessarily reside in steel alone, but in the political system, in the human being.

Su That (*Truth*) *magazine 1958.*

The force which attacks and defeats imperialism is not the atomic weapons but the revolutioanry activities of the masses which, under a correct political and revolutionary leadership, stand up and destroy all oppressive fetters. Even at the time when the U.S. had the monopoly of atomic weapons, the revolutions in China and in Vietnam were successful. This was due to correct political and revolutionary leadership.

Su That, *1964.*

In countries with well established democratic structures, the struggle to gain power must pass through revolutionary struggle in which the main effort should be directed to political struggle, even to the use of election machinery. But in a fascist regime such as exists in the south of Vietnam, the struggle to capture fundamental powers must be an intensified armed revolutionary struggle and this regardless of the fact that it must be principally based on the politically organized masses. But this political army must be allied and coordinated with the revolutionary armed forces. Without the revolutionary armed forces, it is impossible to seize power, even power at the village level.

Su That, *1965.*

The present struggle is a great opportunity to build a new human being, to build new values and feelings in our people.

Su That, *1965.*

The experiences of the Vietnam Revolution are: parallel political and military struggles, relying on the forces of workers and peasants; establishment of liberated zones to conduct guerilla warfare in the countryside (the peasants are the main force for guerillas); uprisings in the cities (relying on the main forces of the proletariat and other working classes) . . . . It is necessary to have a strong Marxist-Leninist party, a strong political and armed force, a broad united front based on the alliance between workers, peasants, soldiers; liberated zones in the countryside, bases in the cities.

Su That, *1965.*

We greatly appreciate the aid given us by our brotherly nations. Now and in the future, we will receive these aids. But no matter how important these aids are, they cannot replace the efforts of our peoples. To rely on the brotherly nations is totally contrary to the principle of proletarian internationalism. Each communist party has a double responsibility, towards its own nation and towards the international proletariat. Only in fulfilling our duties to our people can we well discharge our duties to the international proletariat . . . . Only communists, only communist parties can possess the genuine patriotism and the genuine international spirit.

Su That, *1965.*

At the present time, we produce and fight at the same time. These two tasks are closely related. Only by preparing well and fighting well can we protect our production and only by increasing production can we support the war. We must make all efforts to produce and fight.

Tap Chi Tuyen Huan (*Magazine for Propaganda and Training*), *1965.*

We fight and we win, not because we are endowed with steel skin and copper bones, but because we are human.beings, real human beings. We are Vietnamese who are moral, loyal, patient, strong, indomitable, but filled with compassion.

Address to soldiers and population in Quang Binh on TET (New Year) of 1973.
(This quote is not from Discussions of People's War and on People's Army.)

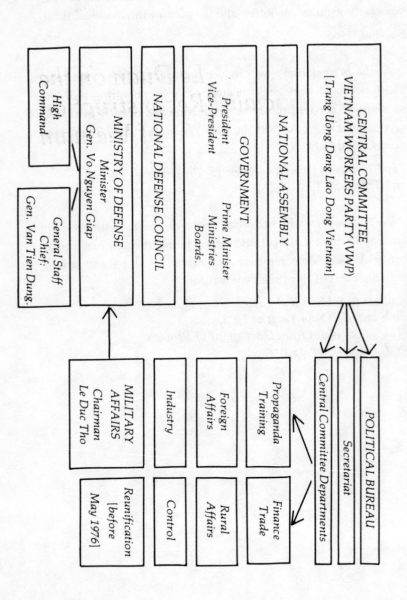

THE PARTY, THE GOVERNMENT AND THE MILITARY
In the Socialist Republic of Vietnam

CENTRAL COMMITTEE
VIETNAM WORKERS PARTY (VWP)
[*Trung Uong Dang Lao Dong Vietnam*]

NATIONAL ASSEMBLY

GOVERNMENT
President · Prime Minister
Vice-President · Ministries
Boards.

NATIONAL DEFENSE COUNCIL

MINISTRY OF DEFENSE
Minister
Gen. Vo Nguyen Giap

High Command

General Staff
Chief:
Gen. Van Tien Dung.

POLITICAL BUREAU

Secretariat

Central Committee Departments

Propaganda Training

Finance Trade

Foreign Affairs

Rural Affairs

Industry

Control

MILITARY AFFAIRS
Chairman
Le Duc Tho

Reunification
[before
May 1976]

*Le Duan on the
Socialist Reconstruction
of Vietnam*

Let Our Entire People Unite To Build Our Reunified and Socialist Fatherland

Dear members of the presidium,

Dear comrade deputies,

On behalf of the Central Committee of the Vietnam Workers Party, I warmly welcome you, comrade deputies, authentic representatives of our people, symbols of our broad national unity, having come here today from all over the country, from Cao Lang (in the north—ed.) to Minh Hai (in the south—ed.) to attend the first session of the National Assembly of reunified Vietnam, held in the heart of Hanoi, at a place where 31 years ago our great President Ho Chi Minh proclaimed the birth of the Democratic Republic of Vietnam.

This session of our National Assembly completes the reunification of our country on the state level. This is an event of tremendous importance in the political life of our country. Our countrymen from the north to the south, from town to country, are following with the greatest attention the important decisions of this historic session. Our brothers and friends throughout the world share our joy of victory.

Our National Assembly is shouldering the tasks entrusted to it by our countrymen at a time when our country is entering the most glorious stage in our nation's history of several thousand years.

Political Report to the reunified National Assembly, Hanoi, June 25, 1976.

In the spring of last year, our people and army won a great victory in the resistance war against U.S. aggression, for national salvation, with an earth-shaking general offensive and uprising, sweeping away the U.S. imperialists' neocolonialist regime, completely liberating the southern part of our homeland. This victory put a glorious end to the war for national salvation and national defence lasting 30 years since the August Revolution (1945), ended forever the 117-year imperialist domination of our country, completed the national people's democratic revolution throughout the country, safeguarded the fruits of the socialist revolution in the north, and opened an era of brilliant development for a completely independent, free, reunified and socialist Vietnam.

Our people's victory in the resistance against U.S. aggression, for national salvation, has shattered the biggest counteroffensive of the imperialist ringleader spearheaded at the revolutionary movement since the Second World War, dealt a staggering blow at the U.S. imperialists' counterrevolutionary global strategy, breached one of their defence lines in Southeast Asia, repelled and weakened imperialism, further strengthened and consolidated the offensive position of the three revolutionary currents of our times and strongly encouraged hundreds of millions of people in the world now struggling for peace, national independence, democracy and socialism.

The glory of today is the fruit of the extremely hard and valiant revolutionary struggle waged by our people for nearly half a century under the correct leadership of the former Indochinese Communist Party, now the Vietnam Workers Party and President Ho Chi Minh. Citizens of an enslaved country, our people have risen up heroically and successively defeated the Japanese fascists, the French colonialists and the U.S. imperialists. We have stood among the vanguard peoples struggling for the noble ideals of mankind, and made an active contribution to the advance of the world revolution.

Today, with deep emotion, the National Assembly turns its thoughts to our beloved and venerated Uncle Ho: Our party, our state, our entire people and army feel boundless pride for having acted upon his sacred testament and fulfilled our pledge to win complete independence and achieve national reunification. To our great president Ho Chi Minh we dedicate our collective exploit and express our eternal gratitude to him who gave leadership to our people and took us from one victory to another and who devoted all his life to the struggle for the liberation of our people and the reunification of our country, to the cause of our party and our nation! We pay respectful tribute to the memory of the heroic men and women who laid down their lives for independence and freedom for the fatherland and socialism. Eternal glory to the members of the armed forces, comrades and other compatriots who have made the sacrifice of their lives to clear the way for the continuous advance and the triumph of the revolution.

In the jubilant atmosphere of this historic session, our National Assembly warmly hails the ardent patriotism and tremendous revolutionary heroism of our compatriots, combatants and all the fraternal nationalities throughout the country of the north—the rear area and the invincible bastion of socialism which brilliantly fulfilled its task as the mighty base of the Vietnamese revolution in the period of resistance against U.S. aggression; of the south—the frontline which for 30 years running struggled in blood and fire, setting an example of loyalty, courage and perseverance and fully deserving the glorious title of "brass wall of the fatherland." We hail our compatriots throughout the country who have, over the past year and more, fully carried into effect their right to be masters of society, shown a stirring revolutionary spirit on the front of productive labour so as to overcome the grave sequels of war, and who have recorded initial achievements of which we can be rightfully proud.

Our National Assembly warmly commends the heroic Vietnam People's Army, those fighters of our revolutionary armed forces who, one generation after another, have continued the long march and fought in all parts of the country, carrying forward the traditions of Bach Dang, Chi Lang, and Dong Da, recording many Dien Bien Phu-type victories both on the ground and in the air, and achieving such springtime exploits as in the spring of 1968, the spring of 1972 and the spring of great victory of 1975 with the campaign named after our great Uncle Ho!

Our victory is also a victory for the solidarity uniting the peoples of the three Indochinese countries, solidarity of exceptional strength which has been tested in the flames of struggle against our common enemies. Our National Assembly warmly acclaims the great historic victory of the fraternal Lao and Cambodian peoples, and conveys to our comrades-in-arms the warmest feelings and the unshakable solidarity of the Vietnamese people.

We take this opportunity to express our profound gratitude to the Soviet Union, China and the other fraternal socialist countries which have extended great and precious assistance to our resistance and are now helping us heal the wounds of war and build socialism. We sincerely thank all our friends in the five continents for their strong support to our people's just cause.

Dear comrade deputies, with the total and complete victory of our fight against U.S. aggression for national salvation, the Vietnamese revolution has moved into a new stage, the stage of socialist revolution throughout the country. This is the stage in which our people set about building on their beloved fatherland the finest society that has ever existed in the history of the nation, taking their homeland forward step by step so as ultimately to reach the radiant peak of civilization, and fully carry into effect the sacred testament of President Ho "to build a peaceful, reunified, independent, democratic and prosperous Vietnam, and make a worthy contribution to the world revolution."

Socialism is the necessary development of the Vietnamese revolution and conforms to the law of development of human society in our era, the era of transition from capitalism to socialism on a worldwide scale. In the present era when socialism is the only solution to all urgent problems facing the various countries on the road forward, national independence and socialism are inseparable, indeed are closely bound together. Our people have become imbued with this truth of our time at an early date because they have always been motivated by ardent patriotism and a deep collective spirit—moral values manifest in our national culture, in our 4,000-year old tradition of national building and national defence, and now aroused by the light of Marxism-Leninism. President Ho, who embodies the quintessence of our nation, was the first Vietnamese to integrate patriotism with socialism. He said: "To save the country and liberate the nation, there is no other way than that of proletarian revolution," and "only socialism and communism can liberate the oppressed nations and the working people throughout the world from slavery."

Deeply imbued with that great thought, the Vietnam Workers Party has, ever since its founding in 1930, always held high the banner of national independence and socialism. Under this banner the party has brought into full play the strength of our nation and, by combining the strength of our nation with that of our time, created the invincible aggregate power of the Vietnamese revolution. That is how the Vietnamese people have won the great honour of having defeated two big imperialisms, the French and the American, opening first the process of collapse of old colonialism and now the inevitable collapse of neocolonialism.

Today, when our fatherland has gained complete independence and when the country has been cleared of all aggressors and has been reunified, nation and socialism merge into one.

Only socialism can make the working people the real and complete masters of society. Only socialism can materialize their age-old dream of being forever freed from oppression, exploitation, cold and hunger and of enjoying a plentiful life, a secure future, a civilized and happy life. Only under socialism can our homeland build a modern economy, advanced culture and science, and powerful national defence, so as to preserve forever its independence and prosperity.

Only under socialism can our homeland enjoy the most complete unity: territorial, economic, cultural, social, political and ideological unity; uniformity in rights and duties for all our countrymen who are closely united and bound by sincere mutual love and affection.

Nation and socialism are one. For us Vietnamese, love of country now means love of socialism; it means devoting all our zeal, strength, intelligence and talent to the building of their socialist homeland.

Dear comrade deputies, the Third Congress of the Vietnam Workers Party held in 1960 laid down the line for socialist revolution in North Vietnam. Afterward, the meetings of the party's Central Committee, step by step summed up practical experiences of the Vietnamese revolution and further developed and concretized that line. Following the complete liberation of South Vietnam, basing ourselves on the experiences of the socialist revolution in the north, and proceeding from the new situation in the country, the party's Central Committee laid down the general line for the revolution throughout Vietnam and concrete tasks for each zone in the new stage.

On behalf of the party's Central Committee, I wish to expound to the National Assembly, that is, to the entire nation, the main features of these revolutionary line and tasks. Entering the new stage, the revolution in our country is developing with the following major characteristics:

—Our entire country lives in peace, independence and unity, under the leadership of the Vietnam Workers Party, with a tested proletarian dictatorship, with a solid worker-peasant alliance serving as basis for the national united front and for the people's revolutionary administration.

—Our entire country is in the process of advancing from small production to socialist production without going through the stage of capitalist development. Thirty years of war have left serious sequels in the economic and social fields. In the north, the exploiter classes have been abolished, socialist production relations have been established, and the initial bases of large-scale socialist production and of an independent and sovereign economy have been built. In the south, exploiter classes still exist, capitalism had begun developing, and private economy and small production are still common. Before liberation, the economy in the south was entirely dependent on imperialism and at present vestiges of feudal exploitation still remain in the newly liberated areas. In the old liberated zones, the social system has a national people's democratic character but the economy is not yet developed and was heavily ravaged during the war.

Our country is advancing to socialism at a time when the revolution in Laos and that in Cambodia have won and are winning great successes, when the world socialist system and the forces of national independence, democracy and peace are growing ever more powerful, when the three revolutionary currents of our time are developing, the prestige and political position of our country in the international arena are rising daily and imperialism is facing ever more crises and weakening.

The strategic task of the revolution in our country in the new stage is: *to achieve the reunification of our homeland, and to take the whole country rapidly, vigorously and steadily to socialism.*

The north must give a strong impulse to the building of socialism and perfect the socialist production relations; the south must at the same time carry out socialist transformation and socialist construction.

Socialist transformation and socialist construction are two closely related aspects of the socialist revolution. "On the one hand, it is necessary to set up socialist transformation with the aim of converting the nonsocialist production relations into socialist ones, of which the keystone is the transformation of the system of individual ownership and that of capitalist ownership of the means of production into different forms of the socialist system of ownership so as to liberate the productive forces and clear the way for the development of production. On the other hand, it is necessary to push ahead socialist construction with the aim of developing the liberated productive forces, to build the material and technical foundations of socialism, to abolish the state of backwardness, to transform small production into large-scale socialist production and unceasingly to develop and perfect the new production relations."

Proceeding from the fact that our land is a former colonial and semifeudal country now advancing directly to socialism without going through the stage of capitalist development, our task is to create a socialist society from the base to the top: We must at the same time create new productive forces and new production relations; create new economic bases, a new superstructure and new social relationships; create a new material life and a new spiritual and cultural life. For these reasons, the process of socialist revolution in our country is a process of continuous, comprehensive, extremely profound and thorough revolutionary changes. This process involved firmly grasping proletarian dictatorship, developing the working people's right to be the collective master of society and carrying out the triple revolution: revolution in production relations, scientific and technical revolution, and ideological and cultural revolution, with the scientific and technical revolution as the keystone. Through these three revolutions, the working people's collective mastery of society, large-scale socialist production, and new socialist people will gradually take shape. The central task is socialist industrialization. The above three revolutions are inseparable. They do not occur separately, but take place and must be carried out simultaneously and in a closely associated way. Likewise, collective mastery of the socialist society, large-scale socialist production and the new, socialist type of man are very closely related and exert deep influence on one another. The close combination of the three revolutions enables us to advance directly from small production to socialism without going through the painful historical stage of capitalism.

The central task of the entire period of transition to socialism is to carry out the *socialist industrialization* of our national economy and to take it to large-scale *socialist production*. The highest goal of large-scale socialist production is to ensure the satisfaction of the daily growing material and cultural needs of our entire society, according to a system of distribution that clearly expresses the people's right to collective mastery of society, by unceasingly developing and perfecting production on the basis of ever more advanced techniques.

The line for building the socialist economy in our country is as follows: To give priority to a rational development of heavy industry on the basis of great efforts to develop agriculture and light industry, to combine industry and agriculture, to build the whole country into a modern industrial-agriculture structure; simultaneously to build the centrally run economy and regional economies, to combine economy with national defence; to widen economic relations with the socialist countries and other nations on the basis of firmly maintaining our independence and sovereignty and provided they are beneficial to the building of an independent and sovereign economy. We must have a good grasp of planning work, considering it a key instrument for managing our economy; at the same time we must make proper use of market, prices, wages and credit within the framework of the state plans. We must attach importance to both use-value and value and make a judicious application of the law of value. We must make a very close combination of the revolution in production relations with the scientific and technical revolution. As each step in the process of development, we must closely associate production relations and productive forces, and make them accord with each other, and stimulate each other. We must unceasingly increase labour productivity. Every year each production base must set to itself targets for increasing labour productivity while each production base must set to itself targets for increasing labour productivity while paying adequate attention to the quality and economic effect of its products; we must step up the socialist emulation movement, organize our work well, especially now when it is still mostly done by handicraft methods, carry out standardization and set economic and technical norms for production, correctly solve the relationship between accumulation and consumption, and work out a rational policy with regard to consumption.

We will strive to complete in the main the task of laying the material and technical basis of socialism in our country within 15 or 20 years.

In following this economic line, it is necessary to continue to perfect the socialist production relations in the north while stepping up the transformation of the production relations in the south with a view to integrating the production relations in the two zones, as soon as possible on the basis of socialism. For this purpose, it is necessary now, in the north, to make great efforts to develop and strengthen the state economic sector, consolidate the collective economic sector, and closely associate them; to manage well small individual production and family subsidiary economy in the south; at the same time to rapidly do away with the bureaucratic and militarist comprador bourgeoisie as well as all vestiges of the feudal landlord class. We must firmly punish and eliminate speculators and hoarders who are upsetting the market and who, banking on the temporary difficulties of the country after liberation, are enriching themselves at the cost of the sufferings of the people.

It is necessary to create, develop and strengthen the state economic sector and make it strong in all fields—in industry, agriculture, building, transport and communications, commerce, etc. It is necessary to carry out socialist transformation of the private capitalist economy in production, transport and communications and building, this transformation being effected through the use of different measures to suit concrete situations. Private enterprises may be turned into joint state-private ones, or they may be allowed to continue in existence and encouraged to serve socialism under the guidance of the socialist state and within the framework of state plans.

It is necessary to turn individual farming into large-scale socialist production by means of collectivization to carry out collectivization alongside irrigation and mechanization; to reorganize production at the district level along the line of intensive farming, all-round development and specialization; to combine industry with agriculture and associate the state with the peasantry;and to cut off all ties between peasants and speculators. It is necessary to direct small industries and handicrafts onto the path of large-scale socialist production by reorganizing them according to trades and by putting them under state management.

This can be done in different ways: Either to set up cooperatives with a view to improved techniques and equipment, enlarged production, higher efficiency and better quality of the products; or to group them into "satellites" which would participate in turning out various groups of products in close association with state enterprises; or to make them operate exclusively to fill orders placed by the state with materials supplied by the state.

In certain cases, private business will be allowed to continue. It is necessary to effect socialist transformation of private capitalist traders and small traders by developing a broad state trading service capable of handling all commodities necessary for everyday life and supplying them directly to the consumers, and by reorganizing the private traders and channeling most of them into the productive sector of the economy.

In the organization and management of the economy, we must strive to build a management and planning system in the south while improving and perfecting the management and planning system in the north, thus building a single management and planning system for the whole country.

In distribution, it is necessary to create a system in which the material and cultural needs of the whole society will be met more and more fully in keeping with the level of development of production, the premise and condition of this being that everybody must fulfil his or her duties to society, society is responsible for the welfare of all its members, today's society is being responsible for the welfare of the society of tomorrow. In this spirit, we must now consistently observe the principle of to each according to his work, with regard to all people of working age and fit for work, strictly enforcing everybody's duty to work and the slogan "more work, more pay; less work, less pay; no pay for those who can but do not work."

On the other hand, we must, as production develops, gradually increase social welfare, step by step broaden the raising and education of children by society, provide health care, education, rest and recreation for everybody, take good care of the old and the disabled, provide women with adequate conditions so that they can discharge their noble duties as mothers, and see to it that all cultural and social organizations function effectively.

We know very well that under the system of socialist collective mastery even newborn babies are masters of society and are entitled to require from society whatever they need to live and develop. It is the responsibility of society to ensure equal opportunities to all children in life, education and development. No children should suffer handicaps because they have lost their parents, or because their parents are sick or disabled.

Those people in the south who, as a result of the U.S. imperialist war of aggression, had attained a living standard much too high for the country's economy and their own working capacity, should understand that this prosperity was a sham one, the cost of which was misery and death for millions of their countrymen, destruction for innumerable villages and towns, degradation for many young people and humiliation for countless women in areas under enemy occupation, and enslavement of the country. They should know that the frantic needs and vulgar tastes of that "consumer society" are the complete opposite of a truly happy and civilized life. Such people today can and should come back to reality and the life of the nation, and live by their work. This is the way to a happy, beautiful life with meaning and dignity, a life of true and lasting happiness for themselves and their children.

To take our economy from small-scale production to large-scale socialist production, we must grasp our central task, which is socialist industrialization; we must strive to step up the scientific and technical revolution, and turn our present production, a largely manual, scattered production, in which the division of labour is not yet developed and output, efficiency and quality are still low, into mechanized, automated, electrified and chemicalized production highly concentrated and specialized with advanced coordination and cooperation; we must reorganize work on a large scale, turn to account the achievements of advanced science and technology, bring into play and use in a rational way all the potentialities of our country in terms of manpower and materials.

Great efforts must be made to create a new material and technical basis by providing good equipment, first of all to those key branches of the economy in which most of society's work force is engaged, like agriculture, fishing, forestry, industry, small industry and handicrafts producing consumer goods, capital construction, and transport and communications.

New and useful materials must be created, technical means must be amply provided, adequate energy must be obtained for the national economy, and advanced industrial processes must be widely applied. For this purpose, alongside reorganization and the improvement of technique, and a full use of what is already at hand, the most decisive task is to strive to build a network of key heavy industries.

A mechanical engineering and electronic industry must be built and made strong enough to supply machinery and partial or complete equipment to the other economic branches and to cultural branches. There must be an industry of ferrous metals, first of all, iron and steel, to meet the needs of mechanical engineering, building and transport and communications. Then there must be a nonferrous metal industry chiefly to produce copper, aluminum and tin, and an industry of precious metals. Great efforts must be made to develop the electric power industry through a combination of hydroelectricity and thermal electricity with especial attention to the former, while creating conditions for the use of other sources. Along with coal mining, great efforts must be made quickly to exploit natural oil and gas. The chemical industry must be developed in such a way as to satisfy the needs of agriculture for fertilizers, insecticides and herbicides, and those of light industry for artificial and synthetic fiber and plastic products . . . . It must make full use of natural rubber, ensure adequate supplies of necessary chemicals for use in medicine and other sciences and other fields of activity, and for export.

Special efforts must be made to build a petrochemical industry as soon as possible; we must quickly strengthen capital construction, increase the material basis of, and rapidly develop the industry of building materials especially cement, lime, bricks and tiles . . . organize well the labour force, heighten the capabilities of statistical work and apply new construction methods with the aim of meeting the great needs of national reconstruction, in a country just emerging from a long hard war, with many cities and villages to be rebuilt and with a material and technical basis to be laid for socialism, on a growing scale.

We must develop communications and transport vigorously and comprehensively and harmoniously so as to serve well the economy and the people's needs for transport.

Agriculture must advance vigorously to meet, together with fishing and forestry, our society's demand for food, and to provide adequate supply of raw materials to industry and for export. Agriculture, in particular, must serve as the basis for the development of industry, especially in this initial stage. We must see to it that agriculture, animal breeding, fishing and forestry are well developed in all respects.

Zoning must be carried out for a harmonious development of the plains, the midlands, the highlands and the coastal areas, with full use of the advantages of each region, and with a view to a prompt formation of zones of concentrated and specialized production. Attention must be paid equally to intensive farming, the multiplication of crops, and the expansion of arable land. Within a short time we must reclaim or restore to cultivation several million more hectares. We must step up irrigation and soil improvement while perfecting the irrigation system on large areas; actively make use of new strains giving high and stable yields; and actively apply new achievements of science and technology and turn to full account the advantages of tropical agriculture. While breeding, we must step up mechanization for a sharp increase in efficiency and redeploy the work force in all parts of the country in a rational way. State farms must be set up in newly opened areas, and a fillip must be given to the reorganization of agriculture along the line of large-scale socialist production, this reorganization being effected from the grassroots up with each district to be turned into an agro-industrial economic unit.

We must strive to achieve a rapid development of light industries, among them the food industry, so that before long we can produce all necessary commodities in growing volume, and with greater variety and usefulness in order to better serve the material life and improve the cultural life of the people, effectively serve the deployment of the social work force on a growing scale, and for export. Efforts must be concentrated on the development of the textile, leather-making, paper-making, wood-processing, porcelainware, earthenware and crystalware industries, the production of household utensils, teaching aids, appliances for hospitals and kindergartens, and cultural articles. Existing light industries and the food industry must be rearranged and reorganized on a nationwide scale, and must be made to work in a planned way along the line of large-scale socialist production, with a combination of the large, and individual sectors of production. At the same time, we must actively build more establishments of the kinds deemed necessary. Very great attention must be given to the improvement of technique and the assimilation of advanced technology in order to raise the quality of products, especially those destined for export.

We must strive to develop science and technology to attain the level now prevailing in the world; we must actively learn from the achievements of modern science and technology and apply them to production and everyday life; we must carry out effective technical management regarding all processes and standards, in measurements, in technical and quality control, and in discoveries and inventions. It is necessary to go on training technical workers in sufficient numbers and with high professional standards for whole branches of activity; training scientists, technicians, and economic managers capable of mastering advanced science and technology and resolving problems arising from production activities and everyday life.

Besides economic transformation and economic construction, there is another very important task. We must actively step up the socialist revolution in ideology and culture, and train a new, socialist type of man.

The purpose of the socialist revolution in ideology and culture is to create for everybody a rich moral and cultural life, in keeping with the highest goal of socialism; to meet not only the material but also the growing cultural needs of society. We must make all cultural values the property of the people and enable the people to become direct creators of all cultural values. Our objective is a society with a high culture. The culture of such a society must be one with a socialist content and a national character. It must be built on the basis of Marxism-Leninism and of the sense of collective mastery of society; it must selectively assimilate the achievements of human civilization and of modern culture and science.

At the same time, it must condense and magnify what is best in the national spirit and the national culture, which have a tradition of 4,000 years, a tradition of patriotism, dauntlessness, perserverance and resourcefulness, a tradition of mutual affection and love binding together the working people, a tradition of diligence and optimism. This culture is a harmonious blend of the original cultures of the many fraternal nationalities living on our soil, which are like so many flowers blooming in the magnificent garden of our nation. In this society of high culture human relationships are an expression of this noble motto: "Each for all, and all for each." This happy society will be made up of happy families.

It is necessary at this stage to make great efforts to develop education with both a national and a socialist character and complete preparations for the transformation of education soon to be under way throughout the country. It is necessary to develop science vigorously, improve and strengthen the press, radio, television, and publishing. It is necessary to step up cultural and art acitivites, museum and library work, and folk arts, the movement of physical culture and sports. While doing this, we must aim to attain ever higher quality together with gradual expansion. We must strive to train the staffs, build the material bases, and ensure the supply of necessary means . . . . We must see to it that all parts of our country—cities, villages and even remote mountain hamlets—receive the benefits of culture, education, the arts, and sports, so that the people's moral and cultural needs may be satisfied more and more fully.

The building of a new culture must be undertaken in the context of a struggle to root out all ideological and cultural vestiges of the old regime, particularly to extirpate from South Vietnam all the poisons of the U.S. neocolonialist ideology and culture.

This was an enslaving, mongrel, decadent and utterly reactionary "culture" with backward practices and superstitions. It induced a considerable number of people, especially city dwellers, to indulge in "living at a fast tempo" an individualistic, egoistic life of depravation, and gave stimulation and encouragement to the basest instincts and the most vulgar tastes. The evil intention of U.S. imperialism was to destroy all traditional moral values and the wholesome way of life of our people, to debauch young people and make hoodlums out of them, to destroy in them all that is best in the national character and make them forget about their dignity and their duties to the country, and the nation. Our fellow countrymen in the south have for decades put up a stiff resistance to the neocolonialist "culture" while preserving and developing the fine traditions of our nation.

Since liberation, they have done a great deal to remove the last vestiges and sequels of this "culture." This work must now be continued persistently, actively and resolutely. We must use the light of the new culture to dispel the darkness of the past, save those who have gone astray and bring them back to the people, reunite them with the spirit of the nation and make them join the entire people in working for a brilliant cultural life that is both Vietnamese and socialist.

As President Ho Chi Minh said:"To build socialism, first of all there must be socialist people." New, socialist people in Vietnam must be people working for their collective mastery of society. They must embody and develop what is best in our traditional culture. These new, socialist Vietnamese must fit into the system of socialist collective mastery of society and serve the large-scale socialist production now underway.

They must be highly conscious people, full of determination and will to overcome all difficulties so as to accomplish their tasks. They must be honest working people who hate hangers-on, loafers and liars. They must be disciplined, skilled, efficient working people, people dedicated to work, zealous guardians of public property, and scrupulous observers of all the rules of social life. They must be deeply attached to the working people who are building a new life together with them.

These new people ardently love socialism and harmoniously associate their patriotism with proletarian internationalism. These new people must show all-round maturity and lead a harmonious and rich social and private life.

Man being a product of social relationships, the new type of man must be the combined result of all the three revolutions in which he takes a direct part. Only through practice, struggle and work, can man transform himself and, little by little, attain these moral standards.

To foster a new type of man, a whole series of measures must be taken in all fields, ideological and organizational, educational and administrative, political, cultural, legal and economic. Of these, the conduct of an ideological and cultural revolution and a wide application of criticism and self-criticism, which is the law governing man's evolution, are of particular importance. The fostering of a new type of man must be undertaken and drives launched among specific groups for specific purposes in suitable forms, especially emulation movements in labour.

The fostering of the new man must be actively and carefully undertaken in productive units, offices, schools, kindergartens, research centres, in cultural, artistic, and physical education organizations, in city blocks and streets, in villages and hamlets, in families, in trade unions, in youth and women's associations and other social organizations.

The economic transformation and economic construction, the stepped-up socialist revolution in ideology and culture, and the fostering of the new man have one purpose: to build a system of socialist collective mastery of society. And to build a system of socialist collective mastery means to make our country a society whose authentic, supreme masters are the social community, the highly organized collective of working people with the worker-peasant alliance at the core. Collective mastery involves mastery in every field: political, economic, cultural and social; mastery of society, mastery of nature, mastery of oneself, mastery over the whole country, mastery over each locality. On the basis of full mastery by the collective, full freedom is attained by everyone, for "the free development of each is a condition for the free development of all." (*Manifesto of the Communist Party*)

This is a genuine mastery, mastery in its fullest sense of the word. Socialist collective mastery finds a concentrated expression in the mastery exercised by the working people through the socialist state and under the leadership of the vanguard party of the working class.

To act in a conscious, organized and planned manner, our working class, our working people, and our people in general must be reorganized in a careful, concentrated and comprehensive way into a state. Through the state the people will exercise their mastery over society, engage in social activities, manage society, and manage their own lives. To exercise mastery through the state is the highest and most effective form of mastery. The socialist state is a new-type "state." It is a state of the people, by the people and for the people. It is an administrative organization, an institutional organ and also an economic and cultural body. It is an integral part of the socio-economic structure, pervades it, instead of lying above or on the margin of that structure. It applies all measures—administrative and economic, educational and legal measures, coercion and persuasion, organizational and ideological work—so as to manage the economy and society in all respects. It is responsible for ensuring political security and national defence, for building and managing the economy, building and managing culture, protecting the interests of both the collective and the individuals, conducting diplomatic activities and economic, cultural, scientific and technical exchanges and cooperation with other countries.

The vanguard party of the working class is the social force representing the new regime; it has a firm grasp of Marxism-Leninism and uses Marxist-Leninist methods to discover the rules governing the Vietnamese revolution and the development of Vietnamese society. Science and revolution, revolution and science, these are the twofold essence of the party. Party leadership alone can give the activities of the state and the people a truly scientific character and make them conform to the law of development of Vietnamese society, thereby bringing about the expected results. The party leadership alone can give the activities of the state and the people a strong revolutionary character, and allow the people to fully develop their creativeness. In any given historical period, a nation is best represented by a certain class.

In Vietnam today, when the nation and socialism are one, the best representative of the nation is the Vietnamese working class and its vanguard party, the Vietnam Workers Party. The party's leadership has been the basic factor for all the great victories of the Vietnamese revolution over the past decades. This leadership is now the best guarantee of success for the socialist revolution in the new stage.

The working people's collective mastery of society through the socialist state and under the leadership of the party will unfailingly result in a greater development of the spirit of initiative and boundless creativeness of the working people. It will give rise to one revolutionary movement after another. It will give the activities of the working people a highly organized character in the whole society and make them conform to objective laws. It will communicate to them both a revolutionary and scientific character, thus mustering enough strength to move mountains and fill up oceans, overcome all difficulties and obstacles at any time, any place and in all aspects of life, get rid of the old and create the new, and move history forward at a pace never seen in our country before.

The exercise of collective mastery over society by the working people—whose nucleus is the worker-peasant alliance—through the state and under the leadership of the vanguard party of the working class is proletarian dictatorship. Our state, therefore, is a state of proletarian dictatorship.

The August Revolution, for the first time in the history of our nation, established a new-type state of the working people in our country. With the complete victory of the resistance against U.S. aggression, for national salvation, our people have today become the complete master of the country having a new-type state embracing the whole country through which to exercise their right of mastery.

To strengthen and perfect this state is the duty of the whole country as well as each locality, in the south and in the north alike. The essential point is rapidly to increase efficiency of the state machinery as an administrative body and one for economic and cultural management. Both aspects are important. However, since the conduct and management of economy by the state are the main aspect, one that is relatively new and therefore difficult, we should pay special attention to raising the capacity of the state for economic operations and management.

The state must have an organizational structure suited to its nature. As an organisation for economic operations and management, the state structure must be built on the basis of the principles of management and planning: democratic centralism; combination of management and planning according to branches with management and planning according to localities; combination of planning at the central level with planning at the local and grassroots level; ensuring both good production and good distribution; attaching importance to work productivity, the quality of products and economic efficiency; upholding technical improvement and individual responsibility; and combating bureaucracy.

As an organization responsible for building and managing culture, the state must have a structure commensurate with the requirements of the socialist revolution in ideology and culture. Our state is an organization representing the common interests of the whole country, a unified state of all the fraternal nationalities living on Vietnamese territory.

Firmly holding the banner of unity of all nationalities, ensuring and defending the right of collective mastery and all other legitimate rights of all nationalities, majority and minority alike, ensuring equality among all nationalities in the country—such is a fundamental policy of our state. Proceeding from the duty to defend the happiness and legitimate rights and interests of the people, the socialist state respects the beliefs of religious citizens. For that reason, to ensure freedom of belief is a major policy of our state.

Our state must be strong enough to defend our country's political security and social order and to smash in time all schemes of the counterrevolutionaries. It must endeavor to build a strong and firm all-people national defence, enforce the regime of military service and assign to the army the task of economic construction so as to keep our country prepared to smash all attacks by foreign aggressors.

In our system of state administration, the National Assembly is the highest organ of state power while the people's councils are the local organs of state power. The National Assembly and the people's councils are elected according to the principle of universal, equal, direct and secret ballot. The National Assembly and the people's councils at various levels are responsible to the people. Under the leadership of the party, the National Assembly decides the most important questions of the state while the people's councils decide the important questions of the localities in keeping with the line and policies of the central state administration.

The Council of Ministers is the executive body of the National

Assembly. It is elected by the National Assembly, while the people's committees at various levels are the executive organs of the people's councils and are elected by these councils. The Council of Ministers and the people's committees at various levels are responsible to the National Assembly, the people's councils, and the people. The National Assembly and the people's councils at all levels supervise the activities of the state machinery at these levels.

It is necessary, by means of concrete procedures, to fully carry into effect the responsibility of the Council of Ministers and the people's committees at various levels to the National Assembly and the people's councils at these levels. It is necessary to define rules and create conditions for the deputies to the National Assembly and the members of the people's councils to collect and communicate the opinions of the people to the state organs and see how they solve these problems. It is necessary to institute regular communication between the electors and their deputies and ensure the right of the former to control and dismiss the latter.

It is necessary strictly and scrupulously to control the activities of the various state organs. The mechanism of control includes the system of self-control within the state apparatus, control by the mass organizations, and control by the party.

Supervision and control must become an institution which compels each organization and each individual to comply with the law, to observe the rules and regulations, to fulfil each task, perform each job and turn out each product according to quantitative and qualitative norms. All state organs from the grassroots to the centre must answer questions concerning them posed by the people.

The people make use of their rights guaranteed under the constitution to combat any wrong-doing of the state organs and compel them to respect the right of the people as collective masters of society. The mass media should expand their investigations and researches so as to reflect constructive ideas of the masses and criticize any manifestation of bureaucracy and authoritarianism on the party of state organs.

It is necessary to strengthen legality. We must by means of the law steer the activities of state organs into strict observance of regulations and norms. We must define and safeguard the rights and duties of the citizens and require that every citizen observe the law. We must strictly supervise the observance of the law, use coercion with regard to those who refuse to observe the law, and mete out due punishment to all lawbreakers.

The strength of our socialist legality lies in the fact that its basis and essence are precisely the people's right to collective mastery of society. Along with deciding on the constitution, our National Assembly will adopt the law on the organization of the Council of Ministers and the people's councils and people's committees at all levels and other laws and regulations on the organization and activities of the state. It is necessary to build and enact in time a series of laws and regulations in many fields; timely attention must be given to enacting a system of economic laws and regulations.

The citizens of our society have the right to work, to enjoy the fruits of their labor, to rest, to study, the right to freedom of the individual, freedom of expression, of the press, of assembly, of association, freedom of belief, freedom to adhere to any religion or not to adopt any, the right to stand for election, the right to elect state organs . . . . All citizens are equal before the law. Women and men are equal in all fields, political, economic, cultural, social, and in the family. Children are entitled to proper care and education, the aged and invalids and the sick have the right to receive care from the state. Our state not only recognizes these rights of its citizens, but also ensures the necessary material conditions for the citizens to really enjoy these rights.

Apart from their rights, the citizens have duties toward society. These are the duty to work, the duty to defend the fatherland and the socialist state, and the duty to observe the constitution and the law, labor discipline, public order and the norms of social life, the duty of protecting public property.

It is necessary to see that rights and duties are consistent with each other and are both aimed at ensuring the full exercise of the collective mastery of society and, on this basis, also full independence and freedom to each individual.

We must resolutely oppose loafing, avoidance of work, misappropriation of public property, bribery, corruption and waste. We must severely condemn and resolutely combat such attitudes as irresponsibility, arrogance, authoritarianism, the creation of unnecessary and cumbersome procedures and red tape, indifference, and even callousness in the face of the difficulties and sufferings of the people, and a perfunctory acceptance of criticism. These manifestations encroach upon the people's right to mastery of society and sometimes even cause political harm to citizens. We must also take effective measures to prevent a number of cadres and public employees from becoming a stratum of privileged people who lord it over the masses.

Along with exercising their highest right of collective mastery through the state organs and under the leadership of the party, the working people also exercise their collective mastery through the activities of the broad mass organizations: the trade unions, the cooperatives and the peasants association, the youth union, the women's union, the national united front. On behalf of their members, these organizations take part in the activities of the state, control the state and constitute schools in which the people learn to exercise their right to socialist collective mastery. Under the party's leadership, the activities of the state and of the mass organizations have the same goal and are all aimed at ensuring the working people's collective mastery over society.

The working class is the vanguard class, the leading class of our society. The constitution and the trade union law affirm the leading role of the working class and the right of the trade unions to represent the working class in taking part in state affairs, controlling the state and taking part in the management of the factories. This is one of the important measures to strengthen and perfect the state. It is necessary to develop the role of the front with regard to the state, especially to the National Assembly, such as naming candidates for general elections, following and encouraging activities of the deputies to the National Assembly, proposing the dismissal of deputies who are no longer trusted by the people, and reporting the opinions of members of the front to the National Assembly.

Dear deputies: Above we have presented the suggestions of the Vietnam Workers Party on the main points in the basic content of the socialist revolution and socialist construction throughout the country. This content may be summed up as follows:

Firmly grasp proletarian dictatorship, develop the right of collective mastery of the working people, carry out simultaneously the three revolutions (revolution in production relations, scientific and technical revolution, and ideological and cultural revolution, of which the scientific and technical revolution is the keystone), step up the socialist industrialization of the country, build a large-scale socialist production system, build the regime of socialist collective mastery over society, build a new-type socialist man, abolishing the regime of exploitation of man by man, abolishing poverty and backwardness, constantly heightening revolutionary vigilance, strengthen national defence, firmly maintaining political security and social order, resolutely repressing the counter-revolutionaries smashing in time all their schemes of rearing their heads again, standing ready to defeat all schemes and acts of aggression and sabotage by imperialism and its henchmen, uniting the entire people and striving to build our socialist fatherland, Vietnam, into a country with modern industry, modern agriculture, powerful national defence, advanced culture and science, and a happy and civilized life.

That is also the basic content of the arduous and complex class struggle aimed at solving the question "who will win" between the socialist and capitalist paths in the period of transition to socialism in our country. This struggle is being waged in many forms: transformation and construction, political and economic, persuasion and compulsion, peaceful and violent. It requires that all our compatriots, combatants, cadres and party members have a new determination, new capacities, necessary knowledge and correct methods of work in all domains, the spirit of revolutionary offensive and perseverance to struggle for the complete victory of socialism.

Our working class and working people as a whole must march forward vigorously, endeavour in productive labour and make assaults into science and technology with the same revolutionary zeal and ardour as in the days of fighting against the aggressors to save the country.

In implementation of that line, our people and state should, in a number of years ahead, focus efforts on the following concrete tasks:

To perfect the state administration from the centre down to the regional and grassroots levels in the management of administrative affairs as well as of economy and culture, so as to make our administration really strong and firm, capable of providing effective guidance and management for all spheres of social life throughout the country, and more and more representative of the collective mastery of the people.

We should pay special attention to the building and consolidation of the people's administration at all levels in the south. In order to make this administrative apparatus really pure and clean and capable of shouldering its revolutionary tasks in the new period, we must firmly maintain political security and social order, constantly see to the strengthening and consolidation of national defence, and combine the task of consolidating national defence with that of economic construction.

Step up economic rehabilitation and development: We must firmly grasp the central and long-term task of socialist industrialization, actively build the material and technical bases of all branches of the national economy, build the structures of a modern industrial and agricultural economy. In the south, we must closely associate the task of economic rehabilitation and development with that of socialist transformation. On the basis of countings and assessments aimed at providing a good knowledge of the material bases and productive forces available in each branch of production and for each group of products, and on the basis of an evaluation of the fixed capital in both zones, we must reorganize social production throughout the country according to a unified program and plan, and make effective use of the existing production capacity while endeavouring to build new enterprises.

The main orientation for economic rehabilitation and development is as follows: To concentrate to a high degree the forces of the whole country, of all levels and all branches, and call for intensive efforts from the people; to step up the all-sided development of agriculture, first of all strive to provide a fundamental and firm solution to the food problem in the whole country, through intensive farming and multiplication of crops, reclamation of fallow lands and opening of new land to expand the acreage under food crops and through intensive development of animal breeding and fishing. To strive to quickly solve the question of zoning for planned agricultural production; to devote large areas to the cultivation of industrial crops; to ensure good exploitation of forest in order to supply enough materials for home industries and for export; to make the fullest use of and actively expand the productive capacity of the existing light industries in the country. To pay adequate attention to the great potentialities of handicrafts while building a number of new light industry factories in order to produce enough consumer goods for the people. Under no circumstances should a shortage of the main necessities be allowed to develop.

Along with the reorganization, reequipment, transformation and expansion of the existing heavy industry establishments with a view to serving agriculture, light industry, construction, communications and transport, we must start building a number of key projects of heavy industry in such branches as energy, engineering, metallurgy, chemicals and building materials, in order to lay the groundwork for an accelerated tempo of socialist industrialization.

Actively restore and further expand the various branches of communications, strive to improve the organization and operation of transport services in order to meet the needs in goods and passenger transport; we should strive to increase capital construction in order to meet the increasing demands of economic and cultural development and the post-war improvement of the people's life.

We must take the most active measures to promote export, make good use of the capacity of agriculture, forestry, aquatic products, handicrafts and industry in order to increase rapidly the sources of export goods, expand economic relations with the fraternal socialist countries and other countries with a view to creating better conditions for economic rehabilitation and development in our country. We should attach great importance to using the abundant manpower of our country to produce more wealth for society. In the immediate future we must strive to create enough jobs to make full use of all the social work force while taking steps to redistribute labour among the various branches and areas in the country. We should strive to readjust and improve the organization of labour in order to uphold labour discipline and increase labour productivity; we should mobilize and organize the army to perform its duty of building economy.

To transform the old production relations and build, consolidate and perfect the new production relations in the north, we must continue to consolidate and perfect the socialist relations of production in all fields, especially in management and distribution. In the south, we must immediately abolish the comprador bourgeoisie and the remnants of the feudal landlord class, undertake the socialist transformation of private capitalist industry and commerce, agriculture, handicraft and small trade through appropriate measures and steps, combine transformation with building in order actively to steer the economy of the south into the orbit of socialism and integrate the economies of both zones in a single system of large-scale socialist production. We must strive constantly to build, improve and perfect the system of socialist management and planning, ensure centralized and unified management by the central government in the whole country while safeguarding the democratic rights of various levels and developing the initiative and creativeness of the various localities and production units at the base.

To improve the circulation and distribution of goods and ensure their socialist distribution, we must vigorously develop socialist trade, improve the purchase and sale system in order to turn the socialist trading service into a good housekeeper catering for the people's life and a businessman taking an active part in the promotion of production. We must struggle resolutely to curb speculation and hoarding and all activities aimed at creating disturbances on the market, and strive to stabilize the market in the south. We must improve the price, wages and credit systems and fully enforce socialist distribution which means distribution according to the work done by the recipient. At the same time, we should strive to expand public welfare projects.

We must step up efforts in all fields in order to unify the market, and the price and wage systems throughout the country.

To strive to promote scientific and technical work to serve production and the people's life effectively, we must strengthen technological management, rationalize production and apply the norms of advanced techniques to economic development programs.

We must actively build a network of institutes for research, experimentation and planning, link teaching and scientific research with production activities, strive to train and make good use of skilled workers and scientific and technical cadres.

Our cultural, educational and health services must make special efforts to meet the people's needs in education, health protection and physical training, literature and art and wholesome entertainment and recreation. We must strive to develop socialist education and make good preparations to carry out our educational policy throughout the country, and promote all fields of activity aimed at building and developing socialist culture.

In the south, it is necessary to continue sweeping away the poisons of the enslaving culture of neocolonialism. We must vigorously push forward health work, physical culture and sports and actively eradicate the diseases and social evils left by the war. We must see to the protection of the health of mothers and children.

To improve the people's life step by step, first of all, we should, on the basis of economic rehabilitation and the development of production, meet the needs in food, clothing and education of the people, create more jobs to do away with unemployment left by the old regime, actively rebuild the towns and villages devastated by war, take steps to improve the housing conditions of the working people. We must take good care of wounded and sick armymen and of the families of those who have laid down their lives for the country, bring up war orphans, provide help to the aged and invalids who have lost all means of support and to war victims. On the other hand, we must organize community life in all spheres, including the supply and distribution of goods, the organization of food supply, housing, transport, education, medical care, entertainment and rest, etc. We must strive to improve services, raise the sense of responsibility of the personnel of the branches concerned and help them adopt correct attitudes.

To actively carry out basic surveys in all fields, to prepare for economic development on a large scale in future long-term plans, we must step up geological surveys, intensively accelerate the delimitation of economic zones, the planning of agricultural and forestry production, survey and planning work and take other necessary steps aimed at collecting data and preparing conditions for the drawing up of long-term plans and building the material and technical bases of socialism on a large scale.

To launch revolutionary mass movements, with a view to fulfilling the above-mentioned tasks, we must launch stirring, vigorous and continuous revolutionary movements among the masses, especially emulation movements in productive labour.

As we are entering the period of peaceful construction, the economy of our country is facing splendid prospects of development. But in the immediate future, we shall still meet with many difficulties left by the war of aggression and the neocolonialist policy of the United States and also resulting from the fact that the economy of our country remains essentially one of small producers. We must help our people see clearly the causes of the present difficulties and clearly realize that the only way to overcome the immediate difficulties is for each to march forward on the impetus of our victory and uphold the spirit of self-reliance, to devote all his energies and strength to productive labor so as to rapidly heal the wounds of war and produce more material wealth for society, and to guard himself against reliance on outside assistance.

Besides, we must strictly practice economy: economy of time, fuel, raw materials, food, funds . . . . We must practice thrift both in production and consumption, and resolutely combat waste and corruption. We must help everyone—workers, peasants, intellectuals and other strata of the people—to heighten their consciousness of their duty and right to work, march forward enthusiastically and devote all their revolutionary zeal to productive labour, show courage and abnegation, treasure each hour and each minute of labour, value every ounce of raw materials, every pound of food and every cent so as to build socialism with diligence and thrift and strive for the prosperity of the fatherland, and the happiness of the people.

Comrade deputies, the Vietnamese revolution is an integral part of the world revolution. The complete victory of our people in the war of resistance against U.S. aggression, for national salvation is closely associated with the wholehearted support and great assistance of the fraternal socialist countries and of our friends in all continents. This victory is also a worthy contribution to the common victory and the constant growth of the revolutionary forces in the world. This victory has created new favorable conditions for our state and people to continue fulfilling our internationalist duty and developing our active role in the common struggle of the world's people for the noble goals of our time, namely peace, national independence, democracy and socialism.

The tasks of our party, state and people in the domain of external relations in the new period is: to make the most of the favorable international conditions so as to rapidly heal the wounds of war, restore and develop our economy, develop culture and science, strengthen the technical bases of socialism; to continue to stand shoulder to shoulder with the other socialist countries and the people of other countries in the untiring struggle for peace, national independence, democracy and socialism; to actively support the struggle of the world's people against U.S.-led imperialism and colonialism, old and new; at the same time actively to contribute to strengthening the militant solidarity, co-operation and mutual assistance among the revolutionary forces, to consolidating solidarity among the socialist countries, and within the international communist and workers' movement, and to strengthening the world peoples' front against imperialism.

The fundamental content of our foreign policy is:

A) To endeavour to consolidate and strengthen the militant solidarity and relations of socialist co-operation in all fields between our country and all the fraternal socialist countries, and do everything in our power to contribute together with the other socialist countries and the international communist and workers' movement to restoring and consolidating solidarity and enhancing mutual support and assistance on the basis of Marxism-Leninism and in the spirit of proletarian internationalism in a way conformable to both reason and sentiment in the words of President Ho Chi Minh's testament with a view to making the noble ideal of Marxism-Leninism win ever more glorious successes.

B) We shall do everything in our power to safeguard and develop the relations of solidarity and fraternal friendship between the Vietnamese people and the people of Laos and Cambodia, strengthen the militant solidarity, mutual trust, long-term co-operation and mutual assistance in all fields between our country and fraternal Laos and Cambodia in accordance with the principle of complete equality, respect for each other's independence, sovereignty and territorial integrity, respect for each other's legitimate interests. In this way, the three nations, which have been attached to one another in the struggle for national liberation, will be forever attached to one another in the building and defence of their respective countries, for the sake of their respective independence and prosperity and in the revolutionary interests of the peoples in Southeast Asia and the rest of the world.

C) Fully support the just struggle of the people in Southeast Asia for national independence, democracy and social progress; support the countries in this region in their efforts to become truly independent, peaceful and neutral nations without military bases and troops of the imperialists on their territories. We are ready to establish and develop relations of friendship and co-operation with other countries in Southeast Asia on the basis of respect for each other's independence, sovereignty and territorial integrity, non-aggression and non-interference in each other's internal affairs, equality, mutual benefit and peaceful co-existence.

D) Fully support the struggle of the peoples of Asian, African and Latin American countries against imperialism and colonialism, old and new, racial discrimination, for national independence, democracy and social progress, strengthen the friendship and solidarity and the relations of mutual co-operation and mutual assistance in all fields between our country and the developing countries with a view to the above-mentioned goals, actively contribute to the struggle of the non-aligned countries against the policy of aggression and sabotage of imperialism with a view to safeguarding their independence and freedom, winning back the right of definitive ownership over their natural resources and establishing a new international economic order on the basis of respect for their national rights, equality and mutual benefit.

E) Fully support the just cause of the working class and working people in the capitalist countries who are striving to build a broad united front and directing the spearhead of their struggle at the chieftains of the native and foreign monopoly capitalists, for their vital interests and for democracy and social progress in order to safeguard national independence and world peace, win success step by step and ultimately to gain complete victory for socialism.

F) Establish and expand normal relations between our country and all countries with different social systems on the basis of respect for each other's independence, sovereignty, equality and mutual benefit.

G) Together with the fraternal countries and progressive people throughout the world, resolutely to continue the joint struggle against the policy of aggression and war provocation of the imperialists headed by U.S. imperialism, thus making an active contribution to the safeguarding and consolidation of peace and security in Southeast Asia and in the rest of the world.

The essence of our foreign policy is: to continue holding high the banner of national independence and socialism, closely combine genuine patriotism with proletarian internationalism, to oppose all tendencies of opportunism and all manifestations of bourgeois and petty nationalism, firmly defend independence and sovereignty while strengthening solidarity among the forces of socialism and national independence, direct the spearhead of the struggle at imperialism headed by U.S. imperialism, strive to fulfil our duties toward our nation, and at the same time fulfil our internationalist obligations toward the people of other countries.

With the correct external policy of our party and imbued with the pure revolutionary sentiments which President Ho Chi Minh painstakingly instilled into us, our state and our people will certainly fulfil the international obligations and successfully carry out the external policy which I have just expounded.

Dear comrade deputies, in the process of revolutionary struggle, our state has worked out two constitutions since it came into being.

The first one, the constitution of 1946, was born following the victorious August Revolution of 1945, and the founding of the Democratic Republic of Vietnam. That constitution confirmed and consolidated our newly won independence and freedom and affirmed the will of the Vietnamese people to "defend our territorial integrity, gain complete independence and build the country on the basis of democracy." In the spirit of the constitution of 1946, for the first time in their history our people have built a people's democratic state with the working class and the peasantry as its core, which was also the first worker-peasant state in Southeast Asia, unceasingly strengthened and perfected our state, causing its full impact to be felt in the struggle for liberation against the French colonialist aggressors.

Our people's victory forced the French colonialists to sign the Geneva agreements which recognized the independence, sovereignty, unity and territorial integrity of Vietnam, but the U.S. imperialists, stepping into the French colonialists' shoes, invaded the southern part of our country. The Vietnamese revolution then entered a new stage, the stage in which our people simultaneously carried out two strategic tasts: To build socialism in the north while continuing the struggle for the liberation of the south and the completion of the people's national democratic revolution throughout the country.

To meet that situation and those tasks of the revolution, in 1959, our National Assembly adopted the second constitution of our country.

The constitution of 1959 summed up and consolidated the successes obtained by our people throughout the country, affirmed the will of our people to resolutely take the north to socialism, making it the firm and strong base of the fight to liberate the south and reunify our fatherland. Implementing the constitution of 1959, we basically completed the transformation of the production relations, and started building the material and technical foundations of socialism in the north. Our entire people relying on that revolutionary base for the whole country, fought until the Americans quit and their stooges toppled, and won total victory in their revolutionary struggle for independence and freedom.

At present, our people have entered a new stage of the revolution, the stage in which the whole country is making socialist revolution, the north continuing to promote socialist construction, while the south actively engages in the socialist transformation of the economy and the building of socialism.

The present requirement of the revolution, of our state, is to work out a new constitution for the whole country so as to consolidate the successes already gained and to ensure the rapid, vigorous and steady advance of our entire country to socialism.

The drafting of the constitution is a major work of the state, a political performance of deep significance, relating to all strata of our population. That is why we must make it possible for the broad masses of our cadres and people to discuss and give their opinions regarding the elaboration of the new constitution.

Proceeding from these considerations, we propose that at this session, the National Assembly elect a commission for drafting a new constitution for our peaceful, independent, reunified and socialist Vietnam.

Dear comrade deputies, in the new constitution, the National Assembly will lay down comprehensive principles concerning the structures of the state and the activities of the various state organs. But right now it is necessary to have provisional regulations concerning the organization and activities of the state, which will allow our state to manage the various aspects of life in our country in the immediate future. It is up to the National Assembly to decide upon this matter.

The party's Central Committee proposes that the National Assembly should stipulate that pending the working out of a new constitution, our state will be organized and will work on the basis of the constitution of 1959 of the Democratic Republic of Vietnam. We can take the constitution of 1959 as the basis because this is a socialist constitution, the result of the revolutionary struggle of our entire people. That constitution was discussed and adopted by the first National Assembly, which was a common national assembly for our whole country.

To conduct state affairs, the National Assembly will elect the president and vice-president of the republic, the Standing Committee of the National Assembly, the Council of Ministers, the National Defence Council, the president of the People's Supreme Court, and the director of the People's Office of Public Prosecution.

In the various localities, an administration with three levels will be established:

—The provincial and municipal administration, put directly under the central authorities,

—The district and equivalent levels, and

—The communal and equivalent levels.

At each of these levels of the administration, there will be a people's council and an executive organ of the people's council elected by the people's council and for which we propose a common name in the whole country; the people's committees.

From the legal point of view, right now our state should consider the gradual elaboration of a comprehensive legal system for the whole country. With regard to the laws now in force in the north, we propose that the National Assembly entrust the Council of Ministers with directing their implementation in a manner suited to the new situation, or studying amendments for their enforcement throughout the country.

Dear comrade deputies, the history of our nation has moved into a great turning point. In the new era of our country, we vividly recall the solicitous and earnest recommendations of President Ho Chi Minh: "Our mountains, our rivers, and our people will always be. The U.S. invaders defeated, we will build our country 10 times more beautiful."

We have defeated the U.S. invaders. Our beautiful country has definitively returned to the hands of our people. We are the complete masters of the immense and rich mountains, jungles, plains and seas of our fatherland.

And here we stand, 50 million members of a nation which has written a splendid page of history, raised our country to the level of our times, and made it worthy of enjoying independence, freedom and a fine life.

Certainly we will rebuild our fatherland, making it 10 times greater and more beautiful. Certainly we will turn our homeland into a unified socialist country with modern industry, modern agriculture, powerful national defence, advanced culture and science, with a civilized and happy life. With a worthy international position we have all the conditions necessary to achieve these results.

Our slogan for action at present is: "All for production, all for socialist construction; all for making our fatherland prosperous and powerful; all for the people's happiness."

Let all our compatriots, workers, peasants, intellectuals, young people, women, armymen, turn the revolutionary heroism displayed in the past patriotic war against U.S. imperialism into revolutionary heroism in labour, and march enthusiastically to the front of production, the front of labour, the front of construction!

To fulfil our historical mission in the new stage, the Vietnam Workers Party promises to the National Assembly and the entire nation, to strictly abide by President Ho Chi Minh's teaching: "Our party should preserve absolute purity and prove worthy of its role as the leader and very loyal servant of the people."

For our socialist fatherland, for independence, freedom and the happiness of the present generation and all future generations, let our entire people valiantly march forward!

Appendices

Funeral Oration

Read by Comrade Le Duan,
First Secretary of the Central Committee
of the Workers' Party of Vietnam,
at the Memorial Service for
President Ho Chi Minh
September 9, 1969

Compatriots, combatants throughout the nation, comrades, friends,

Our beloved and venerated Ho Chi Minh is no more!

We have suffered an immense loss. Our grief is boundless.

Our people and our party have lost an inspired leader and a great teacher.

The international Communist movement, the movement of national liberation, and all progressive humanity have lost an experienced fighter, a comrade resolute in battle, beloved of all.

Throughout the nation our compatriots and combatants are thinking of him, their hearts wrung with unspeakable grief. Our brothers and friends throughout the world share our grief and our poignant sadness.

For sixty years, ever since his early youth and until his last moment, President Ho Chi Minh dedicated his whole life to the revolutionary work of our people and the peoples of the world. His life was full of trials and sacrifices; it was one of the noblest, richest, and purest of lives.

Inspired by ardent patriotism, President Ho Chi Minh came early to Marxism-Leninism, which provided him with a beacon to light the way to the national welfare and happiness of the people. He was the first Vietnamese to apply Marxist-Leninist principles, adapting them creatively to conditions in our country; he was the first to trace the route to be followed by the Vietnamese revolution, enabling it to move forward with assured steps, leading from victory to victory.

President Ho Chi Minh was the founder, leader, and educator of our party, the founder of the Democratic Republic of Vietnam and of the unified National Front, the beloved father-founder of the People's Army of Vietnam. He was the soul, the standard bearer of our party, leading our people, our armed forces, uniting them *en bloc* in a heroic combat that is filling the most glorious pages of our history.

Our country, our people, our rivers and mountains gave birth to Ho Chi Minh, the great national hero, and he, in return, enhanced the glory of our fatherland, our people, and our rivers and mountains.

Ho Chi Minh is the symbol of the finest quality possessed by the Vietnamese people: that flawless indomitability the Vietnamese have forged in the course of the four thousand years of their history. Nothing is more precious than independence and liberty. It is better to die than to lose our fatherland and be reduced to slavery. The name Ho Chi Minh is a vibrant appeal for the national well-being of our country at this time; it is the message of our ancestors echoing down the centuries; it is the sacred duty that we have assumed toward future generations.

Ho Chi Minh said: "The Vietnamese nation is one and indivisible." And he said: "The South's flesh and blood is Vietnamese flesh and blood." During his lifetime he followed the liberating revolution of the South step by step, day and night. He thought of our compatriots and combatants of the South and cherished for them a boundless affection.

In bidding him farewell, we pledge ourselves solemnly: *without fail to wave the flag of national independence, determined to fight and conquer the American aggressors, determined to liberate the South, defend the North, reunify the country; we will do all this to realize the hopes he nourished.*

Liberty for the fatherland and happiness for the people—such were the most cherished aspirations of Ho Chi Minh.

He said: "I have but one desire, a passionate desire, and it is to act in such a way that our country will recover its entire independence, our people will enjoy their liberty, our compatriots will have enough to eat, clothes to wear, and be educated at school."

In his lifetime he kept a warm affection for our compatriots: the old, the young, the infants, the men and women in both the North and the South, those of the plains and those of the mountains. Before his death he bequeathed "to all the people, all the party, all the armed forces, all youths and children, boundless affection."

In bidding him farewell, we pledge ourselves solemnly: *to continue to fight with all our strength to accomplish the noble ideals of socialism and communism, ideals outlined by Ho Chi Minh for our worker class and our people, with a view to building the prosperity of our country and the happiness of our compatriots.*

President Ho Chi Minh was constantly preoccupied with and intent on edifying our party, to make of it a solid bloc, firm and powerful, completely unified. He said: "The strength of the party resides in its unity and its singleness of aim." In his person he represented the union of the nation, the ties of blood that unite the North and the South. He said: "To unite, to unite still more, to unite in the largest sense of the word is our goal! To conquer in the most decisive way possible!" He never ceased to recommend and develop our tradition of unity and the affection that binds us to our compatriots and our comrades of the party.

In bidding him farewell we solemnly pledge ourselves: *to apply ourselves wholeheartedly to the preservation of unity of the party and to reinforce the combativity of our party, to make of it a unifying element binding all our people together so as to assure total victory of the revolution of our working class and our people.*

President Ho Chi Minh is the purest symbol of authentic patriotism linked closely with proletarian internationalism. His heart and mind were continually at the service of the Vietnamese people and at the service of the working class and the oppressed peoples of the world. Faithful disciple of Karl Marx and Lenin, he was not only a great patriot but also an experienced combatant in the international Communist movement and the national liberation movement of the twentieth century. President Ho Chi Minh constantly recommended that we preserve unity on the international plane, in the interest of the great revolutionary work of our country, and fulfill our sacred duties to world revolution.

In bidding him farewell, we solemnly pledge ourselves: *to develop constantly the pure internationalist sentiments that always inspired President Ho Chi Minh; to contribute wholeheartedly to reestablish and reinforce union within the Socialist camp and between the Communist powers, on the basis of Marxism-Leninism and proletarian internationalism; to tighten again the bonds of solidarity and friendship with the Indochinese peoples; to sustain with all our strength the revolutionary movements of other peoples; to contribute efficaciously to the world-wide struggle for peace, national independence, democracy, and socialism.*

So long and beautiful was Ho Chi Minh's life that it will always be a radiant example of revolutionary fervor and tenacity, of independence and national sovereignty, of profound love for the people, of total objectivity, of modesty and simplicity. He recommended that we "preserve the party in its total purity, faithful to its role as leader and servant of the people."

In bidding him farewell, we solemnly pledge ourselves: *to devote our whole life to following his example in working methods and revolutionary morality, to strengthen our minds and our revolutionary qualities, not fearing either the difficulties or the sacrifices, to mold ourselves to become faithful combatants for the people and for the party, worthy to be the comrades and disciples of President Ho Chi Minh. In his example, we will persuade our people and our youth to set as their goal to become new men, teachers of their country and of the new society that will plant the flag of Ho Chi Minh.*

President Ho Chi Minh is no more with us in the flesh, but he has left us a particularly precious legacy, the epoch of Ho Chi Minh, the most radiant and glorious epoch in our history—the era of independence, freedom, and socialism in our country.

All the Vietnamese people will forever keep in their hearts the memory of the immense services he rendered.

To the spirit of the departed President Ho Chi Minh we solemnly pledge ourselves to remain faithful to him all our lives; to work wholeheartedly and with all our strength to stand together, firmly united; to fight with total abnegation, determined to fulfill our sacred duties in order to obtain independence and freedom for our country and happiness for the people; and to contribute worthily to the revolutionary struggles of the peoples in the world.

President Ho Chi Minh is no longer with us in the flesh, but he will forever be our guide. His spirit is forever present at our side, for we continue to follow the route he traced, and we will complete the great work he began. He lives eternally with the rivers and mountains of the country, and his name is graven, from day to day, ever more deeply in our hearts.

Beloved comrades and compatriots, before departing, *Bac Ho* left a historical last will and testament for our party, our compatriots, and our fighters in both the North and the South. In that testament are his last recommendations, his last expression of the sentiments and the convictions he cherished toward us of this generation and those of future generations.

Let us continue to seek to be worthy of him!

Let us contain our grief in order to struggle heroically, driving boldly ahead, surmounting all obstacles and hardships, with complete resolve to conquer definitely the American aggressors and to build socialism, thus fulfilling the pledge of honor that we pronounce in these solemn hours of farewell.

President Ho Chi Minh, the great leader, the beloved and venerated teacher of our party and our people, will live forever!

Last Will and Testament of President Ho Chi Minh

Democratic Republic of Vietnam
Independence—Liberty—Happiness

In the patriotic struggle against American aggression, we shall certainly have to endure the greatest tribulations and will have to consent to new sacrifices, but total victory is inevitable.

It is absolutely certain.

When that victory comes, I propose to make a tour of the North and South to congratulate our compatriots, our cadres, and our heroic combatants, and to pay a visit to our old, our young, our beloved children.

Then, in the name of our people I will visit the Socialist countries, the fraternal countries throughout the world, to thank them for having aided and wholeheartedly supported our people in their patriotic struggle against American aggression.

Tu Fu, the well known poet of the T'ang epoch, has written: "In all time, rare have been those who attained the age of seventy."

This year, having celebrated my sixty-ninth birthday, I have become one of those "rare" people. My mind is still lucid, but my health has somewhat failed in comparison with the preceding years. As one lives beyond sixty-nine summers, the more one ages and the more good health withdraws. This is not at all surprising.

But who can predict for how much longer I will be able to serve the revolution, the country, and the people?

For this reason I am writing these few lines in expectation of the day when I shall go to rejoin the venerable Karl Marx, Lenin, and our revolutionary elders; thus our compatriots throughout the country, the comrades of the party, and our friends throughout the world will not be caught by surprise.

To begin with, I shall speak of the party. Thanks to the close union it has realized and maintained within itself, thanks to its complete devotion to the working class, the people, and the fatherland, our party has always organized and directed our people, inducing them to fight with ardor and leading them from one victory to another.

Unity is an extremely precious tradition of our party and our people. Let all our comrades, from the members of the Central Committee to our comrades of the basic cells, cherish the unity of the party.

Within the party the best way to consolidate and develop unity is to practice a liberal democracy by regularly and seriously encouraging criticism and self-criticism. For this there must be a real bond of affection uniting all the comrades.

We are a party in power. Each member, each cadre, should thoroughly imbue himself in *revolutionary morality*, must earnestly show proof of application, thrift, integrity, uprightness, a total dedication to the public cause, and exemplary unselfishness. The party must be preserved in all its purity so as to be worthy of the role it plays as the faithful guide and servant of the people.

The members of the "Worker Youths" groups and our young people are generally of excellent character, eager to carry out *avant-garde* tasks, not at all afraid of difficulties, and tirelessly aiming at progress. Our party should instill in them an elevated *revolutionary morality*, training them to be the continuers of socialism and to be both "Reds" and "experts."

Our working people in the plains as in the mountainous regions have endured countless privations and hardships for many centuries; they have been exploited and feudalized and have suffered colonial oppression, in addition to suffering many years of war.

Nonetheless, our people have shown great heroism and courage, ardent enthusiasm and a great application in their work. The people have always followed the party and have remained faithful to it.

The party should establish a good *plan* for economic and cultural development, in view of *constantly raising* the living standards of the people.

The war of resistance against American aggression may be prolonged. Our compatiots may have to consent to new sacrifices in property and human lives. No matter what, we must be resolved to combat the American aggressor until total victory is ours. *Our rivers and mountains and men will be here forever. The Yankees having been defeated, we will build up our country much finer than ever.*

No matter what the hardships and privations, in the end our people will surely conquer. The American imperialists will surely take to their heels. Our fatherland will surely be reunited. Our compatriots of the North and of the South will be reunited under the same roof. Our country will then have the distinction and honor of being a small nation that, through heroic combat, vanquished two great imperialisms—the French and the American—and brought a worthy contribution to the national liberation movement.

In regard to world-wide communism. Having dedicated my life to the service of the revolution, I am all the more proud to see the international Communist and workers' movement expand, and I suffer all the more because of the dissension that at present divides the Communist powers.

I want our party to do its best to contribute efficaciously to the reestablishment of good relations between the Communist powers, on a Marxist-Leninist and international proletarian basis, always in conformity with the demands of the mind and heart.

I firmly believe that the fraternal parties and countries will one day be reunited.

As to personal affairs. Throughout my life I have served the fatherland, the revolution, and the people with all my heart and strength. Now that I am about to leave this world, I have nothing with which to reproach myself. I merely regret that I am unable to serve longer and better.

I hope there will be no great funeral ceremony after my death. I do not want to waste the time and money of the people.

Lastly, I bequeath my unlimited affection to all our people, to our party, to our armed forces, and to my young nephews and nieces.

Likewise, I address fraternal greetings to my comrades, friends, and the youth and children of the world.

My ultimate desire is that all our party and all our people, closely united in combat, will raise up a Vietnam that is peaceful, unified, independent, democratic, and prosperous. Thus we will make a worthy contribution to world revolution.

(signed) Ho Chi Minh
Hanoi, May 10, 1969

Platform of the Viet-Nam Lao Dong [Workers Party] March 1951

Chapter One: The World and Viet-Nam

(1) The end of the Second World War brought the collapse of German, Italian and Japanese fascism. While capitalism entered a period of grave crisis, the Soviet Union became more prosperous and powerful with each passing day, and the democratic movement daily gained in strength. The world has been divided into two camps: the anti-imperialist, democratic camp headed by the Soviet Union, and the anti-democratic, imperialist camp led by the United States.

The democratic camp has become stronger while the imperialist camp has become weaker day by day. With the victory of the Chinese People's Revolution and with the founding of the German Democratic Republic, the balance of power was changed further in favour of the democratic camp.

At the present time, the American imperialists and their accomplices are making frenzied preparations for a third world war and are expanding their war of aggression. The danger of a new world war has become apparent. The central task of the working class and the peoples of the world at present is to struggle for the defence of peace. Under the leadership of the Soviet Union, the world peace camp is strongly opposing the imperialist warmongers. The peace movement has become stronger and more widespread than ever before in history. If the imperialists ever start a third world war, they will be signing their own death warrant.

(2) After the Second World War, thanks to the victory of Socialism over fascism, the people's democratic revolution spread and achieved victory in several countries of Eastern Europe and the Far East. A number of People's Republics were established and broke away from the imperialist system.

The people's democratic regimes have day by day become more consolidated and are developing and laying the basis of Socialism: People's Democracy, under the present historic conditions of the world, is in many countries a transitional stage towards Socialism.

(3) A striking characteristic of the world scene since the end of the Second World War is the widespread liberation movement which gains in strength day by day and which is shaking the very foundations of imperialism. The liberation movement has become an integral part of the world-wide movement for peace and democracy and against the imperialist warmongers.

The British, French, Dutch and other imperialists are using various cunning means to deceive the colonial peoples, such as granting them pseudo-independence, buying over the reactionary feudal landlords and bourgeois compradores, attempting to split the ranks of these peoples so as to maintain their rule over their colonies. The American imperialists are striving to turn the colonies of other countries into markets for their own goods and into their aggressive military bases.

However, the colonial and semi-colonial peoples are becoming more and more convinced that the only path to national liberation is that of national unity, close alliance with other peoples in the world and unremitting, persistent armed struggle under the leadership of the working class. Experience shows that any oppressed people that faithfully takes this path is assured of victory.

(4) Viet-Nam is an outpost of the democratic camp in Southeast Asia. The Viet-Nam revolution is a part of the world-wide movement for national liberation and for the defence of peace and democracy. In their struggle for their own independence and freedom, the people of Viet-Nam contribute to the maintenance of world peace and to the development of People's Democracy in Southeast Asia.

Thanks to the efforts of all the people of Viet-Nam and the progress of the democratic camp, especially the gigantic victory of the Chinese people, the Viet-Nam revolution will surely achieve success.

Chapter Two: Viet-Nam Society
and the Viet-Nam Revolution

(1) Prior to the French imperialist conquest, Viet-Nam society was a feudal society. After the establishment of French domination, Viet-Nam became an exclusive market, a source of raw materials and man-power, an object of usurious exploitation, and a military base of the French colonialists.

After the First World War, the French mining industry and light industries were expanded in Viet-Nam. The Viet-Nam feudal regime began to totter. The working class of Viet-Nam was formed and matured quickly. Capitalism in Viet-Nam came into being but was unable to develop owing to the domination of French capital.

French colonial policy made Viet-Nam completely dependent on France. It hampered the development of the productive forces of Viet-Nam. It combined the forms of capitalist oppression and exploitation with those of feudal oppression and exploitation, driving the people of Viet-Nam, especially the workers and peasants, into the darkest misery. For this reason, the people of Viet-Nam never ceased to struggle for independence and democracy.

In 1930, the Communist Party of Indo-China was founded. Since then the hegemony of the revolution has been exclusively in the hands of the working class of Viet-Nam.

During the Second World War, the Japanese occupied Viet-Nam. Under the yoke of Japanese and French fascism, the people of Viet-Nam were subjected to untold sufferings. Many uprisings broke out. Guerrilla bases were established and developed. The People's Rule was set up in the liberated area of the uplands of North Viet-Nam after the coup d'etat of March 9, 1945.

As a whole, however, Viet-Nam society was still a colonial and semi-feudal society.

In 1945, under the crushing blows of the Soviet Red Army, the Japanese fascists surrendered. Under the leadership of President Ho Chi Minh and the Communist Party of Indo-China, the Viet-Minh League together with the people of Viet-Nam launched a successful general uprising. The Democratic Republic of Viet-Nam was founded.

But the French imperialists invaded Viet-Nam once again in the hope of restoring their old colonial rule. The nation-wide, all-out and protracted War of Resistance of the people of Viet-Nam began.

The American imperialists made the utmost efforts to help the French colonialists. However, as a result of the unity and single-mindedness of our people and the heroic struggle of our army, the French colonialists were able to occupy temporarily only a part of our territory. In fighting for liberation and in realising democratic reforms in all fields—economic, political, social and cultural—Viet Nam has stepped on to the path of People's Democracy.

Today, Viet-Nam society is, therefore, a society which is popular-democratic and partly colonial and semi-feudal in character.

(2) The people of Viet-Nam earnestly desire a People's Democracy. The colonial regime has been a scourge to the whole of the people. The remnants of feudalism and semi-feudalism hamper the progress of the new Viet-Nam and have been a heavy burden to the peasants who are the majority of the people of Viet-Nam. The entire people of Viet-Nam demand independence and freedom, and are determined never to be enslaved again. The great majority of the people of Viet-Nam—the peasants—need land.

The fundamental task of the Viet-Nam revolution, therefore, is: to drive out the imperialist aggressors; to gain complete independence and unity for the people, to wipe out the colonial regime in the temporarily enemy-occupied areas and uproot the remnants of feudalism and semi-feudalism so that the tillers may have land; to develop People's Democracy; and to lay the foundations of Socialism.

The motive forces of the Viet-Nam revolution at present are the people comprising primarily the workers, peasants, petty bourgeoisie and national bourgeoisie, followed by the patriotic and progressive personages and landlords. The basic mass of people consists of the workers, peasants and intellectual workers (intellectual workers belong to various strata of the people, mostly to the petty bourgeoisie). The leading class in the Viet-Nam revolution is the working class.

From the point of view of the basic tasks it aims to fulfill and because its motive forces are the people led by the working class, the Viet-Nam Revolution is at present a national people's democratic revolution.

This national people's democratic revolution will lead Viet-Nam towards Socialism. The road towards Socialism is a road of protracted struggle which will pass through several stages.

In the present stage, the Viet-Nam revolution is spearheaded against the imperialist aggressors. It is necessary to rally all the forces of the people, to consolidate the national united front to carry on the protracted Resistance against the imperialist aggressors and their lackeys. At the same time, it is necessary to improve the living conditions of the people, especially the working people, so that the people can take a still more active part in the Resistance.

The main task at the present stage is to fight against imperialist aggression. The other tasks must be carried out so as to contribute to the fulfillment of this main task.

Chapter Three: Policy of the Viet-Nam Lao Dong Party

The Viet-Nam Lao Dong Party is resolved to fulfill the mission of liberating the people of Viet-Nam, to curb the influence of feudalism so as to further eradicate feudal and semi-feudal remnants, to develop People's Democracy, to build an independent, united, democratic, free, prosperous and powerful Viet-Nam and lead it towards Socialism.

During and immediately after the War of Resistance, the Viet-Nam Lao Dong Party stands for the realisation of the following policies aimed to give a powerful impetus to the Resistance to achieve complete victory, and to lay the basis for the building up of a prosperous and powerful state.

1. Fighting to Complete Victory.

The people of Viet-Nam are resolved to fight to the end in order to wipe out the French colonialists, defeat the American interventionists, punish the traitors and gain complete independence and unity for the Motherland.

The War of Resistance of the people of Viet-Nam is a people's war, with the characteristics of a nation-wide, all-out and protracted war. It must pass through three stages: a defensive stage, a stage in which the opposing forces approach a balance and a stage of counter-offensive.

The central task of the Resistance from the present time till final victory is to complete the preparations for and to launch a victorious general counter-offensive. In order to win complete victory, it is necessary to mobilize man-power, material and financial resources for the War of Resistance in accordance with the slogan: "All for the front, all for victory!" and continually to replenish the Resistance forces of the people. At the same time, the following strategic directives of the Resistance must be strictly observed:

All political, economic and cultural work must aim at ensuring military victories, and the military struggle must be co-ordinated with the political, economic and cultural struggle;

Fighting at the front against the enemy must be closely co-ordinated with guerrilla fighting and sabotage in the enemy's rear;

The War of Resistance of the people of Viet-Nam must be closely co-ordinated with the armed Resistance of the peoples of Laos and Cambodia and with the world-wide struggle for peace and democracy.

2. Consolidating the People's Rule

The political power in our country is a democratic power of the people, that is, of the workers, peasants, petty bourgeoisie, national bourgeoisie, and patriotic and progressive personages and landlords. The form of this power is the People's Democratic Republic. Its content is the People's Democratic Dictatorship: democratic towards the people, dictatorial towards the imperialist aggressors and traitors.

The People's Rule relies on the national united front based on the alliance between the workers, peasants and intellectual workers, and is under the leadership of the working class.

The organisational principle of the People's Rule is democratic centralism.

Our People's Rule owes its strength to the active participation and support of the people, to the leadership of the working class, and to the assistance rendered by the Soviet Union, China and other People's Democracies. Thus in order to consolidate our People's Rule, we must:

Continually consolidate the links between the state power and the popular masses;

Increase the number of workers, peasants and women participating in the government organisations, particularly in the People's Councils;

Put into effect a genuine People's Democratic constitution;

Strengthen the Party's leadership in government organisations of all levels;

Consolidate Viet-Nam's friendly relations with the Soviet Union, China and other People's Democracies.

3. Consolidating the National United Front

The National United Front of Viet-Nam unites all political parties, organisations and patriotic persons irrespective of class, nationality, religion, or sex in the common struggle for Resistance and national construction.

The National United Front is one of the pillars of the People's Rule. It has the task of mobilising, organising, educating and leading the people to implement the policy of the government, and of informing the government of the people's aspirations and proposals.

The Viet-Nam Lao Dong Party co-operates closely with all the political parties, organisations and personages in the National United Front according to the following principles:

Sincere solidarity and friendly mutual criticism for the sake of common progress;

Joint action and consultation in the struggle for a common programme;

Long-term co-operation during and after the protracted War of Resistance.

In order to consolidate the national united front, we must complete the merger of the Viet-Minh and the Lien Viet; consolidate the alliance of workers, peasants and intellectual workers as a solid basis for the Front; mobilise all circles of the bourgeoisie and the landlords to participate actively in the Lien Viet Front; develop the organisations of the Front in the temporarily enemy-occupied areas, in the areas inhabited by religious groups and by the national minorities; consolidate the Party's leadership in the national united front, etc.

4. Building Up and Developing the People's Army

The Viet-Nam Army is a people's army organised from among the people, maintained and assisted by, and fighting for the people. It is national, popular and democratic in character.

Its discipline is strict and voluntary. While fighting, it carries on deep and widespread political work, strengthening the unity of purpose between officers and men and between the army and the people, and strives to carry out propaganda work among enemy troops with a view to breaking down their morale.

In order to build up and develop the people's army, we must develop the local people's armed militia groups and guerrillas in the villages so as continually to replenish our regular army. At the same time, we must capture the enemy's arms, ammunition and food supplies so as partly to solve our equipment and supply problems.

5. Developing the Economy

Our economic policy now is: to increase production so as to meet the demands of the War of Resistance and to raise the living standard of the people, benefiting both the government and private individuals, and both Labour and Capital.

In the present stage, while special attention must be paid to the development of agriculture, we must develop industry, handicrafts and home trade, we must establish and develop trade relations with friendly countries, and lay the basis for a state economy and the development of co-operative economy. The national bourgeoisie has to be encouraged, assisted and guided in its enterprises.

In the financial field, we advocate increasing the national income through increased production, reducing expenditures through economies and putting into practice the system of democratic contributions.

As regards the enemy's economy, we urge planned sabotage and blockade in ways beneficial to the Resistance and the people, and confiscation of the imperialist aggressors' and traitors' properties and the putting of these properties at the disposal of the People's Rule.

6. Carrying Out Agrarian Reform

Our agrarian policy at present aims mainly at carrying out the reduction of land rent and interest as well as other reforms such as:

Regulation of the land-rent system;

Provisional allocation of the land formerly owned by the French colonialists and traitors to the poorer peasants and families of disabled ex-servicemen and war dead;

Re-distribution of communal lands;

Appropriate use of land belonging to absentee landlords and of wastelands, etc.

These reforms must be thoroughly carried out so as to improve the living conditions of the peasants and to mobilise the majority of the people, that is, the peasants, to participate actively in the armed Resistance, to increase production and ensure supplies.

In order to carry out these reforms thoroughly, our Party must organise and awaken the great peasant masses and give steady leadership to the peasant movement.

We must carry out this agrarian policy step by step, according to local circumstances. In South Viet-Nam where land is more concentrated than in North and Central Viet-Nam, the agrarian policy of the Party must be carried out more vigorously than in North and Central Viet-Nam.

We must prepare the conditions for gradually giving each peasant his own plot of land.

7. Developing Culture and Education

In order to train new men and new cadres and to push forward the war of Resistance and national construction, it is necessary to wipe out the remnants of colonial and feudal culture and education, and develop a national, scientific and popular culture and education.

Thus the task of Viet-Nam culture and education at the present stage is:

To develop the people's hatred for the imperialist aggressors, and to develop their genuine patriotism and spirit of internationalism;

To develop the best of the people's national culture and at the same time to study the progressive culture of the world, especially of the Soviet Union and of China; to develop the culture of the national minorities;

To develop the people's science, technique and art;

To develop a 'new life movement';

To liquidate illiteracy, reform the educational system and develop vocational schools.

8. The Party's Stand Towards Religion

The Viet-Nam Lao Dong Party respects and guarantees the freedom of religious belief of the people.

It opposes the French imperialists' policy of utilising religion to deceive the people and to split the National United Front of Viet-Nam.

9. The Party's Policy Towards the Nationalities

All the peoples living in Viet-Nam's territory are equal in rights and duties. They must unite with and help one another in order to carry forward the armed Resistance and national construction.

Our Party resolutely opposes narrow-minded nationalism and is determined to smash the plots of the imperialists and traitors to sow hatred among the people and divide them.

Our Party seeks to raise the living standards of the national minorities, to help them progress in all spheres of activity, to ensure their participation in the government and the use of their own language for their education in their own areas.

10. The Party's Policy Concerning the Temporarily Enemy-Occupied Areas and the Newly-Liberated Areas

We attach the same importance to the work in enemy-occupied areas as to that in the liberated areas.

The work in the enemy-occupied areas consists in bringing about a broad unity between all strata of the people, intensifying and extending guerrilla warfare, building up and consolidating the People's Rule, destroying the puppet administrations and shattering the ranks of the puppet troops, mobilising the people to struggle against the enemy's oppression and exploitation, and co-ordinating action in enemy-occupied areas and liberated areas.

With regard to the lackeys of the enemy, we recommend the punishment of the leading unrepentant traitors and clemency towards those people who have been misled but who seek to atone for their mistakes and return to the side of the Motherland.

With regard to the newly-liberated areas, we must pay great attention to the realisation of unity among the whole population, to the question of ensuring the people's security, to vigilance against traitors and their extermination, to rehabilitation of the economy.

11. External Policy

Viet-Nam's external policy must be based on the principle of mutual respect for national independence and territorial integrity, equality of rights and defence of world peace and democracy.

Consequently, it is necessary for Viet-Nam to consolidate her friendly relations with the Soviet Union, China and other People's Democracies, actively to support the national liberation movements of colonial and semi-colonial countries and to establish diplomatic relations with all countries that are willing to respect Viet-Nam's national sovereignty on the basis of freedom, equality and mutual benefit.

We stand for broadening the sphere of the people's diplomatic activities.

We stand for the protection of Viet-Nam nationals in foreign countries.

12. Our Policy Towards Laos and Cambodia

The people of Viet-Nam must unite closely with the peoples of Laos and Cambodia and give them every assistance in the common struggle against imperialist aggression, for the complete liberation of Indo-China and for the defence of world peace.

In the common interests of the three peoples, the people of Viet-Nam are willing to enter into long-term co-operation with the peoples of Laos and Cambodia, with a view to bringing about an independent, free, strong and prosperous federation of the states of Viet-Nam, Laos and Cambodia, if the three peoples so desire.

13. Our Policy Towards Foreign Nationals

Those foreign nationals who respect Viet-Nam law are assured of the safety of their lives and properties, and they have the right to reside and carry on business in Viet-Nam.

Foreign nationals belonging to the People's Democracies, especially overseas Chinese in Viet-Nam, are allowed to enjoy the same rights and perform the same duties as citizens of Viet-Nam if they so desire, subject to the approval of the government of their own country and of the Viet-Nam People's Government.

14. The Struggle for World Peace and Democracy

To fight for the defence of world peace and democracy is an international task of the people of Viet-Nam. To fight against the imperialist aggressors is the most active means whereby our people can fulfill this task.

We recommend that the people of Viet-Nam co-ordinate their War of Resistance and the struggles of other peoples of the world, and especially with those of the peoples of France and the French colonies.

15. Patriotic Emulation

The patriotic emulation campaign is a nation-wide movement reaching into all branches of activity and mainly aiming at checking three enemies: illiteracy, famine and foreign aggression.

The army, rural areas, enterprises, schools and offices are the main places where the emulation campaign is to be carried out.

We recommend that emulation heroes and labour fighters be promoted so as to mobilise the entire people to take part in the War of Resistance and national construction.

Political Theses of the Indochinese Communist Party October 1930 (Excerpts)

This important historic document of the Indochinese Communist Party was drafted by Tran Phu and approved at the First Meeting of the Party's Central Committee (October 1930). The Theses applied the universal principles of Marxism-Leninism to the concrete conditions of our country. It analysed the characteristics and laid down the tasks of the revolution, and defined its main motive forces. It charted the Party's general line in the national democratic revolution.

We publish below the first six points:

The World Situation and the Indochinese Revolution

1. Since the end of the imperialist war (1914-1918), the world situation may be viewed as having gone through three periods:

a) During the first period (1918-1923), as a result of the war, the capitalist economy suffered depression and crisis, and in many places in Europe the proletariat rose up and fought for power. Eventually, on the one hand, the Russian proletariat defeated the imperialists who attacked the country from the outside and the counter-revolutionaries who carried out sabotage inside, and set up a firm dictatorship of the proletariat; on the other hand, however, the West European proletariat met with failure (for instance the German proletariat in 1923).

b) During the second period (1923-1928), availing themselves of the recent setbacks suffered by the European proletariat, the various imperialisms acted on the offensive, exploited the proletariat and the colonial peoples to the utmost, and brought temporary stability to the imperialist economy. On account of its previous failure, the proletariat in the imperialist countries acted only on the defensive. The revolution broke out in the colonial countries. Economic consolidation in the Soviet Union helped Communist influence spread all over the world.

c) The third period, the present one, presents the following characteristics: Capitalism has not been able to maintain its temporary stability and has slid back into crisis; the various imperialisms again have to engage in a sharp competition for markets, making a new imperialist war inevitable.

The Soviet economy has surpassed the pre-imperialist war level; successful socialist construction has exasperated the various imperialisms, which seek to overthrow the Soviet Union, the citadel of world revolution.

In the imperialist countries, the proletariat has put up a fierce struggle (large-scale strikes in Germany, France, Poland, etc.); the colonies (especially China and India) are in a revolutionary effervescence. This is due to increasingly harsh exploitation of the masses by capitalism, which is undergoing a crisis; in the world the number of unemployed totals scores of millions and the workers and peasants suffer untold misery. In this third period, proletarian revolution and colonial revolution have reached a very high level; in some places the revolutionaries are ready to seize power.

At present, Indochina has contributed its revolutionary forces to the seething struggle going on in the world, thus broadening the worker-peasant front against imperialism. On the other hand, the intense revolutionary movement in the world (especially in China and India) exerts a strong influence on the struggle in Indochina and gives it an even more vigorous impetus. And so the world revolution and the Indochinese revolution are closely connected.

The Characteristics of the
Situation in Indochina

2. Indochina (Viet Nam, Cambodia, Laos) is a colony of French imperialism. So, its economy is dependent upon that of French imperialism. The following are the two outstanding features of the development of Indochina:

a) Indochina must develop independently, but it cannot do so because of its colonial status.

b) Class contradiction has grown ever fiercer between the workers, peasants and other toiling people on the one hand, and the feudal landowners, capitalists and imperialists on the other.

3. Economic contradictions:

a) Though the bulk of agricultural products is exported by the imperialists, the economy has remained feudal in character. Most plantations (rubber, cotton, coffee, etc.) belong to French capitalists. The greater part of the land is owned by native landlords, who exploit it in the feudal way, i.e. rent it in small plots to poor tenants for a very high rent. Rice yields are, besides, lower in Indochina than in other countries (per hectare paddy output in Malaya: 2,150 kilograms; in Siam, 1,870 kilograms; in Europe, 4,570 kilograms; in Indochina, only 1,210 kilograms). More rice is exported every year, but this is not due to the development of rice-growing, only to increased plundering of the people's rice by the capitalists.

b) The oppressive regime imposed by French imperialism hampers the development of productive forces in Indochina. The imperialists have not built any heavy industries (like iron works, machine building, etc.) for this would harm the monopoly of French industry. They only develop those industries which serve their administration and trade, for instance, railway lines, small shipyards, etc.

The aim of French imperialism is to make Indochina an economic dependency of France, and so it promotes only those industries which it finds more profitable to develop in Indochina than in France itself. Raw materials exploitation is meant not to help Indochina's economy develop independently, but to prevent French industry's dependence on other imperialisms.

c) As exportation is in the hands of French capitalists, internal trade and production is dependent upon the export requirements of the French imperialists. The more exports increase, the more the country is drained of its natural resources by imperialism. Another special feature: French banks (Banque de l'Indochine, Credit foncier, etc.) collect capital from the native people to aid French exporters.

In short: Indochina's economy remains an agricultural one, with predominantly feudal features. All this interferes with its independent development.

4. Class Contradictions:

French imperialism, in alliance with native landlords, traders and usurers, ruthlessly exploits the peasants. It rakes up the country's farm produce for export, imports French goods for sale within the country, imposes high taxation, drives the peasantry to misery and craftsmen to unemployment.

Land is more and more concentrated in the hands of the imperialists and landlords; the existence of numerous intermediaries causes the rent that has to be paid by poor tenants to be all the higher. The latter have to pay such high interest rates to usurers that they are often compelled to give them their lands or even their children in payment of their debts.

The imperialists pay no attention to keeping the dykes in good repair for protection against floods. Irrigation facilities are in the hands of the capitalists, who exact a high price for their use: no money, no water. And so more and more crop failures occur because of flood and drought. Not only are the peasants prevented from developing their economy, but they also grow increasingly dependent upon capitalists and fare worse and worse: unemployment and starvation afflict more and more people.

The old economy is falling to pieces very fast, yet the new industry is developing at a very slow rate; factories, workshops, etc., cannot hire all the poor and unemployed and many starve in the countryside where the situation is truly tragic.

In the factories, plantations and mines, the capitalists cruelly exploit and oppress the workers. Their wages, which are at starvation level, are cut by all kinds of fines. They work eleven, twelve hours a day on an average. Abuse and blows are rained on them. When they fall sick, far from getting any medical attention, they are dismissed. There is no social insurance. In plantations and mines, the owners pen their workers up in camps and forbid them to wander out. They use a system of contracts to recruit labourers and move them to places where they can impose their own law on the workers and even inflict penalties on them. Due to such harsh working conditions, large numbers of workers in Indochina suffer from serious diseases (tuberculosis, trachoma, malaria, etc.) and more of them die at a very young age.

The Indochinese proletariat is not yet numerous, but the number of workers, especially plantation workers, is on the increase. They fight ever more vigorously. The peasants have also awakened and fiercely opposed the imperialists and feudalists. Strikes in 1928, 1929 and the violent outbursts of struggle by workers and peasants this year (1930) clearly prove that class struggle in Indochina is gaining momentum. The most outstanding and most important feature in the revolutionary movement in Indochina is that the struggle of the worker-peasant masses has taken on a very clearly independent character and is no longer influenced by nationalism as it used to be.

Characteristics and Task of
the Indochinese Revolution

5. The above-mentioned contradictions account for the fact that the revolutionary movement in Indochina is growing day by day. In its initial period, the Indochinese revolution will be a bourgeois democratic revolution, for it cannot yet directly tackle the organizational problems of socialism: the country is still very weak economically, many feudal vestiges still linger on, the relation of class forces is not yet tipped in favour of the proletariat; besides, imperialism still holds oppressive sway. For these reasons, in the present period, the revolution will only have an agrarian and anti-imperialist character.

The bourgeois democratic revolution is a preparatory period leading to socialist revolution. Once it has won victory, and a worker-peasant government has been established, industry within the country will develop, proletarian organizations will be reinforced, the leadership of the proletariat will be consolidated, and the relation of class forces will be altered to the advantage of the proletariat. Then the struggle will develop both in depth and in breadth and the bourgeois democratic revolution will advance towards the proletarian revolution. The present period is one of proletarian revolution in the world and socialist building in the Soviet Union; thanks to help from the proletariat exercising dictatorship in various countries, Indochina will bypass the capitalist stage and advance direct to socialism.

In the bourgeois democratic revolution, the proletariat and the peasantry are the two main motive forces, but only if leadership is in the hands of the proletariat can the revolution triumph.

6. The essential aim of the bourgeois democratic revolution is on the one hand to do away with the feudal vestiges and the mode of pre-capitalist exploitation and to carry out a thorough agrarian revolution; on the other hand, to overthrow French imperialism and achieve complete independence for Indochina. The two faces of the struggle are closely connected, for only by toppling imperialism can we eliminate the landlord class and carry out a successful agrarian revolution; conversely, only by abolishing the feudal regime can we knock down imperialism.

In order to reach these essential goals, we must set up worker-peasant Soviet power. Worker-peasant Soviet power alone is the very powerful instrument which will make it possible to overthrow imperialism, feudalism and landlordism, give land to the tillers, and legal protection to the interests of the proletariat.

The essential tasks of the bourgeois democratic revolution are the following:

1—To overthrow French imperialism, feudalism, and landlordism.

2—To set up a worker-peasant government.

3—To confiscate all lands belonging to foreign and native landlords and to religious organizations, and hand them over to middle and poor peasants, the right of ownership of the land being in the hands of the worker-peasant government.

4—To nationalize all big undertakings of the foreign capitalists.

5—To abolish all current taxes and corvees and institute a progressive tax.

6—To decree an 8-hour workday and improve the living standards of the workers and toiling people.

7—Indochina to be completely independent; national self-determination to be recognized.

8—To organize a worker-peasant army.

9—Equality between man and woman.

10—Support to the Soviet Union, alliance with the world proletariat and with the revolutionary movement in the colonies and semi-colonies.

A Circular Letter Sent Out by Nghe Tinh Patriots 24th Year of the Reign of Tu Duc, 1817

The Following is a text of the Scholars' Movement.

Note:

—The regional character of the appeal (there was no national leadership);

—National pride, the evocation of an age-old fatherland, the resolve to fight;

—Attacks on Catholics, the scholars being unable to define a policy of broad national union;

—The programme of restoration of an enlightened monarchy.

Our scholars, our people, standing under the Southern heavens, look towards the North Star.(1)

For many decades, like a beneficent rain, the favours of Nghieu have been bestowed on us;(2)

Under four reigns, we have not been subjected to the fire and water of Kiet.(3)

Thanks to education by Emperor Thanh To, we have rejected the evil doctrine of the West;(4)

In the land of Viet Nam, civilization is more resplendent than ever and the State displays its legitimate continuity.

The Imperial Gate of the Ha and the Court of the Thuong, the founders of the Empire in the eyes of all, still fill everyone with gratitude;

Those of Phan Duong as well as of Ha Phon, in their heart of hearts, continue to harbour boundless loyalty.

The people remain attached to the Nguyen dynasty and ignore the men of the West;

The latter, with their barbarian customs, have shown their dog-and-pig-like faces.

Once already they had dared to display their ratlike visages at our gates, bent on carrying out their perfidious intentions;(5)

Now, they have bared their fangs and are exhibiting their arrogance right in our palaces.

From within and without, they keep nibbling at our country, like silkworms at mulberry leaves;

Churches and conversions; there lies the danger, the ground is giving way under our feet.

Alas, that is the state of affairs, do you know it?

Those who benefited from the Emperor's favours now deceive him;

Those responsible for the destiny of the Fatherland now plan a sell-out.

With the face of a Tu Dao and the heart of a Tan Coi,(6) they form a chain of traitors and shrink from no deceptions to carry through their treason.

They hide the truth to the Emperor, whose lucidity cannot see through the ruses of a Hoan Dau,(7) and, renewing Truong Luong's pretence, simulate loyal ardour.

The true doctrine is in the books of our Saints and Sages: "To attack evil doctrines"—this teaching remains inscribed in our universe; "To forbid all heresies"—this strict rule has existed since time immemorial.

To know and to act are but one thing: why should one divorce one's services to the country from one's own destiny?

Like Thuong Son and Thi Trung, we must live in a worthy fashion and shed our blood for the Empire;

The flesh of Van Dat and the bones of Cao Dong,(8) after their deaths, can proudly face our mountains and rivers.

Like heroes, we shall advance with burning hearts;

We seek no honours, but only to do our duty.

We shall not drift with the stream, we shall not let the wind blow without trying to stop it; once Western ships are driven away, the Perfume River shall again be at peace.(9)

Let rich people donate their wealth, let robust people lend the strength of their arms, and we shall exterminate the Western barbarians; we shall be soldiers when military operations call for it;

between two operations, we shall put aside our coats of mail and again be ordinary people; we shall not blame Heaven for our trials; everywhere our people and our scholars are at one: all of us are enduring hardships for the sake of our native land and we shall reinstate our Fatherland in its former boundaries.

In this Southern land, the right doctrine shall be restored and its limpid stream shall sparkle under the autumn moon;

The imperial power of the Nguyen shall stand as firm as Mount Thai.

This call to arms is addressed to all men of good will.

A poem follows:

Ever since that day when in their citadels,
Our leaders, deceived by the enemy, implored peace,
War has been discussed throughout the land:
Here are three dignitaries who try to sell out the country!
And there's that general, who treats with the enemy!
For centuries, Vo Muc swallowed his anger,
And for millenniums, Di Ngo quivered with rage.(10)
Scholars and commoners, unite your efforts,
Let fidelity and loyalty be engraved in your hearts.

Notes, Chronology
and Bibliography

Notes

Introduction

1. Nguyen Khac Vien: "The Judo Lesson", in *Tradition and Revolution in Vietnam*; The Indochina Resource Center, Berkeley, 1974. Also, my review of the book in *Monthly Review*, October 1975.

2. See my articles: "A Nation that has not Learned to Surrender", in *The Nation*, April 16, 1973; and "Vietnam in the Year of the Dragon", in *Monthly Review*, May 1976.

3. See David Marr: *Vietnamese Anticolonialism: 1885-1925*; University of California Press, 1971. Also, William J. Duiker: *The Rise of Nationalism in Vietnam: 1900-1941*; Cornell University Press, 1976, and my review in *Monthly Review*, October 1975.

4. Central Committee of Propaganda, Vietnam Workers Party: *Thirty Years of Struggle of the Party*; Foreign Publishing House, Hanoi 1960.

5. *Ibid.*

6. *Ibid.*

7. *Ibid.*

8. Published first in *La Correspondence Internationale* in 1924. Reprinted in Bernard B. Fall: *Ho Chi Minh on Revolution*; Praeger, New York 1967.

9. Stefan T. Possony, editor: *The Lenin Reader*; Henry Regnery, Chicago 1966, pp. 224-265.

10. "Lenin and the Colonial Peoples"; *Pravda*, January 27, 1924.

11. The first one was published by the New Moscow Publishing House and the second by Whistle Publishing House.

12. Speaking about imprisonment of ICP cadres, President Ho Chi Minh in his address opening the ceremony commemorating the

thirtieth anniversary of the founding of the Party, January 5, 1960, said: "I wish to remind you that thirty-one of the comrades who are now in the Central Committee were given altogether two hundred and twenty-two years of imprisonment and deportation by the French imperialists before the (1945) Revolution, not to mention the sentences to death in absentia and the years of imprisonment evaded by those who escaped from prison. Turning what was a bad thing into a good thing, our comrades made up for the years in prison in discussing and studying political theory . . . ." Bernard B. Fall: *Ho Chi Minh on Revolution*; Praeger 1967; pp. 339-40.

13. In September 1976, Le Duan revisited his "veritable school of revolutionary nationalism" and was quoted as having said that "once we were in prison, we were able to strengthen our confidence in the victory of the Vietnamese revolution." (Agence France Press; Hanoi, September 6, 1976, reprinted in the *New York Times*, September 7, 1976.) Many prominent Vietnamese revolutionary leaders, Ton Duc Thang (President, Socialist Republic of Vietnam); Pham Van Dong (Prime Minister); Le Duc Tho (who negotiated the 1973 Paris Agreement); spent years on this island which is also known as Con Son Island or Con Dao. During the Nguyen Van Thieu regime in the late 1960's, "tiger cages" were built to keep prisoners in the most inhumane condition. See my "Con Son: School for Revolutionaries"; *The Christian Century*, September 23, 1970.

14. In a recently published memoir, it was revealed that Le Duan, then code-named Anh-Ba (brother Ba), "on the last ship for repatriation to the North in 1955 tearfully waved to his compatriots . . . . At midnight, when the ship was about to leave, he embraced Le Duc Tho. Then by a sideway, he descended into a small sampan, rowed by comrade Vo Van Kiet (now a member of the Central Committee, VWP, and Chairman, People's Revolutionary Committee, Ho Chi Minh City, ed.). He was brought to Ca Mau and there he built the liberated zone of U Minh. He also secretly visited the workers in Saigon. *Doan Ket* (Unity) *Weekly*, Paris, April 30, 1976. The memoir was by Thep Moi.

15. No LD 1NV of October 1969.

16. *The Vietnamese Revolution*, International Publishers, New York 1971, p. 25.

17. See my: "The Vietnam People's Army" in *The Indochina Chronicle*; The Indochina Resource Center, Berkeley, California, February 28, 1974.

18. See my: "Vietnam in the Year of the Dragon", in *Monthly Review*, May 1976.

19. The last Congress was in 1961.

"Revolution is the Work of the Masses"

1. The Trung Sisters: In 40 A.D. these two national heroines led an armed insurrection against Chinese domination and liberated the country. Trung Trac, the elder proclaimed herself Queen and set up her capital at Me Linh (Vinh Phuc province, North Vietnam). In 45 A.D. defeated by Ma Yuan's army, the two sisters committed suicide by throwing themselves into the Hat River.

2. Trieu (true name: Trieu Trinh Nuong): Native of Thanh Hoa province (Central Vietnam), in 248 she led, with her elder brother Trieu Quoc Dat, an insurrection against Chinese domination. She was known for her courage and initiative. Her army being outnumbered, she committed suicide in Bo Dien village (Thanh Hoa province) at the age of 23.

3. Ly Thuong Kiet: Famous general of the Ly dynasty which ruled over Vietnam from 1010 to 1225. He performed brilliant feats of arms by defeating, on the very Chinese territory, the Soong army which was preparing an invasion against Vietnam.

4. Tran Hung Dao: National hero of the Tran dynasty who resisted the aggression of the Chinese Yuan dynasty in 1257, 1285 and 1287-1288, and won brilliant victories.

5. Le Loi: National hero who rose against the domination of the Ming, a Chinese dynasty. After ten years of resistance war, he freed Vietnam from the Chinese yoke and proclaimed himself emperor in 1428.

6. Quang Trung (1752-1792): Leader of the greatest peasant insurrection in Vietnam in the 18th century and founder of the Tay Son dynasty (1788-1802). In 1788, he proclaimed himself emperor; he led the resistance against the Tsing, a Chinese dynasty, and marched to Hanoi where he cut to pieces a 200,000 strong army of the Tsing.

7. At present the population of North Vietnam amounts to 15,916,000 (1962).

8. Mao Tse-tung, *On The Correct Solution of the Inner Contradictions of the People*; Su That (Truth) Publishing House, Hanoi, 1957, page 24.

9. 1 sao : 360 square miles.

10. Now 30 dongs.

"Principles and Methods of Revolutionary Action"

1. V.I. Lenin, "Guerrilla Warfare," in *Guerrilla Warfare and Marxism*, William J. Pomeroy, ed., International Publishers, N.Y., 1968, pp. 85-86.

2. V.I. Lenin, *Two Tactics of Social Democracy in the Democratic Revolution*, International Publishers, N.Y., 1963, p. 72.

3. V.I. Lenin, "Against Boycott," in *Collected Works*, Vol. 13, Moscow, 1962, p. 36.

4. V.I. Lenin, "On Slogans," in *Selected Works*, International Publishers, N.Y., 1967, Vol. 2, p. 179.

"Some Problems of Cadres and Organization in Socialist Revolution"

1. V.I. Lenin, *Collected Works*, Progress Publishers, Moscow, 1964, Vol. 33, p. 296.

2. V.I. Lenin, *op. cit.*, Vol. 5, p. 384.

3. F. Engels, *The Origin of the Family, Private Property and the State*, in Marx-Engels, *Selected Works*, Foreign Languages Publishing House, Moscow, 1958, Vol. 2, p. 170.

4. Karl Marx, *Capital*, (in Vietnamese), *Su That* Publishing House, Hanoi, 1960, Vol. 2, pp. 22-23.

5. K. Marx, *op. cit.*, Vol. 2, p. 27.

6. V.I. Lenin , *op cit.*, Vol. 27, pp. 262-263.

7. V.I. Lenin, *op. cit.*, Vol. 33, p. 226.

8. V.I. Lenin, *op. cit.*, Vol. 5, p. 467.

9. V.I. Lenin, *op. cit.*, Vol. 7, p. 415.

10. V.I. Lenin, *op. cit.*, Vol. 27, p. 55.

11. V.I. Lenin, *op. cit.*, Vol. 27, p. 237.

12. V.I. Lenin, *op. cit.*, Vol. 27, p. 409.

13. V.I. Lenin, *op. cit.*, Vol. 30, p. 428.

14. V.I. Lenin, *op. cit.*, Vol. 32, p. 144.

15. V.I. Lenin, *Selected Works*, (in Vietnamese), *Su That* Publishing House, Hanoi, 1960, Vol 2, pp. 441, 444.

16. V.I. Lenin, *op. cit.*, Vol. 30, pp. 457-458.

17. V.I. Lenin, *op. cit.*, Vol. 31, p. 295.

18. V.I. Lenin, *op cit.*, Vol. 29, p. 338.

*"The New Stage of Our Revolution
and the Tasks of the Trade Unions"*

1. Revolution in relations of production, technical revolution, and ideological and cultural revolution.

2. K. Marx, *Capital*, (in Vietnamese), *Su That* Publishing House, Hanoi, 1960, Vol. 3, p. 288.

3. V.I. Lenin, *Collected Works*, Progress Publishers, Moscow, 1965, Vol. 27, p. 298.

4. V.I. Lenin, *Selected Works*, Progress Publishers, Moscow, 1967, Vol. 3, p. 656.

5. V.I. Lenin, *op. cit.*, p. 655.

6. Instructions given by President Ho Chi Minh at the Conference of trade union cadres (March 14, 1959).

*"Role and Tasks of the Vietnamese Woman
in the New Revolutionary Stage"*

1. V.I. Lenin, *Collected Works*, Progress Publishers, Moscow, 1964, Vol. 23, p. 329.

2. V.I. Lenin, *op. cit.*, Vol. 3, p. 221.

3. Women's army. (*Ed.*).

4. Attack on the political and military planes, and agitation work among enemy soldiers.

"Problems of Revolutionary Strategy"

1. Ngo Dinh Diem headed the regime in South Vietnam from 1954 to November 1963, when he was assassinated, together with his brother Nhu, during the generals' coup.

2. In June 1929, the Indochinese Communist Party was founded in the North. Then followed the formation of the Annamese Communist Party in the South and the Tan Viet Communist League in Central Vietnam. Under the direction of Ho Chi Minh, the three organizations were amalgamated into the Vietnam Communist Party in 1930.

3. This insurrection had been staged by the Quoc Dan Dang nationalist party in February 1930.

4. V.I. Lenin, "Report of the Central Committee, Ninth Congress of the R.C.P. (B)," in *Selected Works*, International Publishers, N.Y., 1967, Vol. 3, p. 317.

5. V.I. Lenin, *"Left-Wing" Communism, an Infantile Disorder*, International Publishers, N.Y., 1940, p. 53.

*Appendix—"A Circular Letter Sent Out
by Nghe Tinh Patriots"*

1. The Southern heavens: Viet Nam's location was stated in relation to China. The North Star: The Emperor.

2. Nghieu: a mythical Chinese emperor, renowned for his virtues.

3. Kiet: a notoriously cruel Chinese emperor.

4. Catholicism.

5. An allusion to the French attacks on Tourane, then on Hanoi.

6. Tan Coi: a defeatist official in Chinese history.

7. Hoan Dau, Truong Luong: personages of Chinese history.

8. Names of patriots.

9. River crossing Hue, the capital city.

10. Two generals of ancient Chinese history who opposed treason by the Court.

Note the abundant allusions to Chinese history, as usually happens in the scholars' writings. With the exception of Van Dat and Cao Dong, two Vietnamese patriots killed in the struggle against the French conquerors, all other proper names were taken from Chinese history.

Chronology of Events

1929:	The first communist cell was set up in Hanoi.
1930	
February 3:	Conference of delegates of three Vietnamese communist parties, held in Kowlon (Hongkong) and presided over by Ho Chi Minh: unification of the communist movement and founding of the Dang Cong San Viet Nam (Vietnam Communist Party).
October:	The First Plenum of the Viet Nam Communist Party Central Committee adopted the name of Dang Cong San Dong Duong (Indochinese Communist Party, ICP).
September 12:	Nghe-Tinh Soviet Movement. After a savage repression by the French colonial administration, it died out in mid-1931.
1930-1931:	Nation-wide strikes, peasants' demonstrations broke out in many parts of Vietnam.
1935:	Big strikes in Saigon.
1936:	Decision of the ICP Central Committee on the founding of a broad people's anti-imperialist front and the launching of a vast campaign for the holding of an Indochinese Congress.
1936-1938:	A period of seething struggle by the Vietnamese working class.
March, 1938:	Decision of the ICP Central Committee on the founding of an Indochinese Democratic United Front.

1939:	Decision of the Sixth Plenum of the ICP Central Committee on the setting up a united anti-imperialist front of the Indochinese peoples with a view to directing the spearhead of the revolutionary struggle against fascism.

1940

June:	French defeat in Europe.
September 27:	Bac Son Insurrection
November 23:	Nam Ky (Cochinchina) Insurrection

1941

January 13:	Do Luong (Nghe An) uprising.
May 10:	Eighth Plenum of the ICP Central Committee presided over by Ho Chi Minh: it decided to accelerate preparations for an armed insurrection and found the VIET MINH Front.

1944

December 22:	Founding of the Propaganda and Liberation Army commanded by Vo Nguyen Giap.

1945

March 9:	The Japanese disarmed the French. The ICP Central Committee met in Hanoi suburbs.
March 11:	Armed uprising in Ba To (Quang Ngai).
April:	Merging of revolutionary armed forces into a Liberation Army.
August 13:	Capitulation of the Japanese.
August 19:	Huge demonstration in Hanoi. Triumph of the Revolution.
September 2:	Proclamation of the Declaration of Independence by President Ho Chi Minh.
September 23:	French troops led by Leclerc landed in Saigon.

1946

December 19:	In answer to a French ultimatum, President Ho Chi Minh called on the people to stand up against colonialist aggression. Beginning of the First War of National Resistance.
1951:	The Dang Lao Dong Viet Nam (Vietnam Workers Party: VWP) was formed to replace the Indochinese Communist Party, officially dissolved in November 1945.

1954

May 7:   Opening of the Geneva Conference. Defeat of the French at Dien Bien Phu.

July 24:   Signing of the Geneva Agreements. Temporary division of Vietnam at the 17th parallel.

1956:   The general elections provided for in the Geneva Agreements for the reunification of Vietnam are rejected by Saigon.

1960:   Formation of the National Liberation Front (NLF) of South Vietnam.

1963:   Assassination of South Vietnam President Ngo Dinh Diem.

1964

August 7:   President Johnson orders American bombing of North Vietnam.

1965:   Beginning of massive bombings of North Vietnam by US Air Force.

1968:   TET (New Year) offensive by liberation forces. Beginning of Paris Peace Talks.

1969

September 3:   Death in Hanoi of President Ho Chi Minh.

1970

May 1st: U.S. invasion of Cambodia.

1971

February 8:   U.S. invasion of Laos (route 9).

1972:   Offensive by liberation forces. Christmas bombing of Hanoi by USAF.

1973

January 27:   Signing of Paris "Agreement on Ending the War and Restoring Peace in Vietnam."

March 29:   The last U.S. soldier leaves Vietnam.

1975

March 12:   The Battle of Banmethuot.

April 30:   Liberation of Saigon.

1976

April 25:   General elections for a unified Vietnam National Assembly. Le Duan elected in District 2, Hanoi with 99.76 per cent of votes.

June 25:   Le Duan delivers his Political Report to the unified National Assembly.

Selected Bibliography
In English Language

Cameron, Allan W. Ed., *Vietnam Crisis: A Documentary History*, Vol I—1940-56 (Cornell University Press, Ithaca, 1971).

Chaliand, Gerard, *The Peasants of North Vietnam* (Penguin, Baltimore, 1969).

Cole, Allan B. et al, *Conflict in Indochina & International Repercussions: A Documentary History: 1945-1955* (Cornell University Press, Ithaca, 1955).

Duiker, William J., *The Rise of Nationalism in Vietnam: 1900-1941* (Cornell University Press, Ithaca, 1976).

Fenn, Charles, *Ho Chi Minh* (Charles Scribner's, New York, 1973).

Hammer, Ellen J., *The Struggle in Indochina* (Stanford University Press, Palo Alto, 1954).

Honey, P.J., *Communism in North Vietnam* (MIT Press, Cambridge, 1963).

Lacouture, Jean, *Ho Chi Minh, A Political Biography* (Random House, New York, 1968).

Lamb, Helen B., *Vietnam's Will to Live* (Monthly Review Press, New York, 1972).

Le Duan, *On the Socialist Revolution in Vietnam* (Foreign Languages Publishing House, Hanoi, 1965, 2 vols.).

————,*The Vietnamese Revolution: Fundamental Problems and Essential Tasks* (International Publishers, New York, 1971).

————,*Some Present Tasks* (Foreign Languages Publishing House, Hanoi, 1974).

Marr, David, *Vietnamese Anticolonialism; 1885-1925* (University of California Press, Berkeley, 1971).

Nguyen Duy Trinh et al, *In the Enemy's Nest: Memoirs from the Revolution* (Foreign Languages Publishing House, Hanoi, 1962).

Nguyen Khac Vien, *The Long Resistance: 1858-1975* (Foreign Languages Publishing House, Hanoi, 1975).

_____, *Tradition and Revolution in Vietnam* (Indochina Resource Center, Berkeley, 1974).

_____, *Vietnam: A Historical Sketch* (Foreign Languages Publishing House, Hanoi, 1974).

Ngo Vinh Long, *Before the Revolution* (MIT Press, Cambridge, 1973).

Pham Van Dong, *President Ho Chi Minh* (Foreign Languages Publishing House, Hanoi, no date given).

Pomeroy, William J., Ed., *Guerilla Warfare and Marxism* (International Publishers, New York, 1970).

Porter, Gareth, *A Peace Denied: The United States, Vietnam and the Paris Agreement* (University of Indiana Press, Bloomington, 1975).

Scalapino, Robert A., *The Communist Revolution in Asia* (Prentice-Hall, 1965).

Sainteny, Jean, *Ho Chi Minh and his Vietnam* (Cowles Publishing, Chicago, 1972).

Sweezy, Paul et al, *Vietnam: The Endless War* (Monthly Review Press, New York, 1970).

Stetler, Russell, Ed., *The Military Art of People's War: Selected Writings of General Vo Nguyen Giap* (Monthly Review Press, 1970).

Terzani, Tiziano, *Giai Phong! The Fall and Liberation of Saigon* (St. Martin's Press, New York, 1976).

Truong Chinh, *Forward Along the Path charted by K. Marx* (Foreign Languages Publishing House, Hanoi, 1969).

_____, *Primer for Revolution* (Praeger, New York, 1963).

Thompson, Virginia, *The Left Wing in Southeast Asia* (William Sloane, New York, 1950).

Trager, Frank N., *Marxism in Southeast Asia* (Stanford University Press, 1959).

Turner, Robert F., *Vietnamese Communism: Its Origins and Development* (Stanford University Press, 1975).

Vo Nguyen Giap, *People's War, People's Army* (Foreign Languages Publishing House, Hanoi, 1974).

_____, *To Arm the Revolutionary Masses to Build the People's Army* (Foreign Languages Publishing House, Hanoi, 1962).

———, *How We Won the War* (Recon Publications, Philadelphia, 1976).

Van Dyke, Jon M., *North Vietnam's Strategy for Survival* (Pacific Books, Palo Alto, 1972).

For an extensive bibliography on Vietnam, refer to: *A Bibliography of Western-Language Publications Concerning North Vietnam in the Cornell University Library; 1966.*